T0026921

THE
HIGHER HELP
METHOD

ALSO BY TAMMY MASTROBERTE

The Universe Is Talking to You

THE
HIGHER HELP
METHOD

STOP TRYING TO MANIFEST AND LET THE UNIVERSE GUIDE YOU

TAMMY MASTROBERTE

sounds true
BOULDER, COLORADO

Sounds True
Boulder, CO

This book is not intended as a substitute for the medical recommendations of physicians, mental health professionals, or other health-care providers. Rather, it is intended to offer information to help the reader cooperate with physicians, mental health professionals, and health-care providers in a mutual quest for optimal well-being. We advise readers to carefully review and understand the ideas presented and to seek the advice of a qualified professional before attempting to use them.

Published 2024

Cover design and image by Huma Akhtar
Book design by Rachael Murray
Illustrations by Jennifer Miles

Printed in the United States of America

BK06830

CIP Data Library of Congress Cataloging-in-Publication Data

Names: Mastroberte, Tammy, 1977- author.
Title: The higher help method : stop trying to manifest and let the universe guide you / Tammy Mastroberte.
Description: Boulder, CO : Sounds True, Inc., 2024. | Includes index.
Identifiers: LCCN 2023039932 (print) | LCCN 2023039933 (ebook) | ISBN 9781649632104 (paperback) | ISBN 9781649632135 (ebook)
Subjects: LCSH: Self-actualization (Psychology) | Spiritual life.
Classification: LCC BF637.S4 M2293 2024 (print) | LCC BF637.S4 (ebook) |
    DDC 158--dc23/eng/20231206
LC record available at https://lccn.loc.gov/2023039932
LC ebook record available at https://lccn.loc.gov/2023039933

FSC
www.fsc.org
MIX
Paper | Supporting
responsible forestry
FSC® C103098

To my nephew, Steven; niece, Alyssa; and stepson, Mason.

May you rely on the method and the tools in this book to guide you through any challenge you face, and may it assist you in creating a life beyond your wildest dreams—filled with unending joy, happiness, love, and peace. All my love, always.

Contents

Conclusion
It's Time to Create a Life You Love   285

List of Exercises

List of Rituals

Introduction

STOP TRYING TO MANIFEST . . . DO THIS INSTEAD

IT WAS THE SUMMER OF 2012, exactly one year after I left my job as an executive editor for a magazine in New York City so I could pursue my own business full time, which back then was an online spiritual magazine. I remember leaving the office for the last time with a huge smile on my face, and I practically skipped out the door with excitement for my future. Fast forward twelve months later, and I was struggling. Neither the business nor my finances were growing the way I had hoped. I felt defeated, frustrated, and alone, and the thought of going back to a full-time job, working for someone else, scared me even more than going broke.

I finished my morning meditation in front of the small altar I had built in my bedroom, and my heart felt heavy. In front of me were statues of the Blessed Mother and Buddha along with a variety of crystals, a lit candle, and the strand of rosary beads my mother received as a gift from a friend who visited Jerusalem years ago. My eyes rested on the rosary beads, and I thought about how special they were to my mother because of how special the Blessed Mother was to her and her mother, my grandmother Rose. I thought about how I used them to pray for my mother when she was on life support after a brain aneurysm three days after Christmas in 1999—and then again when she died a day later. I asked that she be guided on her journey to the other side and that I be given the strength to survive her death.

Growing up Catholic, prayer had always been a part of my life. I remember my mother sitting at the edge of my bed on more than one occasion during my childhood, offering me a prayer card for Padre Pio, the patron saint of stress relief, or Saint Jude, the patron saint of hopeless cases, and telling me to call on them for help with a challenge I faced at the time. During my childhood, I was taught that when you couldn't find something, you prayed to Saint Anthony, the patron saint of lost things, to help you find it. If we wanted to sell a house, we buried a statue of Saint Joseph in the ground outside and asked for his help because he is the patron saint of house sellers and buyers. When we wanted nice weather for an outdoor event, we placed the statue of the Blessed Mother in the window and asked her to bring it. In my family, when crisis hit, we prayed for help and guidance.

On that summer morning in 2012, I looked at those rosary beads, and instead of blowing out the candle and starting my workday like I always did, I decided to do something different. I decided to say a prayer asking for help with my business.

I closed my eyes and silently called in my angels, guides, loved ones who have passed on, and all those in my soul society, which is what I call all the higher helpers on the other side, assisting me on my path whether I know them or not. I asked to be directed through signs and synchronicities to the ideas, opportunities, people, and resources that could help me move forward, and I asked for help in recognizing them when they arrived. Then I started my day. Less than two weeks later, after repeating my prayer each morning, I started noticing help arrive.

It began with an email inviting me to sign up for a free online summit for entrepreneurs, featuring more than twenty experts sharing ideas on increasing prosperity. I attended and enjoyed listening to the advice, but soon realized I was guided to this summit for so much more. The format grabbed my interest, and as I was listening each week, I started thinking about how I could replicate it to create my own summit. I did research and found someone who helped people run them, and when

I saw the person's name, I remembered them working with a woman named Dana Wilde, whose emails I received in the past on a summit teaching mindset strategies. I decided to reach out and ask if she would be willing to chat.

I still call Dana one of my Earth angels because not only did she help me by advising against hiring the person she worked with because of a disastrous experience she had with them, but she also became instrumental in helping me launch my first-ever "Living an Elevated Existence Mind, Body, and Soul Summit" in only a matter of months. This summit helped me add thousands of people to my email list, and through it I earned more money in three months than my business had since its launch four years prior. It also introduced me to others as a spiritual teacher and not just a magazine owner. I taught my first class on how to notice signs and synchronicity from the Universe and loved ones on the other side—which years later led to my bestselling book, *The Universe Is Talking to You*.

That is what happens when you ask the Universe for help and allow it to guide you forward. As soon as I asked, the Universe got to work directing my attention, dropping ideas into my mind, lining up synchronicities, and moving me beyond what I could have imagined at the time. And prayer is only one aspect of my Higher Help Method, which you will learn in this book.

WHY YOUR MANIFESTING ISN'T WORKING

I know there are areas of your life you want to change for the better. You want to make more money, find a new partner, improve a relationship, start a business, change your career, or heal your body, and my guess is you've been trying hard to manifest these changes in your life for a while. You've probably read books, taken classes, worked on your mindset and beliefs, recited affirmations, sat for meditations, created vision boards, and written in a gratitude journal. If you have been doing any of these things, take a minute to pat yourself on the back because they are amazing tools to help you create change in your life.

But let me ask you a question. Have these tools worked for you consistently, or are you still struggling to see the changes you desire?

If you are still struggling, and my guess is you are because you picked up this book, I have good news for you. There is another way. There is a less stressful and more joyful way to create positive changes in your life, and it starts with a critical piece you've likely been missing. Most people are doing a lot of trying, but they are doing it alone without the help of an all-knowing, all-seeing, creative powerhouse filled with magic and miracles available to every single human being in this physical world. I'm talking about the Universe and its boundless, loving energy radiating all around you. It's there right now, waiting for you to tap into it. Instead of trying to create change on your own, wouldn't it be easier to partner with that energy and allow it to guide you toward what you desire—or even something infinitely better?

Whatever it is you are trying to manifest, whatever changes you are trying to make in your life, and whatever problems you are trying to solve, I want you to stop trying so hard and, more importantly, I want you to stop trying to do it alone. You were never meant to manifest, solve problems, make decisions, or figure anything out in life by yourself. You have direct access to the Divine, along with a supportive and specialized team of higher helpers, to assist you. The Universe, your angels, guides, loved ones who have passed on, and an infinite amount of other higher guides are standing by ready to help. And they are the ultimate psychic team because they know and see everything you don't. They access the higher plan for your life, see the best path to take, arrange meetings with the perfect people to assist you in getting there, and help you avoid roadblocks along the way. In my own experience, and from what I've witnessed with my students and clients, without Divine help and guidance, it's much harder to make progress and in many cases we find ourselves stuck or going in circles.

I know this because I've been there. I've felt the frustration, hopelessness, and stress of not making progress while longing for the changes I wanted to see in my life. In fact, there was a time in my life when I was stuck in almost every area. I was working at a job that paid the bills but made me miserable. I started my own business on the side, but it wasn't turning a profit. I had been single for years, and my health and chronic symptoms just kept getting worse. I would beat myself up thinking I was obviously doing things wrong since other people were manifesting what they desired while I watched from the sidelines wishing it could be me. It was from this place of unhappiness that I began creating and combining spiritual tools in an effort to manifest the changes I desired, and while I had no idea at the time, I was formulating what I now call the Higher Help Method. Using this method, I consistently and deliberately began asking the Universe for help and using specific spiritual tools to harness its energy and manage my own.

That is when things finally started to flow into my life with more ease. I met and married my amazing husband, my business took off and continues to grow in exciting ways, I wrote and published a bestselling book, and my health keeps getting better, despite doctors telling me it wasn't possible. And I know the method will do the same for you.

It's time to take a deep breath and drop the burden you've been carrying on your shoulders. You are not doing it wrong. You are not alone. Creating the changes you want to see in life is not a solo job. You are meant to be part of a team, and you are only one piece of that. It's time to bring in high vibrational partners to support and guide you in this process so you finally start moving toward the life and circumstances you desire—and in many cases, moving even further forward than you could ever dream possible. When I asked the Universe for help growing my business in 2012, I had no clue it would lead me down the path of teaching others how to ask the Universe for help and how to receive the guidance it sends. I just wanted to bring in more money. The Universe always knows better than we do. When you start trusting and allowing it to take the reins, it will lead you beyond your wildest dreams and into a life you love waking up to each day. Are you ready for that? Let's go!

A NEW WAY TO CREATE CHANGE

The Higher Help Method is a brand-new way to solve problems, make positive changes, and move toward health, happiness, and love in all areas of your life with more ease. This method creates a partnership with the Universe by consciously asking it for help, using tools to harness its powerful and positive energy, and then allowing it to guide you toward the changes you desire—or something even better. Instead of panicking, stressing, worrying, and working yourself into a frenzy of negativity when an unexpected challenge pops up in your life that you don't know how to handle or solve, ask the Universe for help. Instead of obsessing about things not changing or getting better in some area of your life, turn it over to the Universe and allow it to guide you to the solution. You can even call in assistance to shift your mindset so you hold more positive thoughts, and stay at a higher vibration to remain open to the guidance coming through.

We are always talking to the Universe and asking it for help through our thoughts, emotions, beliefs, and actions, but often these requests are coming from the subconscious mind with its unending programs of fear and worry about the future, its incessant stream of negative thoughts, and its tendency to focus on the problem or what is missing in life rather than a solution or what is going right. The Higher Help Method allows you to deliberately and consciously communicate with the Universe and access its guidance, and it counteracts the subconscious mind. It also puts the Universe and your higher help team in the driver's seat so they can guide you to the best possible solution instead of you struggling to figure it out on your own.

It's important to note that when asking the Universe for help, whether through prayer or one of the other tools you will find in this book, there is a specific approach I find works best, and it may be different from things you've tried in the past. A lot of people say a prayer asking the Universe to grant them a wish—to bring them exactly what they want or to make a problem or issue disappear. They want to be in a relationship with a specific person, so they say a prayer asking for that person to love them. They want a certain job at a particular company and ask the Universe to make it happen. They are struggling with a health challenge and pray for it to be gone when they wake up the next day. And sometimes this works. Sometimes problems suddenly disappear, and things work out exactly as they had hoped. The Universe is truly miraculous, and anything is possible. However, there are many times when it doesn't work this way. They don't get the guy, the job, or the spontaneous healing, and they end up thinking the Universe doesn't care, isn't listening or, even worse, that they must be doing something wrong.

The Universe doesn't usually work like Santa Claus, where you ask for a gift and wake up one morning to find it waiting for you. Creating positive change in your life is meant to be a partnership with the Universe, and that means you need to do your part. When asking for help, instead of saying, "Please bring me what I want," and then standing by and waiting for it to arrive, I always say, "Please show me where I need to go." When I do that, the Universe responds with guidance and answers, bringing through new ideas, signs, and synchronicities. Then it's my job to act on them to move forward.

In order for this partnership to work, you need to trust that the Universe is always leading you to your highest good, even when it may not initially look or feel like it. The Universe and your higher help team have access to knowledge and resources you don't. If you ask for help to create a specific change in your life, and it doesn't happen, it's not because the Universe doesn't care or isn't listening. It's not because you are doing something wrong or don't deserve it. It's often because there is something even better waiting in the wings. Think back to the people you've dated in the past—those who, at the time, you thought were "the one." Think about the people who broke your heart and how you believed you would never find love like that again. When I look back on my past relationships, I'm very grateful the Universe didn't deliver on what I thought I wanted. I may have waited until I was thirty-seven to find my husband, but he was worth the wait. If I had ended up with someone else, I wouldn't be with him, and I wouldn't be the stepmother to an amazing eleven-year-old boy. The same is true for the jobs I didn't get and other opportunities that seemed to pass me by. If I got everything I thought I wanted at the time, I would not be where I am in my life right now. And neither would you. The Universe doesn't make mistakes, and you can't make mistakes either because it always guides you back to your higher path if you allow it. What you want right now might not be the best option for your future, and while you may not know exactly what that best option is, the Universe always does.

When my husband and I were planning to buy a house together, we would drive around on the weekends looking at different towns in New Jersey to see where we wanted to move. We agreed on the areas we loved, and those we did not, and I was specifically against more rural towns, especially those that didn't have sidewalks in front of the homes. I even printed out a picture of a beautiful two-story house and visualized myself pulling up to it in my car and walking inside. I asked the Universe for help, thinking we would buy a house in a year or so, but a few months later a unique opportunity presented itself. The house for sale looked nothing like the one in my picture. It was a ranch-style home, set 500 feet back from the street, and completely surrounded by woods. And it was in one of the towns without sidewalks. My immediate thought was, "Absolutely not—this is not what I want. I don't care how good of an opportunity this is, the answer is an immediate no."

My husband continued to talk about how the house made sense financially, and because he did home improvement work, he could transform it into a home we would love. He even volunteered to build me a home office and meditation room in the large open basement. I still wasn't happy about it, but I eventually agreed to buy it, thinking we could always sell it in a few years.

It's been five years and I've never regretted purchasing this home. We've made a lot of changes, and still have visions for what we will do in the future, but all of the things I thought I didn't want, I now love. Walking outside and being surrounded by nature is a dream. We have a barn on our property that is home to four goats whom I adore, and my office and meditation room are better than I could have imagined.

And because our home is set back off the street, I don't even notice the missing sidewalks. It was not what I wanted. It was actually much better.

When you consciously ask the Universe for help, it always responds by lining up the perfect people, opportunities, and resources to guide you where you are meant to go—and sometimes that is beyond what you envision at the time. It may even appear as something you don't initially want. But when you partner with the Universe, trust it, and follow its lead, everything becomes easier, brighter, and more magical.

If you are stuck in one or more areas of your life right now, you are not alone. Everybody is trying to improve some area of their life, including me. Becoming stuck or unhappy is not only normal, it's also necessary. It's what pushes you to make changes, look for new solutions, try new things, and create circumstances in your life that would not have happened if you were content and happy. Life is truly a cycle of getting stuck and moving forward, so if you feel stuck right now, I want you to celebrate because it means major progress is ahead of you—and after reading this book, you will have my tried-and-true method to help you create it.

INTRODUCING THE METHOD

Whatever you are trying to improve or change for the better in your life, using the Higher Help Method detailed in this book will help you get there and open you up to possibilities you never dreamed possible. It does this by combining specific spiritual tools to ask the Universe for help, to create a conscious partnership with it, and to harness its energy. It also takes the stress and pressure off your shoulders, which actually block you from creating what you want, because it allows the Universe to take the lead and guide you forward. While this partnership does require some work on your part, none of the tools or exercises in this book takes hours to do. In fact, every tool, exercise, meditation, and ritual is done fairly quickly, and the daily routine outlined in the introduction to part 2 takes less than ten minutes each day.

I created the Higher Help Method for myself, based on my own background and experience, including growing up in the Catholic faith, and you will notice elements from that within the method, combined with other belief systems and faiths I've been exposed to and studied over the years. As it unfolded, I had no idea it would become something I would teach other people. This method has allowed me to foster an intimate relationship with the Divine that guides me through life, and as I was creating it, I discovered the combination of tools you will find in this book that began to make a big difference in my life. Creating positive change became easier because I wasn't relying only on myself to do, say, or act the "right" way in order to manifest what I wanted. I had an entire team supporting and guiding me.

You are the CEO of your life, and if you talk to the CEO of any company—large or small—they will tell you how they rely on a team of advisors, or a board of directors, to help them make decisions and grow their organization. And they will likely tell you it allowed them to grow in ways they could never have on their own. Some of the most ground-breaking companies of our time had founders and CEOs who relied on help, including Steve Jobs at Apple, Howard Schultz at Starbucks, and Mary Barra at General Motors. While final decisions are left to the CEO of a company, just like you have free will to decide what actions to take in your life, there is always a team behind the scenes doing research, making phone calls, setting up meetings, and offering guidance.

As a soul inhabiting this physical body, you also have access to a similar team of advisors—what I call higher helpers—who are ready and willing to offer their assistance any time you ask, but your team is even better because it's filled with all-knowing and all-seeing partners. They send you the ideas, line up the perfect opportunities, arrange run-ins with the right people, and guide you to the best resources so you move forward toward success in all areas of your life. The Higher Help Method calls in that team of advisors to help guide you forward, and it offers you tools to utilize the creative and powerful energy of the Universe around you to make your path easier.

Also, throughout the book I use the term *Universe*, which is another way of saying Source, God, Spirit, or any other name you choose to call your higher power. When I refer to "the Universe," I'm including all the higher helpers available to assist, including angels, guides, ascended masters, gods, goddesses, saints, loved ones who have passed on, and other experts on the other side. The reason I include them all together is, regardless of the belief system you grew up with, or what you hold today, you have the ability to call on any higher helpers from any religion or tradition to assist you. When your soul returns to the other side, or the nonphysical world that is your true home, you reenter a space in which there is no separation. We are all one, and we are all connected. Religion is a concept that exists in the physical world, but not in the spiritual world. You don't have to be a Buddhist to call on Buddha. You don't have to practice Hinduism to call on Ganesha, who is known as the remover of obstacles, and you don't have to be a Catholic to ask Jesus or Mother Mary for help. Throughout the second part of the book, you will find lists of higher helpers representing a variety of faiths and belief systems, and it's up to you whom you choose to work with in your life. I've created lists to get you started based on my own research as well as people I've called on for help in my life, but know you have the ability to call on any of them, either alone or in combination, or to leave out those with whom you don't resonate. And, of course, feel free to add any not listed as well.

The Higher Help Method consists of four steps designed to work together so you consciously communicate with the Universe, harness its energy, receive the guidance being sent, and act on it to create a life you love. This is my go-to method when I need help making decisions, finding solutions to a problem or challenge, or when I'm feeling stuck in some area of my life and want to move forward faster. I hope after reading this book and using its tools, it will become your go-to method, too. It's a brand-new way of living your daily life and one that I know will bring more ease, peace, clarity, happiness, and success into it.

Here is an overview of the four steps in this method. We'll dig deeper into each one in the chapters that follow within part 1.

Step 1 is Clarity and Intention, where you get clear on what changes you would like to see in your life, and then set an intention with yourself and the Universe to create either what you desire or something even more amazing.

Step 2 is Ask the Universe for Help, where you use a variety of spiritual tools in conjunction, including calling in higher helpers through prayer and using gratitude exercises, rituals, and crystals to ask the Universe to partner with you and harness its energy in your life to create positive changes.

Step 3 is Shift Your Energy, and this is where you use simple tools and techniques throughout the day to maintain a higher vibration so that you notice the signs and answers coming to you from the Universe to guide you forward, and to stay aligned with the positive changes you desire.

Step 4 is Receiving and Acting on the Guidance, where it's your job to open up to and receive the answers the Universe sends to guide you and then take action on the ideas, signs, and synchronistic experiences that come to you.

HOW TO USE THIS BOOK

In part 1 of this book, I walk you through my four-step Higher Help Method. Chapters 1 through 4 take you step-by-step through the process of applying it to your life. I recommend reading part 1 and doing the exercises before jumping into part 2.

In part 2 you will find a customizable spiritual toolbox filled with lists of higher helpers from all backgrounds and belief systems, crystals, customized prayers, focused gratitude exercises, and rituals based on seven major life areas: money and abundance; physical healing; emotional healing; relationships; career and purpose; fertility, pregnancy, and parenting; and spiritual connection. As I've said, I've been collecting this information from a variety of sources over the years, including cross-checking with online resources and then making my own lists. I've done all the work for you to get started, but feel free to add in your own resources to further customize anything you find in the book. After reading part 1, choose one area of your life to start with—two at the most—so that you focus your energy for the greatest impact. Also, be sure to go back and do the clarity exercises in chapter 1 before starting to work on any new life area.

This book is meant to be a resource you return to again and again to create positive change and find solutions in life. I created this method to help myself, and it's my honor to share it with you so you create the same magic, miracles, peace, joy, and love in your life that it's allowed me to create in mine as well as in the lives of my students, clients, friends, and family members who have used it. In fact, I hope it helps you create even more.

Resources

To further assist you on your path to creating a life you love, you can access audio versions of the meditations in this book, additional prayers and rituals, and other bonus content at higherhelpmethod.com. The indexes at the back of the book also list the higher helpers and crystals mentioned so you can easily navigate to the correct pages if searching for one in particular.

Are you ready to dive into a new way of walking through your life—with a team of higher helpers at your disposal? It all starts in the next chapter, where you will get clear on what you desire and then hand it over to the Universe to help you create it or something better.

Part 1

THE FOUR STEPS OF THE
HIGHER HELP METHOD

IN PART 1 OF THIS book, there are four chapters that walk you through each step of the Higher Help Method. You will discover in detail how to use each one, as well as easy exercises, spiritual tools, and techniques to assist you. But first, here is a brief overview of the steps, why they are important to the overall process of creating positive change in your life, and how they work together to help you move forward.

STEP 1: CLARITY AND INTENTION

The Universe needs direction. In order to provide you guidance, line up the people and opportunities to help, and send the ideas and resources to create positive changes, the Universe needs to know where you want to go so it can help you get there—or somewhere even more amazing. It needs a clear intention from you to get the ball rolling. If you got into a taxi and didn't tell the driver where you wanted to go, the odds of you getting where you need to be are slim to none. It's the same with the Universe. It can't guide you if you don't tell it where you want to go. Without a conscious intention, your subconscious mind runs the show, sending out mixed signals, and you end up with mixed results, making little to no progress forward.

This is the first place people get stuck because the majority of their thoughts are focused on what they don't want, which is usually what they are currently experiencing. And because one of the ways we talk to the Universe is through our thoughts, doing this essentially asks it for help to create more of what we no longer want. That is why the first step to creating positive change is getting clear on what you want to see *in place of* what you have now. Then set an intention and ask the Universe to help you create it or something more spectacular. You learn exactly how to do this in chapter 1.

STEP 2: ASK THE UNIVERSE FOR HELP

Once you are clear on what you would like to create, and you set an intention to manifest it or something better, it's time to consciously call on the Universe to partner with you. There are a number of spiritual tools in chapter 2 to assist you in asking the Universe for help and in utilizing its energy to create positive change. These tools include specialized higher helpers, prayer, focused gratitude, crystals, and rituals. While many of these tools are used on their own to help us move forward, I find combining them creates the best and fastest results.

STEP 3: SHIFT YOUR ENERGY

Once you ask the Universe for help and ignite its energy to start working with you and for you in any area of your life, it immediately starts to respond. Your higher helpers quickly get to work dropping new ideas into your mind, lining up the right people to cross your path, and presenting the perfect opportunities to assist you. The third step in the Higher Help Method is to become aware of your own energy throughout the day and actively shift it when it starts to dip into negativity. Doing this helps you maintain a higher vibration so you receive the guidance being sent to you and also releases any resistance blocking it from coming through. When you begin feeling frustrated, worried, overwhelmed, stressed, anxious, or any other negative emotion, or when your thoughts start drifting toward what is going wrong or might go wrong in the future, that's your sign to shift and elevate your energy. In chapter 3, you discover simple spiritual tools and techniques to do this.

STEP 4: RECEIVING AND ACTING ON GUIDANCE

The last step of the Higher Help Method is recognizing the guidance sent to you from the Universe and your higher help team and acting on it when it arrives. There are specific ways the Universe talks to you, sends answers, and gets your attention, and chapter 4 helps you become familiar with them so you recognize them when they arrive. Then it's your job to take action on what comes through. Taking action sends a signal to the Universe that you are ready for it to guide you to your next step. It's crucial in order to move forward in any area of your life. The good news is there are no "wrong" actions because the Universe is always guiding and rerouting you if you make a wrong turn.

Chapter 1

CLARITY AND INTENTION

DO YOU REMEMBER THE GAME "Pin the Tail on the Donkey"? It was a staple at so many of the kids' birthday parties I went to when I was younger. Every child got a tail, and in front of them was a poster of a donkey who was missing one. The objective was to pin the tail on the donkey in the right spot, but the catch was each child would get blindfolded and then spun around a few times before being set free to attempt the task. After the blindfold and the spinning, you would have no clue which way you were facing, never mind where the donkey was and where to pin its tail! Most kids would miss the mark, and I remember laughing as I watched them pin the tail on the head, the back, and even poke the donkey in the eye. In some cases, they missed the poster of the donkey altogether. This is exactly what happens when you try to create without knowing what you want and without setting an intention. You become just like the child who is blindfolded and spun around over and over. You are confused, in the dark, and nine times out of ten, you miss the mark.

The Universe responds to direction, and in order to direct it you need to know what it is you want to create. My guess is you're already clear on what you *don't* want in your life, and it's likely what you are experiencing right now in the areas you feel stuck. You might be unhappy in your relationship or feel lonely because you're currently single. You might be miserable in your job, aggravated by your boss, or feel unfulfilled in your career. Maybe you're struggling to pay bills or save money, and it's a constant source of stress and worry in your life. Or maybe you feel disconnected spiritually from the love and support of a higher power. But what *do* you want? Have you taken the time to think about the new direction in which you would like to move, the new circumstances you would like to create, and how it would make you feel? Without clarity and intention, you continue to create more of what you don't want, and you likely continue to feel stuck.

Achieving clarity on what you would like to see, why you would like to see it, and how it will make you feel sets the wheels of the Universe and its energy into motion so it starts guiding you toward what you want or something even more incredible. You don't need to figure it all out or plan out every detail, and most importantly, you don't have to know how, when, or where it will happen. In fact, I don't recommend doing any of that. Leave the how, when, who, and where to the Universe. When you are too detailed with these aspects of creation, you actually block yourself from noticing the signs pointing you toward an even better option. Clarity and intention around what you want, why, and how you will feel when you get there are all you need to ignite the power of the Universe to propel you forward. Then it's your job to let go and let it guide you— and be open to being led to something even more amazing than your mind can conceive on its own.

THE CLARITY FORMULA

When it comes to clarity, the three ingredients I just mentioned—knowing what you want, why you want it, and how it will make you feel—create the perfect recipe for a clear intention that ignites the spark for positive change in any area of life. Let's start with the first one: knowing what you want. In order to uncover what you want to create that is different from what you currently have, the easiest place to start is with what you don't like about your present circumstances. Ask yourself what don't you like about your current situation, and then ask yourself what you would like to see, be, or have instead. For example, if you are unhappy in your current job, ask yourself, "What don't I like about my job, and what would I like to see or experience instead?"

Here is how this might play out for a job or career:

What don't I like? "I don't like having set hours when I need to be in the office."

What do I want instead? "I want a job with a flexible schedule that allows me to work from home a few days each week."

What don't I like? "I don't like my boss because he keeps taking credit for my ideas, which blocks me from showing my abilities and growing in the company."

What do I want instead? "I want a job where my boss respects me and where my ideas and abilities are recognized and compensated."

What don't I like? "I don't like working in a hospital as a nurse because there is too much chaos and it's emotionally draining."

What do I want instead? "I want a nursing job where I can leave work feeling fulfilled, happy, and at ease."

For those who are unsure about the direction of their career or don't know exactly what field they want to pursue next, this exercise might look like this:

What don't I like? "I don't like my current job or the work I am doing there."

What do I want instead? "I want to spend my time doing something I love that helps other people and pays me X amount per year."

Do this for any area of your life causing you unhappiness, including money, relationships, health, or spirituality. Here are a few more examples:

What don't I like? "I don't like struggling to pay bills every month and never having enough money."

What do I want instead? "I want to have more than enough money to pay my bills and add money to my savings account each month."

What don't I like? "I don't like fighting with my partner and feeling like I can't tell them how I feel without their getting mad."

What do I want instead? "I want a relationship with my partner in which we are open to one another's points of view and communicate and solve problems openly, freely, and with love."

What don't I like? "I don't like living with anxiety and never feeling safe and relaxed."

What do I want instead? "I want to feel safe, at ease, and carefree no matter what is going on in my life or around me."

Most people have more than one thing they don't like about a specific situation or area of life, so I suggest starting with a list of all the things you don't like, and then for each one, asking yourself, "What do I want instead?" until you come up with a list that can be combined into one intention. For example, in your current job, you may not like the hours, the pay, or the situation in which you work, and you might want to change all of those factors. In that case, you combine them into one statement such as, "I want a job with flexible hours that pays me X amount or more each month, in an environment that supports me, my ideas, and my growth."

The clarity formula works the same way for any new problem or challenge that pops up in life, whether it's deciding what type of car to buy ("I want a car that costs me $350 a month or less and is safe, reliable, and one I enjoy driving"); or hiring help for your growing business ("I want to hire a virtual assistant who will do XYZ for me and is reliable, self-sufficient, and exceeds my expectations in all they do for my business.")

The second piece of the clarity formula is knowing your why. Why do you want the changes you desire? When you answer that question, you get to the heart of what you desire, including the deeper meaning and purpose behind it, and this fuels your motivation to continue on your path even when minor mishaps or delays pop up during the creation process. Once you know what you want, just ask yourself, "Why do I want this? What will it provide me with in my life? What will be different once I have it?"

If you want a job that allows you to work from home, maybe your why is it will allow you to pick your kids up from school, help them with homework, and take them to sports practices so you can spend more quality time with them. If you want to earn enough money to pay your bills on time each month and also put money in your savings, the why could be easing your stress, creating more security, and enabling you to give more to your children, family, or charities you want to support. And if you are suffering from a chronic illness making it hard for you to do certain activities, your why might be having the ability to go out with friends, exercise, travel, and enjoy the things you are unable to now.

Finding your why leads you directly to the third and final ingredient in the clarity formula, which is knowing how the change you desire will make you feel once you achieve it. When you are able to work from home three days a week so you can do more with your children, you will feel happier, grateful, and more at ease. When you have enough money to pay your bills, put money in savings, and treat your children to a Disney vacation, you will feel safe, secure, proud, joyful, and at ease around finances. And with a healthy and strong body, you will feel free, alive, and excited about all you do and experience. When you put all of these ingredients together, you end up with a clear intention for yourself and the Universe so it starts partnering with you to create positive changes in your life.

Here is an example of creating an intention using the clarity formula. About twelve years ago, I was working as an executive editor at a magazine in New York City. Things were changing rapidly at my job—mostly for the worse. Our magazine was purchased by a new company whose only priority seemed to be the bottom line. I had been given a raise the prior year for extra work I took on in my role, but the new company took the money away while still requiring me to do the work. Friends I made were being laid off, and I remember sitting on a commuter train with tears in my eyes because I didn't want to go to this job anymore. But, like most people do, I stayed for the paycheck. By this point, I had already started my own online spiritual magazine, working nights and weekends to produce it every quarter, but it wasn't bringing in enough money to pay my bills. I was clear on what I wanted, why I wanted it, and how it would make me feel, and this was my intention: "I want to earn enough money from my own business to leave my job because I want to write about the spiritual topics I love and that will help others, so I will feel happy and fulfilled."

Although this was years before I created the Higher Help Method, I knew the importance of getting clear on what I wanted, and I said many prayers along the way asking the Universe for help. It took months, but eventually the Universe guided me to an opportunity that was so much better than anything I could have dreamed up on my own.

A contracted freelance writer who worked for the magazine suddenly gave her two-week notice, and the company announced they were looking to hire new freelancers rather than full-time employees. That's when it hit me: What if I became a contracted freelancer with limited duties I could do from home? It would be less money than I was currently making, but it would be enough to pay my bills and allow me to spend the majority of my time growing my own business. I explained to my boss what I wanted to do, and while it took six months, I eventually walked out of the office for the last time, and never looked back.

My intention and prayers set things in motion for the Universe to provide the perfect solution. It was not the solution I intended—which was for my business to grow first so I could leave the job. But this solution worked out even better because I could essentially leave the job with enough guaranteed money to dedicate more time to my own business. The Universe always knows best. You just need to decide what you want, ask it for help, and then let it guide you to it, or an entirely better outcome.

DON'T MICROMANAGE

As I mentioned earlier, it is not your job, nor do I recommend you think about, plan, or concern yourself with how you will get where you want to go, who will help you, when it will happen, or where anything will take place. It's not your job to micromanage the Universe and every detail of how your dreams will come to fruition. Your job is to give the Universe a jumping-off point and then follow the guidance it sends to lead you toward your highest good—which is always what you want or something more extraordinary.

Think about it—it feels good to come up with what you desire, to imagine the ways your life will change, and to feel how wonderful it will be once you achieve it. But as soon as your mind asks, "How will this happen?" or "When will this happen?" you open the door for doubt and fear to creep in, and all those good vibes disappear. When you think about how something will happen, and you start playing out scenarios in your mind, the logical part of you kicks in and starts saying, "That's not possible," "Do you know how hard that will be for you to create," "You need more money to do that," "You're are too old," "You don't have that kind of luck," and the list goes on and on. I remember, years ago, sitting and visualizing the outcome of what I desired in my life, and without fail, about a minute into the practice, my mind would inevitably start picturing how I might get there, and instantly my feel-good visualization would take a nosedive directly into stress. I would end up feeling frustrated and panicked, thinking, "Dear God, this is never going to work!" That is when I knew I needed to avoid what I call "How Land" at all costs. And the good news is the how is not your concern. You must leave that to the Universe to figure out, make the necessary arrangements, and iron out all the details for you. Why? Because the Universe and your higher helpers have something you don't have. They have the ability to see all the puzzle pieces of your life scattered on the board so they can start moving them around and putting them together in the ideal order to help you move forward.

The same is true with worrying about *when* things will change. Some manifestation teachers tell you to set a deadline, to give yourself a specific date to achieve your goals. The belief is that this provides motivation and keeps your goals at the top of your mind. I tried this approach. In fact, I tried it multiple times. But every time I set a date, it would stress me out. My mind would say, "How in the world am I going to create this by X date?" Then as I got closer to the date, even more doubt and fear would overwhelm me, and it became entirely counterintuitive to the process of creating positive change and feeling good while doing it.

If setting a date works for you, then by all means do it, but remember that not everything you desire comes to you in *your* timing. You have to leave room for Divine timing. You have to give the Universe the freedom it needs to line up the right people, opportunities, and circumstances at the perfect time for everything to come together. This is true for big dreams you have for your future, as well as for trying to solve everyday problems. Clarity is not about the when and how. Stick with the what, why, and how you will feel, and then leave room for the Universe to surprise and delight you.

Exercise: The Magic Wand Meditation

I created this meditation to help you hone in on what it is you truly want to create in any area of your life, especially when you feel stuck. It's designed to guide you past limited thinking and doubt and into a space of unlimited possibilities. If you are looking to change more than one area of your life repeat this meditation for each area.

Either sitting in a chair or lying down, get into a comfortable position and relax your body. This meditation starts with a pattern of breath called box breathing, which helps to relax the nervous system and increase focus. You will do three cycles of this breathing, counting to four with each step, and breathing in and out through the nose.

Breathe out, letting all the air out of your lungs, and contract the belly all the way in. Then breathe in, two, three, four; hold, two, three, four; breathe out, two, three, four; and hold, two, three, four. Repeat this two more times.

Now, take a deep breath in through the nose, and slowly let it out. Imagine walking down a smooth, stone-lined path surrounded by nature. As you walk, you look to your right and left and notice tall trees on each side with bright leaves gently blowing in the breeze. You also notice the colorful flowers on each side of the road. You see tulips, daisies, roses, and sunflowers, and as you look up, you see a bright blue sky peeking through the leaves on the trees. You hear the birds chirping and singing in the distance, and you feel the warmth of the sun as it touches your skin. You feel peaceful and content here.

As you continue walking along the path, you come across a captivating waterfall with a white bench in front of it. You decide to sit down and close your eyes, and you hear the soothing sounds of the water rushing down the rocks and falling into the pond below it. This is your creative garden. Take a deep breath in through your nose, and slowly let it out. You feel clear and confident here. You are in a space where anything and everything is possible. You are in a space where you are connected to the Universe and its creative energy, and you are surrounded by angels, guides, and other higher helpers who support and love you unconditionally.

Bring to mind the area of your life you would like to create positive changes in now. If you could wave a magic wand that instantly removed all limitations, barriers, and blocks standing in your way, making it easy to have whatever you desire, what would you create? What does it look like? What are you doing when you have it? How does it make you feel? Spend as much time as you need here getting clear on the answers.

Now I want you to physically put both of your hands over your heart, take a deep breath in through your nose, and as you breathe out, ask yourself, "If I had no fear, worry, or limitation around [fill in the blank with the life area you are changing], I would . . ." and then allow whatever comes to mind to flow in. Don't judge it. Just see what your heart has to say about creating change in this area of your life.

Take a deep breath in through your nose, and slowly let it out. Now imagine yourself standing up from the white bench, and begin to walk back down the stone-lined path that brought you to the waterfall. As you continue to walk, everything around you—the trees, the flowers, and the sound of the birds and the waterfall—begins to fade. You keep walking until you are surrounded by pure, sparkling light. Within that light is your higher help team and the unlimited positive energy of the Universe. Feel their loving energy and support now. You are one with the creative force of the Universe, and it's ready to work with you to create what you desire or something even better.

You slowly begin to come back into your body, back to the here and now, and when you are ready, open your eyes.

SETTING YOUR INTENTION

Once you have clarity around what you want, why you want it, and how it will make you feel—leaving room for the Universe to guide you to something even more amazing—set an intention with yourself and the Universe to ignite the flow of creative energy around it. I recommend writing out a simple statement and inviting the Universe to partner with you. We go deeper into asking the Universe for help and specific tools to utilize its energy in the next chapter. For now, just write out your statement of intention and use the Intention Prayer below to release it into the Universe.

Your intention statement should include your what, why, and the feeling you will have once it's created. For someone looking to attract a new romantic soulmate, it might look like this:

I am now creating a new, unconditionally loving relationship with a partner who shares my interests in movies and travel. We communicate lovingly and listen to and respect one another. I am creating this to have the joy of sharing my life with someone who will support me and love me through all the ups and downs. And having this person in my life makes me feel loved, happy, grateful, and content.

For someone looking to change careers, this might be the intention:

I am now creating a career where I make X amount of money or more each month as an energy healer because it allows me to help others and earn money doing something I truly love. I feel fulfilled, joyful, and grateful every day.

Exercise: The Intention Prayer

Once you have an intention written down, release it to the Universe with the following Intention Prayer:

Dear Universe, I call in my angels, guides, loved ones who have passed on, and all those in my soul society, only those of the highest vibration, to be with me now.

[Say the intention statement here.]

I am asking you and all the higher helpers who can assist with this intention to partner with me and guide me now. Please send me the signs, synchronicities, ideas, opportunities, and resources to move me closer to creating this or something even better. I surrender my highest good and the highest good of all involved to you now, and I also ask for your assistance in helping me recognize and act on the guidance when it arrives.

I am open and ready for your help now, and I am grateful for your partnership in this creation process. Amen.

SURRENDER AND TRUST

After you set your intention and recite your Intention Prayer, it's time to let go, to surrender and trust the Universe is on it. Specifically, you have to let go of the outcome. This is where a lot of people get stuck. I often have students ask me, "How do I want something and focus on it, but let go at the same time?" The answer is in the statement "Help me create this *or something better*." The "something better" is how you surrender and let go of the outcome. In order for the Universe to guide you toward positive changes in your life, you have to leave room for the unexpected, for new ideas, and for twists and turns that lead you to unimaginable and incredible places. There is so much uncertainty in life, and that often leads to fear. But there is one thing you can be certain of: when you ask the Universe for help, and then surrender and trust it's working for your highest good, it always guides you to a better place.

That doesn't mean you do nothing in the meantime. The other three steps in the Higher Help Method, along with all the tools and resources in the second part of this book, help you do your part in this Divine partnership. But it does mean you surrender the outcome to a higher power. When you become laser focused on what you want, you are more likely to block or miss the signs guiding you toward what you truly need, or something that makes you even happier in the long run. Let's say you decide you want to marry a man who is 6' tall, with dark brown hair, who wears a suit to work every day, and is in his thirties. If you are only looking out for this guy, you might not notice the one with the blond crewcut, who is 5'10", owns his own construction business, just turned twenty-nine, and will bring love and happiness into your life. If you only want to work in the corporate offices of Starbucks, you might ignore a headhunter's proposal to interview at Tim Hortons—and maybe that is where you will meet a friend who would introduce you to the love of your life. Missing these signs doesn't necessarily mean the Universe won't reroute you to people if they are truly meant to be in your life, but you will miss key opportunities and clues along the way and could prolong the process.

Consider the example I shared earlier about wanting to grow my business first and then quit my job when I had enough money. If I was only focused on that and not open to other possibilities, I would have ignored the opportunity for me to become a contracted freelancer. That opportunity allowed me to quit my job before my business grew and still have enough money to support myself. Looking back, I know the Universe lined that up for me, and it worked out even better because I was able to quit my job much sooner.

The moral of this story, and this chapter, is you need to get clear on what you want so the Universe starts partnering with you to create it, but you need to let the Universe take the lead because when you do, everything flows more smoothly and easily. In the next chapter, you will discover how to start consciously asking the Universe for help and using its energy to move forward toward positive change, make decisions, and uncover the ideal solutions to handle any problem or challenge life throws at you.

Chapter 2

ASK THE UNIVERSE FOR HELP

EVERY SINGLE SOUL LIVING IN this physical world has unlimited and direct access to the creative energy of the Universe. And every single soul has the ability to consciously tap into it and request its help for anything they face or want to create in life. This energy is within you and around you, and it includes a vast team of specialized higher helpers ready to assist and guide you 24 hours a day, 7 days a week, and 365 days a year. You were never meant to figure anything out or navigate this life on your own. Whether you need to find something you've lost, fix something that's broken, make a critical decision, find a solution to a sudden problem, manifest something you desire into your life, or even manage your mindset, all you need to do is ask for help.

We are all in constant communication with the Universe, but most people are not in *conscious* communication. As I mentioned previously, the majority of what you say to the Universe comes from the sub-conscious mind, and it's causing you trouble. When you allow the subconscious mind to run the show, it broadcasts into the world your negative limiting beliefs, along with your thoughts and emotions filled with worry, doubt, and fear, and hinders your ability to manifest positive change. However, when you become conscious about what you are saying, and deliberately ask the Universe for help, you take back control of the narrative.

This is the missing piece for so many people who have been trying to manifest more happiness, better health, loving relationships, and unlimited abundance but keep bumping into roadblocks and walls. Instead of manifesting alone and relying on only yourself, there are simple spiritual tools to partner with the Universe and allow its infinite wisdom to lead you forward. In this chapter, we explore these tools so that you create a life you love waking up to each day with more ease.

YOUR CURRENT CONVERSATIONS

What have you been saying to the Universe, and what are you saying to it right now? To find the answer to these questions, all you need to do is look at what you've already created in your life. Are you in a job you love or one that just pays the bills? Are you in a loving and fulfilling relationship or are you single and longing for a romantic partner? Are you paying your bills with ease each month or are you in debt and living paycheck to paycheck? Is your body making progress and healing or are your symptoms getting worse?

Your current life right now tells you all you need to know about the conversations you've been having with the Universe, and it also helps you uncover where you most need to shift the narrative. In what areas of your life do you feel stuck? Where are you unhappy? Where do you wish things were different? That is where your subconscious mind has been running wild, and it's time for the conscious mind to step in. Many people feel stuck or unhappy in more than one area of life, and that is actually common. Your mindset, including your thoughts, emotions, and beliefs, affects every aspect of your life, so your unhappiness in one area often spills over and affects others. But the same is true for positive progress. When you start to make positive changes in one area, it's not uncommon for the others to follow. The tools in this chapter, and the second half of the book, help you shift in ways you never thought possible. My advice is to start consciously working with the Universe to change one area at a time—two at the most—so you focus your energy for the greatest impact.

Before you jump into consciously asking the Universe for help and guidance, the following exercise will support you in uncovering what you've been asking the Universe for help to create in the past. It highlights the areas of your life most in need of a shift so you can identify where to start applying the Higher Help Method first.

Exercise: Inventory Your Life

Read through the list of statements for each life area below and answer True or False.

Money and Abundance

1. You earn more money than you spend each month. TRUE FALSE

2. You have money in a savings account that you don't need right now. TRUE FALSE

3. You have no debt or worry around money you owe. TRUE FALSE

4. You feel financially secure now and for your future. TRUE FALSE

5. Money comes to you easily and effortlessly. TRUE FALSE

Health and Healing

1. Your body is healthy and functions perfectly in all areas. TRUE FALSE

2. You eat whatever you desire and digest it with ease. TRUE FALSE

3. Your body is pain free. TRUE FALSE

4. You are a healthy weight and feel good about it. TRUE FALSE

5. Your body is symptom free and does not limit you in any way. TRUE FALSE

Emotional Healing

1. You are happy and content more often than not. TRUE FALSE

2. You are free from anxiety more often than not. TRUE FALSE

3. You easily handle negative circumstances that come your way. TRUE FALSE

4. You quickly rebalance yourself when something throws you off center. TRUE FALSE

5. You are able to easily give love and receive it from others. TRUE FALSE

Relationships

1. You have supportive friends you rely on who bring you joy. TRUE FALSE

2. The majority of your current relationships are harmonious, supportive, and loving. TRUE FALSE

3. You are in a loving, intimate relationship with another person or are happy being single. TRUE FALSE

4. Your current relationships do not trigger, anger, or upset you often. TRUE FALSE

5. You have not recently suffered the loss of a loved one, or the end of a relationship causing you pain. TRUE FALSE

Career and Purpose

1. The work you do each day brings you joy. TRUE FALSE

2. You are happy with your current employment situation (field of work, employer, workload, etc.). TRUE FALSE

3. You feel fulfilled by and passionate about the work you do. TRUE FALSE

4. You feel the work you do is part of your purpose and don't have any desire to change it. TRUE FALSE

5. You would continue to work in the field/job you have even if you didn't get paid for it.   TRUE FALSE

Parenting

1. You are content with the number of children you do or don't have right now.   TRUE FALSE

2. If you have a child or children, you have happy and loving relationships with them.   TRUE FALSE

3. You know exactly how to help your child/children with any issue they are currently facing.   TRUE FALSE

4. You feel confident in your abilities as a parent to nurture, guide, and provide for your child/children.   TRUE FALSE

5. You feel content more often than worried when it comes to your child/children.   TRUE FALSE

Spiritual Connection

1. You trust and know the Universe is always leading you toward your highest good, even when it doesn't look like it.   TRUE FALSE

2. You feel connected to the Universe.   TRUE FALSE

3. You have a strong intuition and are confident in using it.   TRUE FALSE

4. You recognize and receive signs and synchronicities from the Universe and loved ones on the other side.   TRUE FALSE

5. You consistently use spiritual tools and practices to manage your energy and mindset.   TRUE FALSE

In each area, if you answer mostly "True," that means you are currently communicating positively with the Universe in that area. If you answer mostly "False," it indicates an area in which you are asking for more of what you don't want, and you need to make a shift.

HOW TO ASK THE UNIVERSE FOR HELP

Once you have a clearer picture of what you've been saying to the Universe in the past, narrow down the areas most in need of positive change and apply the Higher Help Method. This chapter is dedicated to the second step in the four-step process—consciously asking the Universe for help to create the changes you want to see. There are simple spiritual tools you can use, some on a daily basis and others as needed or desired, to call in higher help and utilize the energy around you to manifest change and find solutions to unexpected problems. These tools are specialized higher helpers, prayer, focused gratitude, crystals, and rituals. When used alone, each engages the energy of the Universe to begin supporting you, but I find that when you use them in combination with one another, it supercharges your results. Let's take a deeper look at each of these tools now.

HIGHER HELPERS

Do you realize how much help you truly have from higher sources? Imagine walking into a room filled with beings of light sitting around a big conference table working together on only one thing—to help you solve problems and move forward toward your highest good in every area of your life. These light beings—archangels, guides, gods, goddesses, ascended masters, saints, and more—see your life from a higher perspective and viewpoint, and can set up opportunities to assist you in creating more joy, happiness, and love in this lifetime. They know which roads you should take and which you should avoid, and will guide you to the perfect people, situations, and resources to help you achieve what you desire or something even more spectacular. If you could walk into a room like this created just for you and your life, would you do it? Or would you continue trying to manifest and solve problems on your own?

It would seem foolish *not* to accept this help, right? You have higher helpers just like this who are standing by and ready to assist right now. And just like the specialized experts you have to assist you in this physical world—the car mechanics, real estate agents, doctors, dentists, lawyers, electricians, and landscapers, all dedicated to helping you fix specific problems, create results, and find solutions in life—you have higher helpers who specialize in certain areas as well. There are higher helpers to assist you with abundance, relationships, health challenges, career, purpose, intuition, mindset, emotional well-being, creativity, confidence, parenting, and more. Instead of struggling, worrying, and stressing about what to do next or what path to choose, it's time to start calling in these beings to guide you. Ask for help as often or as much as you need to—you can't overuse them or abuse the privilege. They are there to help every single soul who asks for it, and that includes you. No task is too big or too small. I call in higher helpers every morning, and the list varies depending on what I'm seeking help with at the time. I don't start my day—or leave home—without them! Higher helpers can also be called on in the moment something pops up: before an event such as a job interview, a meeting at your child's school, or a holiday with relatives who trigger you; or even on behalf of another person in your life who needs assistance.

We all have individual guides working with us in this lifetime who are part of our higher help team, but we also have access to archangels, ascended masters, gods, goddesses, saints, and more, and as I've mentioned, you can call on them no matter what religion or belief system you grew up with or hold today. We are all connected, and we are all one. I grew up Catholic and call on Mother Mary and the saints I learned about when I was younger, but I also call on Hindu gods, Greek goddesses, and ascended masters when I need help in an area they specialize in.

You can also call on any expert you know about who is on the other side—whether you knew them in this lifetime or not. Why? Because we all come from the same Spirit or Source, and we are connected to one another both in this physical world and on the other side. This means if you're struggling with an iPhone, iPad, or Mac computer, call on Steve Jobs for assistance. If you are trying to heal your body, ask for guidance from Louise Hay, a spiritual teacher who healed herself from cancer and taught others to heal themselves. When you need to make a decision on financial investments, call on J. P. Morgan, who founded the bank of the same name. If you are an actor looking to nail an audition, ask Lucille Ball to assist you. A student of mine who was a photographer called on George Eastman, the founder of Eastman Kodak, to help her with a camera issue she had been struggling with for two weeks, and within a couple of hours of asking for his help, she suddenly thought of something that fixed the problem!

Sometimes I choose to work with one or two higher helpers on an issue, and other times I call on a group of them to work together on my behalf. A key part of the Higher Help Method is to stack helpers in a daily prayer, meaning call in everyone who specializes in the area you're struggling with or assists with the change you're trying to create. Many of the helpers featured in this book assist in multiple areas of life, so some of them are repeated in both the lists and prayers found in part 2, along with details on how they help in each area.

For example, Archangel Jophiel is my go-to when I need to shift my mindset and thoughts from negative to positive, and this applies to every area of life. Archangel Raphael is the angel to help with healing, so you will find him in the physical healing and emotional healing chapters, along with the money and abundance chapter for those looking to heal fear around finances. And Archangel Chamuel is the angel to call on when trying to find things, whether it's your lost keys, a new romantic partner, a new job, or your life purpose, but he also helps anyone struggling with anxiety.

Additionally, when you call in these higher helpers to assist, you are not only asking them to guide you, but you are also harnessing their energy to work on your behalf throughout the day, which is why I recommend calling them in during the morning hours through prayer (see below). In doing so, you also set your intention every day with both yourself and the Universe, reminding yourself that your higher help team is on it and working with you every step of the way.

PRAYER

The first way to consciously ask the Universe for help and to call in higher helpers to partner with you is through prayer. Prayer is also a way of setting an intention with both the Universe and yourself. When using the Higher Help Method, I recommend starting each day with a prayer for anything you need guidance on at the time. In doing this, you set yourself up for the day, bring those higher helpers with you, and reinforce your intention to create the positive change you seek. It also reminds you to be on the lookout for the answers being sent your way, which you will learn more about in chapter 4.

Prayer is a powerful, spiritual concept used as part of many belief systems today, and you can say prayers for yourself or for another person. Yes, you can call in higher helpers on behalf of someone else. Even when you feel there is nothing you can personally do to help someone, you can always say a prayer to call in their angels, guides, and higher helper team to assist in the ways you can't—and they don't have to know you are doing it for it to work.

There is scientific evidence to back up the effectiveness of this kind of prayer. A study completed by researchers at Columbia University and published in the September 2001 issue of the *Journal of Reproductive Medicine* demonstrates the power of prayer on behalf of someone else, even when they are not aware it's being done.[1] The study took 199 women undergoing in vitro fertilization (IVF) in Cha Hospital in Korea and divided them into two groups—one that had prayer groups in the United States, Canada, and Australia praying for a successful pregnancy based only on the women's pictures, and another group that did not. The women were unaware the prayers were being said. The results showed that the group who received the prayers had a 50 percent pregnancy success rate compared to only 26 percent for the group without prayer.

As I mentioned in chapter 1, the way I use prayer is to ask the Universe and my higher helpers to show me the best path and guide me to the best solutions. It's always a partnership, and I always let the Universe take the lead. Here is my 5-Step Prayer Formula to call in higher help and ask the Universe to partner with you. Apply it to any situation, whether you need to solve a sudden problem or are actively working to manifest something in your life.

The 5-Step Prayer Formula

Step 1: Call in the Collective Team

I start every prayer by calling in my collective team of higher help, which includes my angels, guides, loved ones on the other side, and anyone in my soul society—those assigned to help me from the other side, whether or not I am aware of who they are or knew them in this life. I also ask for only those of the highest vibration to assist. I recommend starting your prayers this way:

> Dear Universe, I call in my angels, guides, loved ones on the other side, and all those in my soul society, only those of the highest vibration, to be with me now [or "today" if you are saying the prayer in the morning].

Step 2: Explain the Situation

After calling in the collective, take a moment to explain what you're struggling with or looking for guidance around at the time. For example, "I am seeking your help in finding the right doctors, healers, or modalities that will help me with my chronic back pain," or "I am struggling with money and need help creating more and spending less." The same is true if you are calling in help for another person. You could say, "I am asking for you to help X move through her divorce with ease and grace, giving her the strength and knowledge needed to move into the better place I know is waiting for her on the other side of this challenge."

Step 3: Call in Specialized Higher Helpers

The third step is to call in higher helpers who specialize in the area of life or type of struggle occurring. If you don't know which higher helper to call on in the moment, stick with the collective from Step 1, and just add anyone on the other side who specializes in [fill in the blank]. In part 2 of this book, there are extensive lists of helpers in seven main areas of life who can be added into a prayer, such as Archangel Raphael for healing, Hindu Goddess Lakshmi for wealth and prosperity, and spiritual leader and best selling author Thich Nhat Hanh, who passed on in 2022, for help with meditation and mindfulness. When I am focusing on improving an area of my life, I often create a prayer that calls in a large group of higher helpers and ask them to work together with me to find solutions and move forward, so feel free to add in as many as you like and know they are happy to work together on your behalf.

Step 4: Ask for the Guidance and Help Noticing

One of the most important steps in my prayer formula is asking the Universe and your higher helpers to not only send the guidance, but also to help you recognize it and act on it when it comes through. The Universe answers you by dropping new ideas into your conscious mind and sending signs and synchronistic experiences. This step of the prayer formula asks it to start lining up the right people, opportunities, and ideas to guide you, and also asks for help in noticing the guidance when it comes through because you don't want to miss it and prolong your movement forward. It's equally important to act on the guidance when you receive it so you start moving forward and the Universe continues to guide you. This is especially needed when the answers or solutions push you beyond your comfort zone—which is where so much amazing growth lies. You don't want fear and doubt holding you back.

Step 5: End in Gratitude

The very last step is to simply say, "Thank you." Thank the Universe and your higher helpers in advance for the guidance and support you know they will send. This immediately puts you into a higher vibration so you notice the signs that come through. It's as easy as saying, "Thank you, thank you, thank you," or "Thank you in advance for all of the guidance and support I know are coming my way now."

Using the Formula

Several years ago, I had a cat named Phoebe who came into my life only two months after my mother passed away, and the way she arrived was definitely orchestrated by the Universe and probably my mother as well. Phoebe spent seventeen years with me, and she brought me so much joy and love. When she got older, and medical issues started to pop up, I went above and beyond to help her, as so many of us do for our animals. After visiting a homeopathic doctor to help her with some minor issues, I had a liquid remedy I needed to dilute with water and give to her by mouth using a syringe. It looked like water and had no taste or smell, but no matter what I did, I could not get her to take it. She had me chasing her all over the downstairs of the house, from the couch to the kitchen to under the dining room table and back to the couch again. After ten minutes of this, I felt so defeated. All I wanted to do was give her something that would help, and I couldn't figure out how to do it. That's when I remembered my higher helpers!

I stopped and called in the collective, along with Archangel Ariel, who assists with animals, and Saint Francis of Assisi, who is the patron saint of animals in the Catholic faith. I asked them to explain to Phoebe that I was trying to help her and what I was doing wouldn't hurt her. I also asked them to help me get this medicine into her more easily, and to send me ideas and signs that would help. Within a few minutes of saying the prayer—and continuing to chase her around the house—she suddenly walked over to me and just laid down on her side in front of me. I was in total shock, and I knelt down beside her and shot the mixture into the side of her mouth. From then on, giving her the medicine became easier and easier. That is the power of prayer and higher help.

Novenas

One aspect of prayer from my Catholic upbringing that I still use and love is the concept of novenas. The word *novena* is the Latin word for nine and, simply put, a novena is a prayer or set of prayers petitioning the Universe and specialized higher helpers for guidance and support around a specific issue or intention over a nine-day period of time.

Novenas are done similarly to rituals, and the prayers are meant to be said over nine consecutive days, without skipping a day. The number nine has significance in the Bible, including the nine days when Jesus's apostles and Mother Mary prayed for him before his resurrection, but it's also a significant number in numerology, which is often credited to Greek philosopher and mathematician Pythagoras, although some say it goes back thousands of years to ancient civilizations in Egypt, India, Greece, and China. Nine energetically represents completion or endings, as well as new beginnings, since it's the last of the single digits before the next cycle of numbers. It also symbolizes wisdom and experience. I often use the concept of novenas in rituals where I call in higher help, and you will find it used in some of these rituals featured in part 2 of this book.

FOCUSED GRATITUDE

Love and appreciation are the two highest energetic vibrations available to you in this physical world, and when tuned into them, you are in flow and alignment with all the positive energy the Universe has to offer. When you consciously choose to focus your thoughts on gratitude for something either going right in your life at the moment, or for something that has gone well in the past, you instantly shift your energy, boost your vibration, and align with a higher source, so you are more likely to notice the guidance coming through and in this way you consciously ask the Universe to help you create more good things in your life.

Many people on a spiritual path practice daily gratitude by writing in gratitude journals to connect with this energy. Generalized gratitude focused on all areas of life is amazing, and its power is undeniable. Scientific studies continue to be done on the practice of gratitude, showing that people who consciously count their blessings have improved mental health and feel happier overall, highlighting its positive impacts on the brain. I love to use gratitude this way, but when I'm stuck in a certain area of my life and want to create positive change, I find focusing my gratitude in that area to be a powerful tool.

When you are stuck in some area of life, whether it's your health, a relationship, or money, you are usually focused on the problems, the things going wrong, essentially the circumstances you don't want in your life anymore. This focus actually asks the Universe for more problems and more of what you don't want. An amazing tool to counteract this is to focus your gratitude on what is going right in that area of your life so you consciously ask the Universe for help creating what you *do* want instead of what you don't.

The practice of what I call "focused gratitude" does exactly that. Instead of ruminating on how you can't pay your bills or highlighting the unexpected expenses that keep popping up, you look for what you already have to be grateful for in this area. Maybe it's a steady paycheck, the clothes in your closet that took money to buy, or the shelter that is protecting you today. These are symbols of abundance already present in your life. Instead of focusing on all the things your significant other does to trigger you, consciously look for the things they do to make you happy, like folding the laundry, taking the garbage out, or going to work every day to contribute to household expenses. A couple of years ago, my husband and I started a practice of appreciating each other every night before we go to bed. We each name at least three things we are grateful for about the other person either in general or from that day. Without a doubt, this has helped us truly appreciate one another in ways we didn't before starting to practice this focused gratitude exercise. It also trained our brains to look for the good in one another and in the relationship.

In what areas of your life are you longing for positive change? Start focusing your gratitude on one or two of them, and watch the shift in you and the circumstances around you. You will also find focused gratitude exercises for each life area in part 2 of this book.

It is important to note that when I talk about practicing gratitude, and looking for the good or what is going right in your life, that does not mean you should suppress negative emotions, force yourself to be happy, or ignore issues that need to be addressed and healed in your life. Doing that, which has been referred to as "toxic positivity," is actually harmful to your emotional and physical well-being and causes more chaos and issues for you in the future. If you find yourself doing any of these things, I recommend working with an energy therapist or other trained professional to help you process your emotions and thoughts in a healthy way.

CRYSTALS

I've always had a love for and been attracted to crystals and gemstones, even before I knew about the energy they held and could bring into my life. When I was working in New York City, I started buying myself jewelry with a variety of gemstones to match my different outfits. I have my mother to thank for my matching obsession. When she was younger, she always had a handbag and shoes to match every outfit, and she definitely passed this down to me. Jewelry has always made me happy, and I'm still a sucker for anything with a bit of sparkle. But once I began exploring the spiritual and metaphysical world, I discovered that the energy these beautiful gemstones held could have a positive effect on my mood, my physical body, and what I draw into my life. I quickly moved from wearing crystals as jewelry to placing every variety, shape, and size of crystal throughout my home, meditation space, office, and desk.

Every crystal, gemstone, or mineral, most created by nature, holds a unique vibration and can be used as a tool to harness the energy of the Universe to help in different aspects of life. There are crystals to calm stress and anxiety, improve communication, ignite the flow of money, attract a new relationship, and open and balance each chakra. The chakras make up the seven main energy centers in the body, starting at the top of the head with the crown chakra and moving down the body to include the third-eye chakra, throat chakra, heart chakra, solar plexus chakra, sacral chakra, and root chakra at the base of the spine (see figure 1). There are also crystals to facilitate connection with angels and guides, protect your energy, and even clear your energy and aura. They are powerful spiritual tools to assist you in creating change, whether you wear them as jewelry, carry them in a pocket, or place them throughout your home, and you will find lists of crystals to help with seven major areas of life in part 2 of this book.

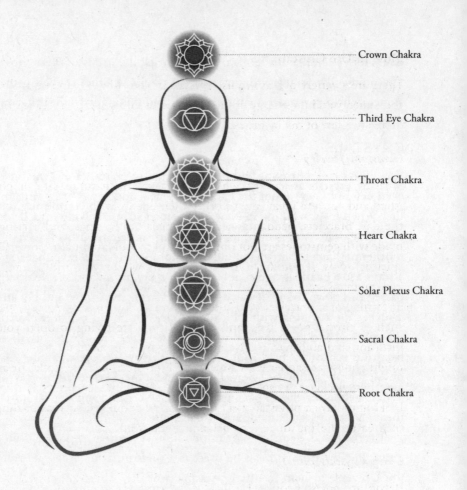

Figure 1. The seven main body chakras.

Additionally, just as higher helpers assist in multiple life areas, many crystals are used in more than one area. For example, clear quartz, which is mentioned in almost every chapter of part 2, is not only a master healer, but is used to amplify the energy of other crystals. As such, I often use it in rituals that involve other crystals to provide an extra boost. Another example is green aventurine, which is a wonderful heart healing stone but is also used to draw in money and abundance.

How to Use Crystals

There are a variety of ways to use crystals in your life to help you utilize their energy and the energy of the Universe to shift yourself and your life. Here are a few of my favorites.

Gemstone Jewelry

Wearing crystals as jewelry, whether in their raw, natural state or polished and cut, is a great way to bring their energy with you throughout the day. Bracelets, pendants, necklaces, mala beads, rings, and earrings made with gemstones are not only beautiful to look at but also powerful spiritual tools. If you are trying to create more abundance in your life, you might wear a pendant or necklace featuring a single stone, such as citrine, or a bracelet containing a group of stones working together, such as citrine, green jade, and pyrite. If you are trying to open your intuition and ability to receive guidance from a higher dimension, you might choose a bracelet with angelite or blue-green kyanite stones or an amethyst necklace. I especially like to wear specific gemstones if I am looking to have a physical effect on my mind and body, such as healing the heart, relieving anxiety, or balancing emotions.

Carry Crystals with You

If you are not someone who likes to wear jewelry, you can evoke the same energy by carrying crystals with you in a pocket or handbag. I especially like placing abundance stones in a wallet to attract more money and prosperity.

Home, Car, Office, or Desk

In Chinese culture, the practice of Feng Shui is a way of harnessing energy forces through the placement and arrangement of furniture, objects, and space in order to create harmony and balance. The practice can be applied to any space, whether it's a home, office, or even the top of a desk at work, and one of the main tools often used in this practice is the Feng Shui Bagua. This is essentially an energy map that originated in China with roots in early Taoism. This map or grid of nine squares (see figure 2) is laid over the floor plan of a home, individual rooms in a home, an office space, or even the top of your desk to see where certain energies fall. For example, when walking in the front door or the door of any room in your home, the far left corner always represents money and abundance, and the far right resonates with love and relationships. And when placed over a desktop, the front door is represented by where you sit. While the practice of Feng Shui offers many principles to balance the energy of a space, including the use of color and the elements of earth, metal, fire, wood, and water, for the purposes of the Higher Help Method, the Bagua is used to identify where to place crystals or perform rituals within a space, combining the energy of the crystals with the energy of the space to target certain areas of your life, such as career, money, family, and love.

For example, to maintain loving energy in my relationship with my husband, I have rose quartz crystals—some in the shape of a heart—in the relationship area of my home, bedroom, and the desk in my home office. For money and abundance, I have a variety of wealth-related crystals strategically placed in the wealth corner of my home, as well as my office, my desk, and my meditation space.

In part 2 of this book, you will find lists of crystals to work with for each life area, and any of them can be programmed and placed in your home, office, or on your desktop based on the Feng Shui Bagua to assist you in creating change and using the energy of the Universe to do it. Instructions on cleansing and programming are coming up.

Use Crystals in Rituals

One of my favorite spiritual tools to ask the Universe for help and apply the energy around me to create change in my life is using a ritual. The rituals I've created, which you find in this book, combine a number of spiritual tools to supercharge intentions and usher in guidance when needed, and crystals are definitely one of those tools.

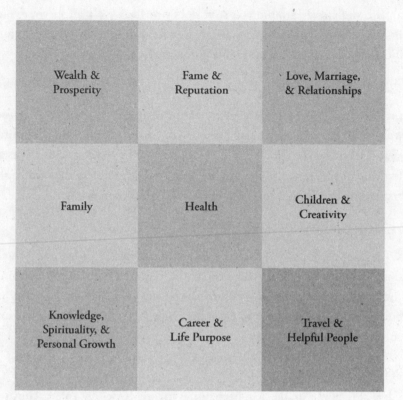

Wealth & Prosperity	Fame & Reputation	Love, Marriage, & Relationships
Family	Health	Children & Creativity
Knowledge, Spirituality, & Personal Growth	Career & Life Purpose	Travel & Helpful People

FRONT DOOR

Figure 2. Feng Shui Bagua Map.

Protecting Energy

In order to create positive change in your life, you must remain as grounded, centered, and clear as possible throughout the day, no matter what you encounter—including the energy of other people and places. Calling in higher help and setting your intentions each day for protection are key, but crystals are another way for sensitive and empathic people to guard themselves against energy and vibrations not beneficial to them. Whether you choose to wear these protective stones or carry them with you, crystals help you stay grounded and, in some cases, absorb the energy around you so it does not negatively affect you, your mindset, mood, or energy. There are a variety of crystals for protection, including one of my favorites, black tourmaline, in chapter 11.

Cleansing Energy

Just as you want to protect your energy throughout the day, you also want to be sure to cleanse it at the end of the day by removing anything that does not belong to you or is not beneficial to you. Crystals are used for this purpose, too, especially kyanite and selenite, as they not only transmute energy, but they also don't hold onto energy.

How to Cleanse Crystals

With the exception of a few crystals, such as selenite or kyanite, which don't hold energy, all crystals need to be cleansed before programming them with an intention to work on your behalf. There are a variety of energy cleansing methods to clear the energy of a crystal, and these are some of the most common.

Smoke Cleansing

Cleansing with smoke has been used for centuries by many cultures worldwide in ceremonies burning a variety of herbs, including sage, sandalwood, and rosemary. In the Catholic faith, frankincense is referred to as a cleansing herb and is one I use as well. There is also a wood called palo santo that comes from trees in Mexico and South America and was historically used by the Incas to cleanse themselves of negative energy. However, if choosing palo santo, be sure to purchase from a company that states the wood is ethically and sustainably sourced. This means it is not cut from live trees but is taken from those already dead and fallen to the ground. When it comes to cleansing crystals, burning these herbs or wood and then passing the crystals through the smoke clears them of any energy they may have taken on before you received or purchased them, as well as anything they absorbed while being worn or used by you in some way.

Essential Oils

Using energy-clearing oils such as sage and frankincense or the oil form of ethically and sustainably sourced palo santo will clear the energy of crystals. Use them in a diffuser and hold the crystals in the mist to clear them. There are also a variety of clearing and energy-cleansing sprays available, featuring a combination of cleansing oils that can be sprayed directly onto the crystals.

Nature

Crystals can be cleansed and recharged in nature by placing them outside at night during a full moon, a new moon, or a rainstorm. However, be careful with placing fragile or porous crystals, such as selenite, pyrite, or black tourmaline, around water.

How to Program Crystals

Once crystals have been cleansed, you can program them to assist you in creating change in any area of your life, amplifying their energy. After choosing a crystal that holds the energy matching the intention you are setting, such as apophyllite to heighten your intuition and open your third-eye and crown chakras, or fire agate to ignite passion in a relationship, program it with an intention by simply holding the crystal in your hands or placing it down on a surface with your hands hovering above it, and then stating out loud:

> I call in the energy of the Universe to clear all unwanted energy and previous programming from this crystal. I command and program it now to [insert your intention].

Every time you cleanse your crystals, whether they were sitting in your home, used in a ritual, or worn on your body, it's beneficial for you to reprogram them with your intention so the energy reactivates to assist you in your life.

Rituals

A ritual is a ceremony consisting of steps or actions done in a certain order and/or for a certain amount of time, and they are often used with the intention of receiving a desired outcome. You might have a morning skincare ritual using your cleanser, serum, and cream in a certain order to keep your skin hydrated and looking young. Maybe you have an evening ritual where you meditate and write in a gratitude journal before bed to calm your mind and body and boost your vibration.

Rituals are also a powerful spiritual tool to help you connect with the energy of the Universe and use it to create the changes you desire in your life. And it's another way to ask the Universe for help and to partner with you. The effectiveness of rituals has even been studied by scientists, and in an article published by *Scientific American* called "Why Rituals Work," which looked at both religious and everyday rituals, the authors stated: ". . . performing rituals with the intention of producing a certain result appears to be sufficient for the result to come true."[2] And that's without adding the benefit of asking the Universe for help with something. Using rituals is a spiritual tool on its own, but the rituals I teach and that you find in this book use a combination of tools for an even more powerful effect. Sometimes a ritual is performed only once, and other times it might be repeated for a certain number of days, or during a specific amount of time. The Higher Help Method uses rituals not only to call in higher help and harness the energy around you but also to set an intention within your conscious mind while simultaneously planting the seed of what you want to create into the Universe so it partners with you to achieve it.

The Energy of Your Home

Everything is energy. Your body, the spaces you inhabit, the items within those spaces, and the people you encounter all resonate at certain energy frequencies and have an effect on you and your life. While you don't have control over the energy everywhere you go, you do have control over the energy of your home. You can also do things to balance that energy and utilize the space to draw in guidance and positive outcomes in your life, and this is where the Feng Shui Bagua mentioned earlier comes into use.

For example, a ritual to create more money and abundance should be performed in the wealth and prosperity section of the home according to the Bagua, and to improve a relationship with a significant other, it should be done in the love, marriage, and relationship section. This is especially true for crystals or crystal grids that are left in the space after a ritual is performed in order to continue harnessing the energy. The Feng Shui Bagua is also used to intentionally program and place crystals in a certain area to draw in help, as explained earlier in this chapter.

These are the main spiritual tools used in the Higher Help Method to ask the Universe for help and to use its energy to manifest the positive changes you desire in life. In the next chapter, we move on to Step 3, which is how to shift your energy so you stay in a higher vibration and be open to receive the guidance and answers the Universe and your higher helpers are sending.

Chapter 3

SHIFT YOUR ENERGY

EVERY DAY, YOUR BRAIN PROCESSES around 60,000 thoughts and 90 percent of them are repetitive, according to research by Dr. Fred Luskin of Stanford University.[1] And because the brain has a negativity bias, you are primed to look for what is going wrong and the negative aspects around you—and also to have a stronger reaction to it—than you are to the positive, according to author and neuropsychologist Rick Hanson.[2] With brains like that, no wonder people wind up stuck and unable to create the positive changes they want to see in their lives! But here is the good news: you can consciously choose to shift your energy, including your thoughts, focus, and emotions, to counteract the negative stream of consciousness often coming from your subconscious mind, which is creating more of what you don't want and blocking the guidance leading you toward what you do want. Living in this physical world, it's impossible to avoid negative thoughts, especially since your brain is literally hardwired that way. But the more you consciously shift your energy to the positive, the more you rewire your brain and shift the circumstances in your life along with it.

Stress, worry, doubt, and fear never lead you to what you desire. These and other negative emotions block you from it and from the solutions and guidance being sent to you from the Universe and your higher help team. However, consciously shifting your energy to feel calmer, happier, and centered boosts your vibration and opens your awareness so you act on the answers when they arrive. The Universe is constantly opening doors and presenting opportunities, but if you are living in a state of chaos in your mind and fear in your heart, you won't notice them.

Solutions to problems are hardly ever found in the midst of stress when you are focused on the problem, desperately trying to figure out what to do. Solutions are found in the shift. As a human being, it's normal to overthink, replay scenarios in your head, rack your brain trying to find answers, and obsess about how things keep going wrong. But all this does is make you feel stressed, frustrated, and overwhelmed, and cuts you off from the answers you so desperately want. As soon as you start feeling these negative emotions, it's your signal to stop and shift your energy. I know it might sound counterintuitive to stop trying to solve your problems, but that is exactly what I want you to do. You have to stop trying to figure it out by yourself, let go, and let the Universe bring you the solution.

Once you ask the Universe for help in Step 2, covered in the last chapter, your job is to shift your energy on a regular basis so you stay in alignment with the answers coming in, and you don't block yourself from the positive changes you desire. You ask the Universe for help, and then you let go. It's not your job to figure it all out or worry about it until you do. It's your job to ask for help and follow the signs that come to you. If you are feeling anything other than good, it's time to stop and shift.

The prayer that follows not only helps shift your energy when you notice your thoughts and emotions going down a negative path, but it also calls in higher help to assist you in doing it. Any time I find myself focusing on what is wrong, becoming easily irritated, worrying about the future, or feeling anything other than good, I call on Archangel Jophiel, the angel of beauty, and I ask her to help me shift my mindset. As soon as you recognize your thoughts and mood going downhill, stop what you're doing and say this quick prayer. In all the years I've been doing this, it's never failed to help me shift into a positive space.

Exercise: The Mindset Shift Prayer

Use this prayer to call in higher help and shift your mindset and energy any time you feel stressed, worried, overwhelmed, or find your mind primarily running negative thoughts.

> Dear Universe, I call in my angels, guides, loved ones who have passed on, and all those in my soul society, only those of the highest vibration, to be with me now. I'm struggling with my mindset and negative thoughts and need help shifting them quickly. I specifically call in Archangel Jophiel to help me shift my thoughts from negative to positive so I may see the good and beauty around me rather than focus on what is going wrong or what I am worried about in the future. Also, I ask you to please help me hold these positive thoughts in my mind now. Thank you, thank you, thank you. Amen.

TWO TYPES OF WORRY

Believe it or not, sometimes worry is a good thing. There are two categories worry falls into—one is productive and the other is destructive. Unfortunately, the majority of our worry falls into the destructive category. Productive worry guides you to productive actions that end the worry, and it also lets go when you can't change something. Let's say you are getting ready to leave for a trip, and your mind starts worrying you might have forgotten to pack something. You immediately check and realize you forgot your laptop charger, so you pack it and then you let the worry go. Or maybe you are worried about a test you need to take, so the productive action would be to study and then let the worry go. In both of those scenarios, the thoughts of worry led you to an immediate action that you took to remedy the situation. And in both scenarios, after the action is taken, the worry stops.

Worry that leads to action is productive and usually doesn't last long. It serves its purpose and then it's done. Destructive worry, on the other hand, is the total opposite. This is when you worry about the future, or about solving a problem, but there is no immediate action to take to solve or control anything. With no action to take, the worry just cycles around in your mind. When you continue to worry about a huge snowstorm hitting your town, but you already filled up the gas tank of your car, stocked up on food at the grocery store, and have a snow blower ready to go, you are engaging in destructive worry. When you are worried about a test result from a doctor but have no control over when they are going to call you, yet you continue to worry and work yourself up, you are engaging in destructive worry.

The easiest way to tell which type of worry you are having is to ask yourself, "Is there an immediate action I can take to help this situation?" If the answer is no, it's time to let go. An action you can always take is asking the Universe for help through prayer, focused gratitude, and other tools found in this book. But once you do, it's time to surrender and trust that the Universe and your higher helpers are on it. All you have to do is be on the lookout for the answers and guidance, and take action on what comes.

Here are three exercises you can use to stop the cycle of destructive worry and shift your energy back into alignment with the positive energy and guidance from the Universe.

Exercise: Surrender Your Worries Meditation

Choose one of your higher helpers to work with you for this meditation. They will take your worries from you and bring them to your higher help team who will assist in finding the solutions you need and creating the best outcomes possible. Choose anyone you resonate with, including loved ones on the other side or anyone from the lists in part 2 of this book. For this exercise, I always choose Mother Mary because I find she offers a comforting energy, and I know she will call in other higher helpers to come to my aid no matter what I am struggling with at the moment. You could also choose the Italian saint known as Padre Pio, who is the patron saint of stress relief, as he is known to assist with letting go of stress, anxiety, and worry.

Close your eyes. Breathe in through your nose slowly for the count of four, and then breathe out through your mouth slowly for the count of six. Repeat this three times.

Imagine that standing in front of you is the higher helper you chose to work with today, and notice how they are surrounded in an aura of sparkling light. Keeping your eyes closed, imagine there is a glowing green light that begins to shine within your chest, specifically in your heart chakra. Watch as it grows larger and then begins to stream outward, leaving your body in a beam of green light. This stream of energy is going to help you release the fears and worries you are holding inside right now, and surrender them to the higher helper in front of you.

Take a deep breath in through your nose, release it out through your mouth, and repeat the following either out loud or silently to yourself:

I am now releasing all thoughts of worry and fear about my life
as it is now, and all the thoughts of worry and fear about what
might be happening to me or coming into my life in the future.
    I release my current worry around my relationships,
specifically [fill in the blank], or I release my current worry and
fear about my career and purpose, specifically [fill in the blank]."

Taking another deep breath in through your nose, and letting it out through your mouth, continue to watch as the energy of your worry and fear continue to leave your body through the beam of green light coming from your heart chakra.

"I release my current worry and fear about my health, specifically
[fill in the blank], or I release my current worry and fear about
my finances and money, specifically [fill in the blank], or I
release my current worry and fear about [insert anything else
you might be worried about now]."

Continue until you have released all the worries you have at the moment. Now, as you watch your higher helper in your mind's eye, accepting all your worries and fears and transforming them into love and peace, state the following:

> "I surrender these worries to you so I no longer need to carry them with me. I ask for you to take them to my higher help team to be resolved for my highest good and the highest good of all involved. Please send me the signs and synchronicities that will guide me to the best solutions, and please help me to recognize them and act on them when they arrive. Thank you, thank you, thank you."

Breathing in through the nose and out through the mouth, take another minute or so to release any extra fear or worry still left in your heart chakra through that green light. When you are done, you will see the green light begin to dissipate until it's completely gone. Notice how you feel physically and mentally lighter. You feel more hopeful. You know your team is working on all your worries and problems now, and you no longer need to stress about anything at all. You know the solutions are coming. And you know you can return to this exercise any time the thoughts of worry and fear return.

Exercise: Release That Thought

As soon as you find your thoughts drifting to the negative, you need to shift them as fast as you can so they don't spiral out of control and drag your energy down with them. However, because you are often completely unaware of your thoughts or what you are saying to yourself at any given time, it is difficult to interrupt and stop them. Something you are more likely to pay attention to are your feelings. How you are feeling in any given moment is often the best clue you have that something is awry with your thoughts.

If you find yourself feeling irritated, stressed, anxious, frustrated, overwhelmed, or anything less than good and happy, it's highly likely the thoughts in your mind are feeding those emotions. Also, any time you find yourself stuck in a cycle of destructive worry, where your thoughts are running wild with negativity, that is also a signal that a shift is needed. As soon as you notice the negative emotions or the thoughts of worry, this exercise can help. Here is how it works:

Step 1: Notice the Thought

If you notice yourself feeling stressed, anxious, depressed, or any other negative emotion, or you realize your thoughts are focused on worry, stop and take note of the thoughts you are having in the moment.

Step 2: Release. Release. Release.

Close your eyes and say to yourself out loud or silently in your head: "Release. Release. Release."

Step 3: Breathe It Out

Keeping your eyes closed, take a deep breath in through your nose, and as you let it out through your mouth, imagine you are breathing out the thoughts of worry and the negative emotions so they completely leave your mind and body. Watch as the energy of them falls into the Earth to be transformed to love and peace.

Step 4: Affirm the Shift

Repeat this affirmation three times: "All is well. I am safe. I can relax and let go because the Universe is on it, and the answers are on the way."

Exercise: 60-Second Retreat

Can you actually shift your energy and tame the chaos in your mind in only 60 seconds? The answer is yes, and you can do it any time and any place. The 60-Second Retreat offers you a break from everyday life, the demands it brings, and the swirling negative thoughts infiltrating your mind. It calms everything down and provides an instant shift. On those days when you can't seem to escape your mind or keep your energy positive, set an alarm on your phone to go off every hour to do this. Do it as often as needed; it literally only takes one minute.

Step 1: Breathe

Close your eyes and take a deep breath in and out through your nose, dropping your shoulders down on the out breath and relaxing your body.

Step 2: Repeat a Mantra

For 60 seconds, repeat any mantra, which is a word, phrase, or sound often used to aid in concentration during meditation that makes you feel good. For example, repeat "Release," as you release the stress from your body, or "All is well. I am safe," to reassure yourself.

Step 3: Breathe

Take another deep breath in and out of your nose, and then open your eyes.

SHIFT WITH EFT

One of my go-to energy-clearing techniques when I need to shift my mind and energy back into a positive and centered state is Emotional Freedom Technique (EFT), also called tapping. Introduced to the public in 1995 with the book *The EFT Manual* by Gary Craig, a Stanford engineering graduate, EFT is based on the Chinese meridian system of the human body often used in acupuncture. Meridians are pathways where energy flows in the body, and by tapping on certain parts of the body with your fingertips (see figure 3), you stimulate those meridians and affect the flow of energy, especially stuck energy. Tapping on these points moves the stuck energy out of your mind and body and brings you back into balance. Use EFT to reduce physical pain, release negative emotions, and transform negative limiting beliefs to more positive and empowering ones.

No matter what you use EFT for, the formula for doing it is always the same. It starts with three setup statements, while tapping on the karate-chop point of one hand with the fingertips of the other hand. Then you continue tapping through all the meridian points, speaking negative statements about a situation and then moving to positive statements. In the end, you can even alternate between the negative and positive, but always end on positive. In addition to the typical

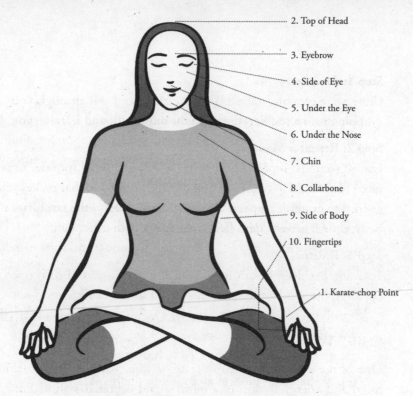

2. Top of Head

3. Eyebrow

4. Side of Eye

5. Under the Eye

6. Under the Nose

7. Chin

8. Collarbone

9. Side of Body

10. Fingertips

1. Karate-chop Point

Figure 3. EFT tapping points.

tapping points, I also include the fingertip points—which is the right-hand corner of each fingernail on either hand.

Tapping dramatically shifts your energy and your mindset. It allows you to release energy stuck or being stored in the body, improves your mood, and rewires your thought patterns or beliefs. Even just five minutes of tapping helps you shift into a better energy space.

Exercise: Restore Peace Tapping Script

Use the following tapping script to release worry, fear, or any other negative thoughts and emotions and to shift your energy back into flow with the Universe and the signs and answers being sent to you. This script is customizable and leaves space for you to fill in specific details around what you are thinking and feeling at the moment. The more specific you are to your situation, the better.

The Setup Statements

Tapping on the karate-chop point: Even though I am feeling stressed, worried, and overwhelmed, and I keep thinking about [fill in the blank], and it's dragging my energy down, I am ready and willing to release this energy now.

Even though I am stuck in a negative thought loop, and I am feeling frustrated and [fill in the blank with other emotions], I am ready and willing to let this energy go now and shift myself to a higher vibration.

Even though I am worried about [fill in the blank], and I am fearful because of the uncertainty I feel, I deeply and completely love and accept myself anyway, and I am ready to release this energy and anything connected to it or triggering it now.

Top of the head: I'm feeling so [fill in the blank].

Eyebrow: I'm really worried about [fill in the blank].

Side of the eye: I'm worried about what's going to happen.

Under the eye: I'm worried I'm not going to find a solution.

Under the nose: I just want an answer now.

Chin: I just want to know what is going to happen now.

Collarbone: I just want to know everything is going to be OK.

Under the arm: I can't take the uncertainty of not knowing what's going to happen.

Thumb: I feel like I can't trust it's actually going to be OK.

Pointer finger: What if it doesn't work out?

Middle finger: What if it doesn't get better?

Ring finger: All these negative thoughts about [fill in the blank] like [fill in the blank].

Little finger: They are causing me to feel [fill in the blank with any negative emotions].

Top of the head: I don't want to feel this way.

Eyebrow: I want to feel good. I want to feel secure and happy and hopeful.

Side of the eye: I want things to change for the better.

Under the eye: I'm just so worried about [fill in the blank].

Under the nose: I want to feel peaceful and calm.

Chin: I want my mind and body to feel at ease and relaxed.

Collarbone: I want to trust it's all going to be OK.

Under the arm: But I'm just not there right now. I'm just too stressed out and overwhelmed.

Thumb: I want to shift this energy.

Pointer finger: Maybe I can choose to let it go.

Middle finger: I want to let it go.

Ring finger: I want to feel good.

Little finger: I want to feel at peace.

Top of the head: I'm ready to release these feelings of stress, worry, and being overwhelmed.

Eyebrow: I'm ready to release [fill in the blank with any negative emotions].

Side of the eye: I'm ready to reconnect with peace.

Under the eye: I'm ready to trust the Universe is working for me on this issue right now.

Under the nose: I know when I ask for help, it always comes.

Chin: It's safe for me to relax and just let the Universe provide me with the answers.

Collarbone: It's safe for me to relax and look for the good around me while I wait for it.

Under the arm: Worrying about [fill in the blank] is not helping me now.

Thumb: I now release any energy or emotions triggering these thoughts of worry.

Pointer finger: I can choose to install peace instead.

Middle finger: I am choosing to install peace now.

Ring finger: Installing peace into my mind and body.

Little finger: Installing the energy and emotions of relaxed, hopeful, peaceful, and loved.

Top of the head: What if this peace doesn't last?

Eyebrow: I know I have spiritual tools to help shift my energy any time I need to, and I'm shifting my energy into a positive space right now.

Side of the eye: I'm still a little worried about [fill in the blank].

Under the eye: But I choose to release this energy of worry now.

Under the nose: I feel like I have no control over these emotions, and that my mind is ruling me.

Chin: But I can choose to relax and take back control.

Collarbone: But what if [fill in the blank] happens/doesn't happen?

Under the arm: I know the Universe is leading me to my highest good right now, but I'm still worried.

Thumb: I choose to relax and let go anyway.

Pointer finger: Letting go of my worry and fear, and anything triggering me right now and causing me to feel unsafe.

Middle finger: I am safe now and always, no matter what.

Ring finger: The Universe has my back and is my unlimited partner.

Little finger: Release, release, release. All is well. I am safe.

Top of the head: I choose peace.

Eyebrow: I choose happiness.

Side of the eye: I choose to shift my energy into the vibration of love.

Under the eye: Installing love into my mind and body now.

Under the nose: I'm letting go of any negative energy, thoughts, or emotions dragging me down now.

Chin: I choose to shift my energy and focus on what is going right in my life right now.

Collarbone: Right now, I am grateful for [fill in the blank].

Under the arm: I am so thankful for [fill in the blank].

Thumb: I choose to tune into that energy.

Pointer finger: I'm already feeling calmer and safer.

Middle finger: I give my body and mind permission to let go and relax now.

Ring finger: I relax and let go.

Little finger: I am peaceful, relaxed, and free.

BELIEFS AS BLOCKS

We all have a variety of energetic blocks in the mind and body that hinder progress toward positive change. There are unprocessed traumas or experiences, unprocessed emotions, and negative energy patterns that keep people stuck. But some of the biggest energetic blocks are negative limiting beliefs. I specify negative because all beliefs are limiting, but if you have a positive limiting belief, such as you deserve to be loved, it's working for you and not against you. Ever since I was a child, I had teachers telling me I was a great writer. I knew it came easily to me, I enjoyed it, and with the positive feedback I formed the belief that I was really good at writing. That belief led me to pursue a college degree in English Writing, land a job at a magazine before I even graduated, and eventually write books to help people on their spiritual paths. It's an amazing belief that I'm definitely keeping. Negative beliefs, on the other hand, limit you in the same way positive beliefs do, but not in a good way. If you have the belief "I'm too old to get a new job," or "I don't deserve to make more money than I need," you hinder your ability to find a new job, and any time you make extra money, some unexpected expense pops up to take it away.

Within your brain there is something called the Reticular Activating System (RAS), which essentially acts as a filter between the subconscious and the conscious mind. Its job is to function as a matchmaker, surveying the outside world looking for evidence that matches the beliefs in your subconscious mind. It only allows the things that match and reinforce your beliefs to flow into your conscious awareness. If you have a belief that you are too old to find another job, your conscious mind will tune into the conversation at the gym in which someone is complaining about how they keep losing job opportunities to younger applicants, but you won't notice the friend on Facebook who is actually older than you announce they just landed the job of their dreams. This essentially keeps you stuck because the RAS reinforces the negative beliefs with proof from outside yourself and ignores anything that would go against them.

When you have a positive limiting belief, your RAS is your best friend because it keeps bringing into your awareness scenarios to bolster that belief. But when you are dealing with a negative belief—even though the RAS is simply doing the job it's designed to do—it blocks you from making positive progress. The good news is you can uncover and change your beliefs, and then reprogram them so your RAS helps create what you want instead of what you don't.

FINDING BELIEFS

Changing your beliefs shifts your energy and opens you up to new possibilities that otherwise would not make it into your awareness. But how do you know what your beliefs are if they are primarily in the subconscious mind? You consciously look for them. The easiest way to do this is through a written rant. You simply pick an area of your life where you feel stuck or where you want to manifest something you have not been able to. Then you sit down with a pen and paper and start writing. Pretend you are complaining to a friend about all the reasons why this thing hasn't happened yet. One of the following prompts can get you started:

I have not achieved/I don't have X yet because . . .

I would love to have X, but . . .

Then you explain all the reasons to this imaginary friend why you can't or have not manifested the changes you desire, and let it all spill out. Keep going until you have no more reasons left. Once you're done, read through what you wrote and pull out each individual reason you gave because each one represents a possible belief. In some cases, it may not be a belief that is blocking you, and in other cases it is something that needs to be shifted. To find out, use muscle testing, also called applied kinesiology, which works with the mind/body connection and uses the body to tap into the subconscious mind. One of the easiest ways to do this on your own is the Standing Method, which is the next exercise. Muscle testing can also be done by using a pendulum if you are familiar with how to get "yes" and "no" answers with one, or by using any other self-muscle-testing method you know how to perform.

Exercise: The Standing Method

This simple muscle-testing method uses your physical body to get answers from your subconscious mind. Start by learning how your body answers "yes" or "no." To determine this, stand up straight with your feet hip distance apart and your weight equally balanced on the heel and ball of each foot. Place your arms by your side, and if you feel comfortable, close your eyes.

Now say out loud, "Show me my yes," and see which way your body sways. Usually it goes forward for yes; it may just be a gentle movement where you feel your weight slightly shift. Alternatively, say a true statement out loud to get your yes, such as, "My name is [fill in the blank]." Once you do this a few times and get clear on your yes, do the same thing for no. Say out loud, "Show me my no," and see which way your body sways. For many people, no is a lean backward. Also, say a false statement to determine your no, such as "I live in Wyoming," if you live in Hawaii.

Once you've established your yes and no, start testing the beliefs. Simply state the belief out loud, such as "I'm too old to find a new job," and see what answer your body gives. If the answer is yes, that means your body resonates with that belief—and if it's a negative belief, you know it's one you need to shift. If you get a no, then that is not a belief you hold, so go on to test the next one until you test all that you have written down.

Once you know how to test beliefs to see if they are true for you or not, another way to uncover them is to go down a list of common belief patterns that show up in any life area, whether it's money, relationships, or health. These include:

- You don't deserve it.
- You will be unsafe if you do or have something.
- You are not willing to do it.
- You can't or are not able to do it.
- You don't believe it's possible.

Applying each of the above to your situation, test them one by one with the Standing Method. For example, if you have a block around money, test the belief by saying, "I don't deserve to make more money," then "Money isn't safe," or "It's not safe to have money." Then move to the next one and state, "I'm not willing to make more money." Continue down the list above, and any that come up as yes, you know you need to shift to a more positive belief.

TECHNIQUES TO EXPLORE FOR REPROGRAMMING BELIEFS

Once you've determined the beliefs you need to change, you want to clear and reprogram them so they no longer have a negative impact on your life and your ability to manifest positive change. For each negative belief, you must uncover the new, more empowering belief to install in its place. This is usually the exact opposite of the negative belief. If you believe something is not possible, you want to shift it to believe it is possible and even easy. If you believe you don't deserve something, you want to shift it to believe that you do. If you believe something isn't safe, you want to install that you are perfectly safe no matter what.

There are a few energy-clearing techniques I use for beliefs, whether I'm working on reprogramming them for myself, students, clients, or friends. Here are some options to explore in case you have interest in learning additional techniques. I recommend muscle testing them for each belief to see which option will help you clear it the fastest. For example, you would start with the first method listed below, Emotional Freedom Technique (EFT), and state, "The best method for me to use to clear the belief [fill in the blank] is EFT." If you get a yes, then use EFT. If you get a no, then continue down the list using the same statement and inserting the next method until you get a yes response.

Emotional Freedom Technique (EFT)

You can use the "Restore Peace Tapping Script" as an example of how to use EFT and the tapping points. You always start with three setup statements, then tap using statements in the negative based on the belief, and then switch to the positive. The setup statements for any belief would start with something like, "Even though I have this belief that [fill in the blank], I am ready and willing to release and change this now."

The Sweep

Another energy-clearing and belief-shifting technique is The Sweep by Amy B. Scher, author of the *How to Heal Yourself When No One Else Can* series of books. This is a script where you fill in the blanks using the old belief in the beginning of the script and the new belief at the end. Use muscle testing to determine the number of times to repeat the script for each belief. This script is also found on her YouTube channel.

The Sedona Method

This "letting go technique," created by Lester Levenson and made popular with coauthor Hale Dwoskin, is used to clear and release beliefs and emotions. Demonstrations of this technique are on The Sedona Method's YouTube channel.

Ho'oponopono

Based on a traditional Hawaiian practice, this clearing method is used on beliefs, memories, and emotions. It uses four main phrases for clearing: "I'm sorry," "Please forgive me," "Thank you," and "I love you." There are many books on the topic, including *Zero Limits,* coauthored by law of attraction teacher Joe Vitale and Dr. Ihaleakala Hew Len, a clinical psychologist who used this method at a hospital in Hawaii to cure patients suffering from mental health challenges. One of my favorite books on this method is *Ho'oponopono Secrets* by Paul Jackson.

Now that you've learned the importance of shifting your energy so you stay in alignment with the positive energy of the Universe and notice the answers being sent from it and your higher help team, in the next chapter, we explore the final step in the Higher Help Method. That step is receiving and acting on the guidance directing you forward toward more joy, love, health, and happiness. It doesn't always come in the exact way you might expect, or on your timeline, but it always comes.

Chapter 4

RECEIVING AND ACTING ON GUIDANCE

WHEN YOU CONSCIOUSLY ASK THE Universe for help to create something in your life, or find a solution, your higher help team of angels, guides, loved ones who have passed on, and any specific higher helpers you call on to assist will immediately get to work. They begin lining up the right people, opportunities, chance meetings, conversations for you to overhear, and ideas to drop into your mind—all with the goal of sending answers to guide you toward what you seek. And they use signs and synchronicities to grab your attention and point you in the right direction. The previous chapter focused on shifting and managing your energy to help you open up to this guidance, and the last step in the Higher Help Method is to actually receive it and act on it when it arrives. Both receiving and taking action are equally important, and that's why part of the 5-Step Prayer Formula shared in chapter 2 not only asks the Universe to send the signs, synchronicities, opportunities, people, resources, and more, but also asks for help to notice and act on them when they arrive. When you do both of these things, you keep the dialogue open so the Universe and your higher helpers continue to direct you.

In this chapter we explore the common ways the Universe sends answers so you recognize them when they show up, and why any action you take is better than none at all.

HOW THE UNIVERSE RESPONDS

The Universe, your higher helpers, and your loved ones who have passed on are always around and ready to assist. Any time you ask for help, they respond with guidance and support, leading you toward the perfect answers and solutions you need to create what you desire or something better. The more familiar you become with the ways they do this, the easier it is to recognize the help when it arrives. Here are the most common ways the Universe and your higher helpers reply to your requests.

New Opportunities

From their higher vantage point, the Universe and your higher helpers see all the moving pieces in the puzzle board of your life, as well as the lives of anyone you come in contact with in the future. As a result, they know how to line up those pieces to create the perfect fit, which appear as opportunities for you. And when you ask for help, these opportunities often seem to suddenly and magically appear before you.

Here is how this might play out: You make the decision to look for a new job because you are unhappy with your current employer. You start calling in your higher helpers through prayer every morning, doing focused gratitude around your current job situation, and you perform a ritual around career. Three weeks later, you get a phone call from a friend that a new job opened up at the company she works for, and it seems like a perfect fit for you. She personally hands your resume to her boss, and you get an interview and land the job.

A year ago, my sister Gina was working as a substitute teacher at a local high school and wanted to find a way to make more money each month. She decided to use the Higher Help Method and began saying a prayer every morning to call in higher helpers who specialized in money and abundance. She also incorporated focused gratitude into her day and did the two rituals found in chapter 5. Two weeks later, a long-term substitute position lasting three months opened up at her school, and they offered her the position. It paid a lot more money, and she would have guaranteed income for months. Then this temporary position ended up lasting for the full year. On top of that, she attended a football game at the school shortly after she started the Method and won $300 in the 50/50 raffle.

Other People

Just as the Universe and your higher helpers work to line up the perfect opportunities to help you, they do the same thing with other people around you. Whether it's a conversation overheard at a restaurant, waiting in line for movie tickets, or through a direct conversation with someone, the Universe arranges situations to bring you and another person together to assist you or provide an answer you need to move forward. Chance encounters are not really by chance.

For example, let's say you have been dealing with stress and anxiety lately, and asked the Universe for help in creating more peace and calm. A couple weeks later, you are at the grocery store for the second time that week because you forgot to get eggs on your last trip. While standing in the checkout line, you overhear two women talking about how much their stress levels improved after taking a meditation class. You ask them about it and realize it's only fifteen minutes from where you live. You sign up and get so much from the class that you end up training to become a meditation teacher. That is not chance or coincidence. There is a reason you forgot the eggs on your first trip, went back to the store at the exact time as those two women, and ended up in the checkout line with them. That is the Universe using other people to get you an answer.

Another example: You decide to call in higher help to heal a chronic illness, and a couple of weeks later you find yourself seated next to someone you don't know at a friend's birthday dinner. You strike up a conversation, and this person tells you about a new healing modality that, when you try it, provides a big improvement in your symptoms. The people the Universe places in your path often don't realize the role they play to help you, but the Universe knows. And once you get the message, you will, too.

New Ideas/Thoughts

One of the most magical ways the Universe and your higher helpers guide you is by energetically placing thoughts and ideas into your mind, or directing your attention to something you might not normally notice. Sometimes these thoughts and ideas are the exact answer you need, and sometimes they're a clue that leads you to the next step on your journey toward what you desire. We often give ourselves credit for these brilliant ideas, but I find the Universe and our higher helpers are usually behind them—especially when we've asked for help.

Before my husband and I bought our current house, we were living in a townhouse and the hot-water heater started leaking gas. We had someone fix it, but when they left, the heat for the house wouldn't turn on. My husband was at work, so I called him on FaceTime to see if he could figure out the issue. Nothing we tried worked, and both of us were frustrated and upset because we just had something fixed and now it seemed like something else was broken. He said he would have to check it when he got home from work, and when I hung up the call, I immediately said a prayer asking for help because I didn't want this to become another big issue, or for him to spend the whole night trying to fix it. About ten minutes later, my husband called back and said to me, "Check the breaker to make sure it didn't trip and cut off the power when they installed the new hot water heater." I checked it, and sure enough, that was it. I flipped the switch and the heat turned back on. I told him I had said a prayer for help, and he laughed because he had done the same thing. Shortly after we both asked for help, checking the breaker popped into his mind and it fixed the problem.

This happens all the time in my life. I ask for help with something—especially a solution to something I can't solve on my own—and it just seems to drop into my mind. And it's usually when I'm doing something else other than trying to figure it out because when we let go and shift our energy, the Universe has room to get through. It's the trying and stressing energy that blocks the answers.

The Language of Signs and Synchronicity

In addition to dropping answers into your mind, another way the Universe alerts or directs you to an answer, opportunity, person, book, doctor, or other resource is by using signs and synchronicities. A sign is usually a single occurrence meant to grab your attention. It could be to wake you up to something that will help or to provide reassurance that you are on the right path.

One of my students shared a story with me illustrating exactly how the Universe used a sign to give her an answer and reassure her at the same time. She had consulted with several doctors for a procedure she needed to have, and although she narrowed her search down to two, she couldn't decide which doctor to choose. She asked the Universe for help and to send her a sign, and shortly after asking, it arrived from an unlikely source. While she was getting a haircut, the hair stylist suddenly mentioned going to one of the two doctors recently. My student had not mentioned anything related to it, but it came up in conversation and she couldn't believe it. The hair stylist raved about the doctor, and my student knew it was the Universe and her higher helpers using this woman to deliver her a sign to guide her in the right direction.

The Universe also uses synchronicity to guide you forward step-by-step. Synchronicity always shows up as two or more events or circumstances meaningfully related to each other. The events don't have to be simultaneous in time—they can happen in the same day, week, month, or even years apart—but when you look back, you can connect the dots relating them to one another.

Let's say you want to attract a new romantic partner, and you ask the Universe for help to draw them into your life. Two months later, a friend calls out of the blue and invites you to a Halloween party, and at the party you meet a woman who works at the same company you do, but in a different department. You realize you have a lot in common and agree to meet up for lunch the following week. At lunch you share how you are single but looking to meet the man of your dreams, and she tells you she has a brother she would love to set you up with and shows you his picture. You end up going out on a date with him, and a year later, you marry him. The Universe used the invitation to the Halloween party to connect you with the woman who works in your building, so she could connect you with your future husband. That is the Universe using synchronicity to move you forward—often without you even realizing it. I find that with synchronicity, it's when you look back at how you ended up somewhere that the magical alignment of events is revealed.

Pay Attention to Repetition

The Universe is always trying to get your attention to help you notice the signs being sent to guide you, and one of the ways it does this is through repetition. Our lives are busy, our world is chaotic, and distractions exist all around us. Because of this, you might not notice or act on the first sign that comes to you. But when it's something important, the Universe keeps bringing it up until you do. It might be a specific book you keep hearing about from different sources or a type of healing treatment like acupuncture or sound healing. It could be a specific supplement, a type of doctor, or anything else that will provide you with a solution, but the Universe will continue to put it in front of you until you get it.

A couple years ago, I was teaching an online class in the month of December and was guiding students through various exercises to help them get clear on what they wanted to create in the new year. As I was guiding them through a specific meditation to ask their higher selves for advice on what they needed to do differently to create the changes they desired, I found myself getting answers, too. When it came to improving health, the answer I got was to start exercising again. I've had a Pilates machine for more than fifteen years, and although it's in my basement and easily accessible, I hadn't used it in a long time. I made a note of it during the class but didn't do anything about it.

A week or so later, I was on the phone with my sister, who said she was on her way to a Pilates class. I knew she belonged to a gym, so I assumed she was taking a class there, and thought to myself, "I really need to start exercising again." Shortly after that, I came across a woman on TikTok who often filmed her routine of waking up at 4:00 am to go running. She got up before her family woke up for the day, and I started following her because I admired her determination and commitment. She literally made me want to exercise, too! But I still didn't start exercising again. Then my sister mentioned Pilates again, and I finally asked her where she was going. I found out she had joined a new Pilates studio near her that was actually a chain with locations all over the United States. I looked into it and found a location only ten minutes from my home. It was then, finally, after all the hints the Universe had been sending, that I decided to join so I could have more motivation to actually exercise. And now I'm using my home machine again, too.

Even though I got the answer dropped in my mind when I asked about improving my health, the Universe had to keep bringing the theme of exercising into my consciousness through various ways—and people—until I acted on it and got the message. Any time you see something repeating in your life, it's a clue to pay attention because it's likely an answer or something that will eventually lead you to an answer.

BRANDING MY BUSINESS

A perfect example of how asking the Universe for help works faster and easier than trying to create change or find an answer by yourself—and one that illustrates how the guidance comes through in a variety of ways—happened to me two years ago when I needed help with my business. I was struggling to rebrand myself based on how my teachings had evolved over the years. I wanted to create a cohesive brand and marketing strategy to clearly explain what I taught and how. Although I had tried several times in the past to rebrand on my own, none of the ideas really captured the work I was putting out into the world.

I felt frustrated, stuck, and overwhelmed, and I knew I needed to stop trying to figure it out myself. I created a prayer for myself using my 5-Step Prayer Formula and called in my collective team, along with specialized higher helpers, asking them to guide me to the right answer, opportunity, or idea. I started saying the prayer every morning and practicing focused gratitude around my business. I had already been working to shift my energy throughout the day on a regular basis, even starting my day with breathwork and meditation, so I knew I had that part covered. Within one week—yes, it only took one week—the guidance started flowing in. First, I noticed an email in my inbox from someone I had been following for years, but whose emails I had not actually opened in a very long time. On this day, however, something in the subject line caught my attention, and I opened it.

I read the email, which was about her course on copywriting, and though I didn't purchase the course, I decided to follow her on Instagram, thinking she might be helpful to me in the future. A few days after following her, I noticed one of her Instagram stories mentioned how she was working with an expert to rebrand her business, and she tagged the expert in the post. That was exactly what I had asked the Universe for help with—rebranding! I immediately recognized this as guidance and started following the branding expert on Instagram. Shortly afterward, I booked a discovery call with her, and during the call I found out she had previously worked for a spiritual publishing company and was very familiar with my market. It all lined up so perfectly, quickly, and almost effortlessly. This woman was my answer, and the Universe led me straight to her by directing my attention, dropping in ideas, setting up synchronicities, and using signs. I hired her and she became instrumental to rebranding my business and setting it up for the future.

That's how the Universe directs you when you ask for help. It makes you take notice of an email from someone you usually ignore. It gives you the idea to follow the person on Instagram because it knows (even though you don't) that she will tag the exact person in her story who can help you. And it makes sure you see that story within the twenty-four hours before it expires on Instagram. Now, I could look at these events and think, "What a coincidence!" But because I know how the Universe speaks, and I know "coincidence" is actually guidance, I received these messages and took action on them. I booked a discovery call based on the guidance, and the Universe provided me with another sign—this time of reassurance—when I discovered that the woman knew my market because she had worked for a spiritual publisher.

That is how your Divine partnership with the Universe works. You ask for the help and the Universe guides you. You receive the messages, act on them, and the dialogue continues as you move forward easier and faster than you ever would on your own.

YOUR TIMING VS. DIVINE TIMING

Time and space only exist in the physical world. On the other side and in higher dimensions—which is where your soul came from and where it will return when it leaves your current physical body someday—there is no time or space. Everything happens in a Divine timelessness, and what you see as taking three months or three years is instantaneous there. Of course, knowing that doesn't help when you're waiting for things to change in your life, and nothing seems to be happening. You want to rub a lamp and have a genie pop out who blinks and grants your wishes immediately, but the Universe doesn't work that way. Although calling in higher help speeds up the process compared to solving problems and creating positive change without it, it doesn't always happen as quickly as you might prefer.

You need to let go of your timing and surrender to Divine timing. Why? Because when you ask for help, the Universe needs a beat or two to set things up in the physical world. It needs to connect you with the right people, put you in the right place, line up the perfect opportunities, and set up seamless scenarios that unfold at the exact right time. Those are a lot of moving parts to organize, and when other people are involved, and they often are, their timing and lives come into play too. You might ask the Universe for help finding a new job, and it could take six months for the person who has your dream job to leave so you can take their place. When I was at an event years ago, I heard Michael Bernard Beckwith, bestselling author and founder and CEO of the Agape International Spiritual Center, say, "A delay is not a denial." I remember writing it down, and I remind myself of that every time I feel like progress isn't happening fast enough. When we ask the Universe for help and change doesn't happen as fast as we would like to see it, it doesn't mean it's not going to happen. It's often just a delay in Divine timing.

Nearly nine years ago, I asked the Universe for help finding love. It had been years since I dated anyone, and at thirty-seven, I thought it was probably time to start looking. This was before I created the Higher Help Method, but I was using and creating spiritual tools that would eventually become part of it, and for help with finding love, I performed a ritual on the back porch of my home on the night of a new moon in February. You will actually find an updated version of the ritual I used, Attract New Love, in chapter 8. It took eight months to meet my husband, and that is because when I performed the ritual, he was still married to someone else. But eight months later, he was free to fall in love again. Divine timing isn't always your timing—but it's always the perfect timing.

Exercise: A Sign of Reassurance

The Universe sends you signs to direct you forward, but it also sends signs to provide reassurance when you are on the right path. And it always sends you signs when you ask for them. When Divine timing seems to be taking too long, and you start to worry the Universe isn't listening or helping—or even worse, you start to think the changes and solutions will never come—ask for a sign of reassurance from the Universe. This will allow you to relax and trust that when the time is right, the perfect solution or opportunity will appear—and also to release the fear and worry that blocks the solutions from coming.

For this exercise, you are going to assign a sign to the Universe and your collective higher help team, and ask them to send it to reassure you that all is well and the answers you seek are on the way. Choose any sign you would like, and also ask the Universe to help you notice it at some point over the next three days.

Step 1: Pick a Sign

What sign would you like the Universe and your higher help team to send to reassure you? It could be a type of flower, a number sequence, an animal, a song on the radio, or an object, such as a purple balloon or a white feather. Decide on a single sign you want them to use, and then move on to Step 2.

Step 2: Assign the Sign

You are going to call in your collective team of higher helpers, give them the sign you would like them to use, and ask for their help in recognizing it. Use the following prayer to do this:

> Dear Universe, I call in my angels, guides, loved ones who have passed on, and all those in my soul society, only those of the highest vibration, to be with me now. I know I've called on you for help with [fill in the blank], but I'm starting to drift into worry and doubt, and it would be helpful to me and my mindset if you could send me a sign of reassurance that you are working on my behalf, and that I should keep going because the answers and guidance are on the way.
>
> I would like you to please use the sign of [fill in the blank] within the next three days, and help me remain open so I recognize the sign when it arrives. Thank you so much for your continued support and guidance and for providing this sign of reassurance for me now. Amen.

Step 3: Stay Open and Aware

Once you assign the sign, it's your job to shift and manage your energy so you stay open to receiving it. It's also important to be open to the sign coming in unexpected ways. For example, if you give your higher help team the sign of a rose, that rose doesn't have to show up as an actual flower. You might sit down at a restaurant and notice a rose on the front of the menu or walk into a restroom that has roses on its wallpaper.

During a podcast interview, I shared how to assign a sign. The woman interviewing me picked a red balloon in the sky. I told her to be open because it might not come through as an actual red balloon floating in the sky when she looked up. For instance, she might be watching a movie or a television show and see it on the screen. A week later, she emailed me and said she was flipping through old photos and was shocked when she saw a photo of a red balloon in the sky. Keep your mind open to all possibilities.

Also, if three days pass and you haven't seen the sign, I want you to ask again. It's likely the sign came and you missed it. Don't give up, thinking the Universe didn't reply. It always replies. Just ask again.

UNEXPECTED ANSWERS

Not only is the timing of the Universe often different from what you desire, but there are also circumstances where the answers you receive are unexpected or in some cases the exact opposite of what you asked for help in creating. For example, you might ask for help to increase money and abundance in your life, and shortly after you lose your job. At first, you might be frustrated or even angry because you asked for help increasing money and now it seems like the Universe took it away from you instead. But what you don't know is two months later you will land a job that makes you happier than the one you had and pays you more money. Not only that, but if you were still at the old job, you would never have looked for or pursued it. Whenever you get an unexpected answer or one that looks like the opposite of what you are trying to create, you might automatically think the Universe is not listening or that you are doing something wrong. But I assure you, the Universe always has a plan. Often while that plan plays out, you have no idea what it is, and it might not make any sense, but nothing gets worse unless it's leading you to something better.

This exact scenario played out in my life when I asked for help with my health and it got worse instead of better. I've suffered with allergies since I was an infant. I was unable to digest dairy and had to be switched to a soy-based formula, and by five years old, I developed a constant cough that would wake me up in the middle of the night as I gasped for air. I spent my childhood taking allergy medication and sleeping with a humidifier in my room because I tested allergic to dust and mold. By the time I entered high school, I had chronic sinus pressure that would often lead to sinus infections. I'd seen general practitioners, allergists, ear, nose, and throat (ENT) doctors, and more, but nobody had an answer for me. At age thirty, I started getting monthly migraines and randomly breaking out with hives on my chest. By thirty-six, I had reached a breaking point and decided it was time to call in higher help. A friend gave me a very detailed novena for Saint Jude, the patron saint of hopeless cases. It included multiple prayers and hymns and the whole thing took ten minutes to complete each day. As I was waiting for the answers to come in, within a week my health started to get worse. Instead of just hives on my chest, I was getting rashes down my arms and stomach, and my entire digestion tanked. I couldn't eat anything without stomach issues, and it seemed to just keep getting worse. I called my friend and asked what kind of wacky prayer she gave me because this was not the help I was looking for, and it obviously wasn't working.

But it was working. It just took a while for the Universe to guide me to the answer, and my health getting worse is actually what led me straight to it. Shortly after starting the prayer, I began eating cultured foods such as kefir, sauerkraut, and kombucha. Because of my allergies, I thought I needed to put more good bacteria into my gut, and cultured foods do that. That's when my rashes started getting worse. I did some online research about cultured foods and realized they were fermented and very high in histamines. I also noticed that after eating tomato sauce, I would break out in a rash, and I discovered that was another food high in histamines. Further research led me to something called histamine intolerance, which led me to a woman online who spoke about low-histamine diets. I reached out to the woman, and although she was based in the United Kingdom, she recommended an allergist in New York state who specialized in histamine intolerance and a condition related to it called mast cell activation disorder—something at the time not many doctors knew existed. I immediately made an appointment, and sure enough, I was diagnosed with mast cell activation disorder.

She immediately put me on a low-histamine diet, and all of the symptoms I had been accumulating for years calmed down.

At first glance, it seemed like my prayers for help were being ignored. But if I had never tried those cultured foods—an idea that came to me suddenly—and made the connection to the rashes and histamines, I would never have reached out to the woman who connected me with a doctor who finally diagnosed me after more than thirty-five years. I asked the Universe for help, and it lined up signs and synchronicities to get me to an answer. Was it an easy, straightforward journey? No, it was not. But it was the best thing that ever happened to my health.

When you ask for help, you need to trust that it's coming—even when everything seems like random chaos or things temporarily get worse. These are the times to remind yourself that the Universe is always working for your highest good—especially when you ask it to partner with you and provide guidance. And these are the times to ask for a sign of reassurance to keep you going. You will eventually land in a better place and look back in awe of the miraculous way the Universe works. You will also have more faith the next time unexpected answers arrive, because you saw the proof in your own life that the Universe and your higher helpers don't make mistakes.

ACTING ON THE GUIDANCE

In a tennis, volleyball, or ping-pong match, two people are needed to keep the game going. One person serves, the other responds by hitting the ball back to the sender, and the game continues until someone misses the ball. Partnering with the Universe and allowing it to guide you works the same way. It's an endless volley of back and forth, of sending and receiving messages, until you reach your goal—unless someone drops the ball. The Universe never drops the ball or misses a hit, but if you don't take action on the guidance being sent, the game ends before it even gets started.

Asking the Universe for help is the first action step that starts the conversation. You've served the ball, and the dialogue between you and your higher help team begins. The Universe always responds when you ask and replies to you through new ideas, signs, and synchronicities. Once you notice the messages, it's your turn to respond back to the Universe, and you do this by taking action. Action helps you move forward toward what you desire, or something better, which sends a message back to the Universe that you're ready for the next step. The game continues with your higher help team sending another sign or synchronistic experience, and plays out until you reach your goal or hit your target.

Without action, you can't move forward or make progress. You simply remain stagnant and stuck, wondering why nothing is changing. The Universe can't continue to guide you if you don't take the steps that will get you there. It could be buying a book, doing research, talking to an expert, booking an appointment, joining a membership, or making a phone call, but you have to act on the guidance to keep the conversation going and keep yourself moving forward.

When I was looking to rebrand my business, if I hadn't booked the discovery call with the expert I found through all the synchronicities sent to guide me, I might still be stuck wondering how to brand myself and my work. The Universe might have continued to send me signs pointing me to the same person, but it's up to me to act on it. When I did, the Universe sent another sign to reassure me—the woman had experience in the spiritual market.

One of the biggest things that stops people from taking action is fear of doing the wrong thing or making the wrong choice. What if I quit my job and the next job is even worse? What if I start my own business and it fails or I end up bankrupt? What if I get into a relationship with the wrong person and end up hurt? The uncertainty of the future coupled with the fear of something even worse waiting for them around the corner stops people in their tracks and essentially keeps them frozen where they are—which might initially feel safer than jumping into the unknown, but the unknown is where manifestation unfolds.

If you are someone who worries about taking the wrong action, it's important to understand that there are no "wrong" actions. The Universe is always guiding and directing you, and more importantly, it's always redirecting you if you happen to make a left instead of a right. Just like the GPS in your car does, the Universe continues to reroute you until you head in the right direction toward more happiness, joy, love, and ease in all areas of your life. If you happen to take an action that isn't the best one, it puts up a roadblock so you turn around. Let's say you need to choose between two naturopathic doctors to help you on your healing journey, and you decide to go with Dr. A instead of Dr. B. If you are truly meant to go to Dr. B, when you call Dr. A, you either have a bad experience with the staff that turns you off, or you aren't able to get an appointment for two months. Then you call Dr. B and discover he can get you in right away, and has a very helpful and kind receptionist.

This actually happened with my rebranding journey. Even though I received all the signs that pointed to the expert I eventually hired, I initially had the idea to reach out to someone else. A friend recommended a marketing expert, and I sent an email explaining how I got her contact information to see if she might be able to help. She had a staff member reply simply pointing me to a link to book a $400 appointment. That was a big enough roadblock for me. The woman I ended up hiring got back to me personally and offered a free thirty-minute discovery call, and the rest is history.

No matter what action you take, by taking it you are moving forward toward your goal and keeping the dialogue open with the Universe so it continues to guide you. Even wrong actions eventually lead to the right ones. But no action leads you nowhere, and you are likely to stay exactly where you are—stuck and unhappy.

Now that you understand the four steps involved in the Higher Help Method, it's time to put it to work in your life. In part 2, you will discover customized tools to ask the Universe for help broken down by seven different areas of life. Using these tools, you will create a routine to partner with the Universe and allow it to guide you, and it will take less than ten minutes each day.

Part 2

THE SPIRITUAL TOOLKIT

WELCOME TO YOUR NEW SPIRITUAL toolkit! This section of the book is broken into seven chapters filled with spiritual tools specifically designed for each life area, including lists of higher helpers and crystals, specific prayers, customized rituals, and focused gratitude exercises. Before you jump into the tools, here is a reminder summary of the Higher Help Method, followed by recommendations and tips for how to work with each of the spiritual tools.

AN OVERVIEW OF THE FOUR STEPS OF THE HIGHER HELP METHOD

When you make use of the Higher Help Method, you are applying the following steps, tools, and practices:

Step 1: Find Clarity and Intention

- Use the clarity formula to get clear on what you would like to create.
  - What don't I like?
  - What do I want instead?

- Set your intention to manifest what you desire or something better.
- Surrender and trust.

Step 2: Ask the Universe for Help

Consciously call on the Universe to partner with you.

- Call on your higher helpers.
- Make use of crystals.
- Learn to use prayer (5-Step Prayer Formula).
  - Step 1: Call in the collective team.
  - Step 2: Explain the situation.
  - Step 3: Call in specialized higher helpers.
  - Step 4: Ask for the guidance and help noticing.
  - Step 5: End in gratitude.

- Perform rituals.
- Incorporate focused gratitude into your day.

Step 3: Shift Your Energy

Shift and elevate your energy. Become aware of your own energy throughout the day, and use the exercises found in chapter 3 (and listed below) to actively shift your energy when it starts to dip into negativity. Doing this helps you maintain a higher vibration so you recognize the guidance being sent to you, release any resistance blocking it from coming through, and stay in alignment with the Universe and what you desire.

- The Mindset Shift Prayer
- Surrender Your Worries Meditation
- Release That Thought
- 60-Second Retreat
- Restore Peace Tapping Script
- Reprogramming Beliefs

Step 4: Receiving and Acting on Guidance

Recognize the guidance sent to you from the Universe and your higher help team and then act on it when it arrives. Here is a reminder of how the Universe guides us, as detailed in chapter 4:

- New Opportunities
- Other People
- New Ideas/Thoughts
- The Language of Signs and Synchronicity
- Pay Attention to Repetition

SPIRITUAL TOOLS TO ASK THE UNIVERSE FOR HELP

Here is an overview of the tools you will use to ask the Universe for help in each life area detailed in the following chapters.

Higher Helpers

In each chapter of part 2 there are lists of higher helpers who specialize in issues within that life area, and you can also add in any not listed here, including your own family members on the other side. Choose one or more to work with depending on your needs and you can also create your own customized prayer using my 5-Step Prayer Formula from chapter 2 on page 42. I recommend working with them daily through prayer to call them in and remind your conscious mind to look out for signs and answers.

Crystals

Each chapter offers a list of crystals to help in the life area covered. Choose one or more to work with that resonate with you depending on what you are looking to change. To work with crystals, be sure to cleanse and program them with your intention (see chapter 2, page 52), and then either wear them as jewelry, or carry them in a pocket or handbag, to draw in beneficial energy. Additionally, place them in the area of the home matching their life area (see the Feng Shui Bagua in chapter 2, page 51) to draw in energy from the Universe.

Prayers

There are customized prayers in every chapter of this section for the most common issues in each life area. Feel free to combine them if you are working on more than one issue, add higher helpers to customize them, or create your own prayer. You can also omit any higher helpers who don't resonate with you. I recommend repeating a chosen or created prayer every morning until you begin to see progress.

Rituals

I've included specific rituals in each chapter that combine a variety of the tools mentioned here to supercharge your intentions and harness positive energy. Feel free to do more than one in the area of life you are working to change, and customize the crystals and prayers to meet your needs.

Focused Gratitude Exercises

There are focused gratitude exercises in every chapter, and I recommend choosing one or more to do daily.

SAMPLE DAILY SCHEDULE

Here is a sample daily schedule to incorporate all of the tools together in only minutes each day. Remember as you follow this schedule to refer back to Step 1 of the Higher Help Method, which is clarity and intention, prior to diving into the tools in this section of the book or any time you switch your focus to a new life area. You may also perform a ritual or place crystals around the home or office space at any time you wish.

Morning

- Recite prayer to call in higher helpers.
- Set alarm for any gratitude exercises.
- Do your first focused gratitude exercise.
- Put on any crystal jewelry you want to wear, or put crystals in your pocket or handbag, after cleansing and programming them to harness the energy for the life area you are working on.
- Shift your energy as needed by using the exercises in chapter 3.

Afternoon

- Do your focused gratitude if repeating more than once or twice a day.
- Shift your energy as needed by using the exercises in chapter 3.

Evening

- Do your focused gratitude, if repeating more than once or twice a day.
- Cleanse your energy.
- Place any crystal jewelry or loose crystals you carried that need to be cleansed on a selenite or black kyanite wand or selenite charging plate.
- Shift your energy as needed by using the exercises in chapter 3.

Chapter 5

MONEY AND ABUNDANCE

THERE ARE SO MANY MISCONCEPTIONS and false beliefs around money and abundance that people have unknowingly taken on, and they block more of it from flowing into their lives. My guess is you have at least one—especially if you feel stuck around money and abundance. Despite what you may have heard or believe, money is not the root of all evil. Having money does not make people bad or good. You don't have to have money to make money. It is not unspiritual to want or have money, and most of all, it's not greedy or selfish to ask the Universe for help creating more of it in your life. Money is neutral. It's simply energy, and when you use it to buy something, or earn it for work you've done, it's an exchange of that energy.

And here is the best part: even though it might not feel like it right now, there is an endless supply of money available to each and every one of us because there is an endless supply of energy. Whether you need to pay off debt, stop overspending, save more money, earn more money, or create some fast cash, all you need to do is ask the Universe for help to create more of it. In this chapter, you will find spiritual tools dedicated to helping you do that.

HIGHER HELPERS FOR MONEY AND ABUNDANCE

These higher helpers can be called on to create money and abundance, save the money you have, and shift your mindset around it.

Andrew Carnegie

A leader in the expansion of the steel industry, Andrew Carnegie became one of the richest Americans in history. Call on him for help as an entrepreneur, for guidance in business decisions, and for ideas to create more money and abundance. He also assists in keeping thoughts aligned with prosperity and success and directs you to helpful resources.

Archangel Chamuel

Often referred to as the angel of peaceful relationships, Archangel Chamuel also helps you find peace within yourself. Call on him to calm anxiety and fear regarding money.

Archangel Haniel

Known as the archangel of joy and Divine communication, Archangel Haniel opens your awareness to notice signs and synchronicities the Universe is sending, and assists with the creation of new beginnings and positive change. She also helps you stay centered no matter what is going on around you.

Archangel Hope

This female archangel helps manifest desires into physical form and keeps you in the vibration of hope that what you are trying to create—or something even better—is on its way. Call on Archangel Hope for anything creative, as she helps give birth to new ideas.

Archangel Jophiel

The archangel of beauty, Archangel Jophiel helps you see the beauty in all things, even struggle. Call on her to assist in quickly shifting your mindset from negative to positive and to help hold more positive thoughts around money and finances.

Archangel Michael

This is the archangel to call on for any type of protection and also to alleviate fear. When it comes to money and abundance, Archangel Michael will protect your energy and dispel any fears connected to it.

Bob Proctor

Bestselling author of *You Were Born Rich* and teacher on manifestation, Bob Proctor shifts your mindset so more wealth can flow in, as well as the creation of new ideas to create more success.

Charles F. Haanel

New Thought teacher, successful businessman, and author of *The Master Key System* (published in 1912), Charles F. Haanel taught on a variety of metaphysical subjects, including the law of attraction, the power of the mind, and achieving success and prosperity. He helps with manifestation, maintaining a positive mindset, abundance, and success.

Dr. Wayne Dyer

A spiritual teacher and speaker who taught others to align with the energy of the Universe and manifest desires. Call on Dr. Wayne Dyer to stay in alignment with this energy. He also sends ideas and resources to help.

Ernest Holmes

Author of the bestselling book, *The Science of Mind* (published in 1926), Ernest Holmes taught how to cocreate your life using the "Universal Mind," or universal consciousness, along with your own thoughts, and how to stay focused on the positive aspects of situations. He helps you direct thoughts in this way around money and abundance and sends ideas and resources to help.

Florence Scovel Shinn

An American artist and metaphysical teacher, Florence Scovel Shinn wrote a number of books on prosperity and success, including *The Game of Life and How to Play It* and *Your Word Is Your Wand*. Call on her for help with money and abundance, success, and shifting your mindset to the positive, as she taught the use of affirmations for the mind.

Ganesha

Ganesha is the Hindu god known as the remover of obstacles. Call on Ganesha to remove any obstacles around money and abundance— known or unknown—that are preventing you from creating more of it in your life, as well as saving it once created.

Geneviève Behrend

A New Thought and mental science teacher, Geneviève Behrend authored a number of books, including *Your Invisible Power* and *Attaining Your Heart's Desire*. She lectured about the power of the mind and the use of visualization for success, and founded New Thought schools in New York and Los Angeles. She helps in shifting your mindset and energy to stay in alignment with what you want to create.

Goddess Abundantia

This Roman goddess's name means "overflowing riches," and Goddess Abundantia is a goddess of prosperity, success, abundance, and good fortune. She provides guidance and assistance around financial investments and savings, as well as creating more prosperity.

Goddess Fortuna

Fortuna is a Roman goddess of chance, luck, abundance, and fate, and she lines up ideal opportunities, chance meetings, and synchronicities to lead you to more prosperity and abundance.

Goddess Kali

Call on this Hindu goddess when you are stuck in the negative energies of fear and attachment, are afraid to move out of your comfort zone to step into the unknown, or are afraid to stand in your own strength and power. Goddess Kali also assists with releasing what is no longer serving you, including addictions or unhealthy habits connected to money. Additionally, she offers guidance and strength to spend less, especially since spending money has an addictive quality to it.

Goddess Lakshmi

The Hindu goddess of prosperity, wealth, fortune, and power, Goddess Lakshmi assists with acquiring money and wealth and also helps preserve and save what is already acquired. She symbolizes good luck, and you can call on her for any financial worries that arise in life.

Holy Amethyst

Holy Amethyst, the twin flame to Archangel Zadkiel and an archangel herself, is one of the keepers of the violet flame, which can transmute energy from negative to positive. Call on her if you are struggling with a compulsion or addiction to spending money, and she will transmute and clear energy that is keeping you stuck in this cycle.

John Pierpont (J. P.) Morgan

An American financier and investment banker, J. P. Morgan was the head of the banking firm of the same name. Call on him when making financial investment or savings decisions and when trying to grow money already earned.

Napoleon Hill

Bestselling author of the book *Think and Grow Rich* (published in 1937), Napoleon Hill was taught by Andrew Carnegie and spent years interviewing successful businessmen to create universal laws of success. You can ask him to help shift your mindset around money to create more.

Neville Goddard

New Thought teacher and author of *Feeling Is the Secret,* Neville Goddard taught about the law of attraction, specifically how to create physical reality using the mind through visualization or imagining, combined with feeling or emotion. He assists in gaining control over negative thoughts and provides direction on resources to help.

Saint Anthony of Padua

Known in the Catholic faith as the patron saint of finding lost items, Saint Anthony of Padua was also known for advocating on behalf of debtors during his life by lobbying the Council of Padua in Italy to pass a law in favor of those who could not pay off debts. Call on him for assistance with debt.

Saint Expedite

As the Catholic patron saint of urgent matters, Saint Expedite assists in emergency situations that need a quick response, whether financial distress, job hunting, or legal matters. Known for the quick delivery of money, Saint Expedite can be called upon for urgent help around finances, income, business, and even health.

Saint Matthew

The Catholic patron saint of finances, bankers, tax collectors, and accountants, Saint Matthew was a tax collector himself, and intercedes on your behalf to assist with any issues concerning financial hardships or debt.

W. Clement Stone

Mentor to bestselling author and law-of-attraction teacher Jack Canfield (known for *Chicken Soup for the Soul*), W. Clement Stone built a very successful insurance company and taught others about manifestation. Not only can you call on him for assistance when creating a business, but also to help you earn more money in your career.

CRYSTALS TO ATTRACT MONEY AND ABUNDANCE

There are specific crystals and gemstones to work with when trying to create more money in your life, and in the following list you will find those to help increase funds, pay off debts, or hold onto the money you earn.

Amazonite

This stone of success and abundance helps you navigate financial and business goals. Amazonite helps provide focus and clarity to make better decisions around money and curb impulse purchases.

Bloodstone

This green jasper stone, with dots of iron oxide creating red splotches throughout it, helps retain money earned. You can place bloodstone in the cash register of a business or carry it in a pocket, wallet, or handbag.

Citrine

Often referred to as the abundance stone, citrine aligns your energy with prosperity and financial success, and is a powerful manifestation stone to bring financial goals into reality.

Clear Quartz

This master healer stone is universal and clear quartz amplifies any intention it is programmed with. It also amplifies the energy of any stone it is placed near or on.

Garnet

For those looking to overcome poverty, financial struggles, or debt in life, garnet assists in freeing you from financial burden and also attracts more wealth.

Green Aventurine

Known as the stone of opportunity, the energy of green aventurine brings good luck, opening you up to new opportunities to find and create wealth.

Green Jade

Considered a lucky stone, green jade ignites the flow of prosperity and has been used throughout Chinese culture and history to attract wealth and harmony. Associated with the heart chakra, it also helps you remain calm and assists in thinking clearly during financial hardships.

Iolite

This gemstone assists in both abundance and freedom from debt. Iolite helps eliminate debt and also helps you manage money better in the future. It also produces a steady flow of money and leads you to the perfect opportunities.

Pyrite

Often referred to as "fool's gold" because of its color and appearance, pyrite is associated with money and good luck and helps summon the energy of wealth and abundance.

Yellow (or Honey) Calcite

Yellow (or honey) calcite increases prosperity, abundance, and positive blessings by removing old, limiting beliefs and energy patterns that prevent them from streaming into your life.

PRAYERS FOR MONEY AND ABUNDANCE

When calling in higher help around money and abundance, I've included prayers for six areas most people struggle with around this topic, including earning more, spending less, saving, and clearing any fear around finances.

Prayer: Ignite the Flow of Money

Dear Universe, I call in my angels, guides, loved ones who have passed on, and all those in my soul society, only those of the highest vibration, to be with me now. I am open, ready, and willing to allow the flow of more money and abundance into my life, and I am asking for your assistance in doing this now.

I call in Goddess Abundantia and Goddess Lakshmi to help me create more prosperity and abundance in all areas of my life with ease and grace. Please work with Goddess Fortuna to line up ideal opportunities, chance meetings, and synchronicities to lead me to the perfect people, resources, and ideas to help me now. I also ask Archangel Haniel for assistance in opening me up to notice the signs and synchronicities showing up in my life, pointing me in the direction of creating and attracting more prosperity.

Archangel Hope and Archangel Jophiel, please help me keep my mindset, thoughts, and emotions positive around money and abundance, and guide me toward new ideas that will lead me in the right direction. I also call on all those authors and experts who taught on the topics of manifesting, positive thought, and abundance, who are now on the other side, including Andrew Carnegie, Bob Proctor, Charles F. Haanel, Dr. Wayne Dyer, Ernest Holmes, Florence Scovel Shinn, Geneviève Behrend, Napoleon Hill, Neville Goddard, and W. Clement Stone. I ask for your help to keep me and my mindset in alignment with the flow of abundance and send me any resources and tools to help me do this.

Lastly, I call in Ganesha to remove any obstacles, known or unknown to me now, that are standing in the way of my creating more money and abundance right now.

Thank you for all the help you provide me now and in the future. Amen.

Prayer: Curb My Spending

Dear Universe, I call in my angels, guides, loved ones who have passed on, and all those in my soul society, only those of the highest vibration, to be with me now.

I am asking for guidance and assistance with my intention to spend less money in my life. I'm also asking for help in clearing any energy patterns or beliefs that are keeping me stuck in a pattern of overspending.

I call in Archangel Haniel to help me create this positive change in my life and assist me in staying centered no matter what is going on around me or triggering me. I also call in Archangel Jophiel to please help me shift my mindset from negative to positive around money so I save rather than spend and also to help me maintain these positive thoughts.

Goddess Kali and Holy Amethyst, I call on your joint assistance to help me release any addictive qualities around or contributing to my spending habits, and Holy Amethyst, please transmute any negative energy keeping me stuck in a cycle of overspending so I may move forward and begin to save more money.

I ask that all my angels and guides please assist me with this and send me any signs, synchronicities, resources, people, and opportunities to help me accomplish this, and please help me recognize and act on them when they arrive.

Finally, I call in Ganesha to remove any obstacles, known or unknown to me, standing in the way of my shifting my mindset around money and spending so I may spend less and save more now.

Thank you, thank you, thank you. Amen.

Prayer: Grow My Savings

Dear Universe, I call in my angels, guides, loved ones who have passed on, and all those in my soul society, only those of the highest vibration, to be with me now as I am seeking help with my goal of not only creating more money, but also saving more of the money I create. I am asking for guidance in helping me save this money, choose the right options to save, and multiply it, and to spend less where needed to accomplish this goal.

Archangel Haniel, guide me forward to easily make this positive change in my life, and please work with Goddess Fortuna to illuminate the path toward uncovering more money to save each month. Archangel Hope, I ask for your assistance in opening me up to new creative ideas to both create and save more money, and I ask Goddess Lakshmi to assist me with this, as well.

Goddess Abundantia and J. P. Morgan, I ask for your guidance around any financial investments and ways for me to save and grow my money, and please bring into my consciousness the most beneficial ideas, people, and opportunities to do this now.

Finally, I call in Goddess Kali to help me emotionally let go of fear and attachment, as well as anything holding me back from saving money now, and Ganesha to remove any other obstacles, known or unknown by me, standing in my way now.

I ask for you to send me the signs, synchronicities, ideas, people, opportunities, and resources to guide me forward now, and please help me recognize and act on them when they arrive.

Thank you in advance for your guidance and assistance with this matter. Amen.

Prayer: Accelerated Money Alignment

Dear Universe, I call in my angels, guides, loved ones who have passed on, and all those in my soul society, only those of the highest vibration, to be with me now, as I ask for help in creating money quickly for [explain the situation here].

I specifically call on Goddess Lakshmi to help me acquire more money and alleviate my worry around finances, as well as Saint Expedite, to answer my plea quickly and intercede on my behalf with other higher helpers while also sending any Earth angels my way who can assist me in this matter now.

Goddess Fortuna, I ask for your help to line up the opportunities, people, and situations that bring in money quickly and in unexpected ways, and Archangel Haniel, please help me recognize the signs and synchronicities that are leading me toward this when they arrive. I also call on Archangel Jophiel to help me shift my mindset, specifically to shift me from negative thoughts and fear around money to positive and hopeful thoughts as I wait for this financial assistance to flow into my life—and please help me maintain these positive thoughts. I also ask Andrew Carnegie, Bob Proctor, Charles F. Haanel, Dr. Wayne Dyer, Ernest Holmes, Florence Scovel Shinn, Geneviève Behrend, Napoleon Hill, Neville Goddard, and W. Clement Stone to assist me in staying tuned into the energy of abundance, and send me to any resources that may help me to do so during this time.

Lastly, I ask Ganesha, who is the remover of obstacles, to please remove any and all obstacles preventing me from manifesting this money quickly.

Thank you, thank you, thank you. Amen.

Prayer: Eliminate Debt

Dear Universe, I call in my angels, guides, loved ones who have passed on, and all those in my soul society, only those of the highest vibration, to be with me now. I am asking for help in paying off and eliminating my debt.

It is my intention to save more money and spend less, and I ask both Saint Matthew and Saint Anthony to please intercede on my behalf with other higher helpers and those on the Earth plane to work your magic when it comes to helping me alleviate my financial debt. Please help open doors and assist me in finding new ways of dealing with and removing this debt. Also, please work with Saint Expedite to allow more money to enter my life as quickly as possible.

I also ask Holy Amethyst to clear and transmute any negative energy around money and debt I may be carrying or that is keeping me stuck in a cycle of debt. Goddess Kali, please assist me with this as well, and help me release any and all fear around money, in addition to unhealthy habits keeping me in debt now.

Goddess Lakshmi and Goddess Abundantia, I call on you both to assist me in drawing more money into my life so I may pay off the debt, and Ganesha, please remove any and all obstacles standing in my way of attracting more money or paying off my debt quickly.

Thank you, thank you, thank you. Amen.

Prayer: Clearing Fear Around Money

Dear Universe, I call in my angels, guides, loved ones who have passed on, and all those in my soul society, only those of the highest vibration, to be with me now as I am seeking assistance in overcoming and clearing any fear I have around money—both fear of not having enough and fear, negative thoughts, and beliefs that may be blocking me as well.

I ask Archangel Michael, Archangel Chamuel, and Archangel Raphael to work together on my behalf to clear any fear energy or anxiety around having or creating more money, as well as not having enough of it to pay bills and live my life comfortably. I also ask Holy Amethyst to work with my energy and transmute my fear into love and positivity around money, and to also clear the energy cycle of fear that may be playing out in my life and keeping me stuck around abundance.

Archangel Jophiel, I call on you to help me shift my thoughts from negative and fearful to more positive and peaceful when it comes to money and abundance, and please help me maintain this mindset as much as possible. Goddess Kali, help me clear any fear I may have related to stepping out of my comfort zone when it comes to creating or making more money, or any fear around my standing in and owning my power to do so.

Lastly, I call in Ganesha to remove any known or unknown obstacles in my path preventing or blocking me from releasing and clearing this fear around money now.

Thank you, thank you, thank you. Amen.

RITUALS TO CALL IN HELP WITH MONEY AND ABUNDANCE

Whether you need money quickly or are just looking to ignite a steady flow of it into your life, these two rituals can help.

Ritual: Accelerated Money Alignment

In need of money for something specific, and the faster the better? This is your ritual! It calls in Saint Expedite, who is known in the Catholic faith for helping people manifest money quickly, and the Goddess Lakshmi, who is the Hindu goddess of wealth and prosperity.

If possible, perform this ritual in the wealth section of your home, which is the far left from the vantage point of walking through the front door of the home, according to the Feng Shui Bagua (see chapter 2). All steps should be done on Day 1, and then repeat Step 4 for eight more days in a row.

Items needed:

- One sage bundle or incense, piece of palo santo wood, or frankincense incense to burn, or your favorite energy-clearing spray
- One green candle (to represent money) or a flameless candle
- One $1, $5, $10, or $20 bill
- One pyrite gemstone crystal (any size or shape)

Step 1: Clear the Energy

Burn the sage, palo santo, or frankincense (or use your clearing spray) to cleanse the energy in the room where you perform this ritual, as well as to cleanse the energy of the pyrite crystal. Clear the crystal by passing it through the smoke or spritzing it directly with a cleansing spray.

Step 2: The Setup

Place the candle on a table within the room that represents the wealth corner of your home and in an area where it won't be disturbed for the nine days of the ritual. In front of the candle, place the money, and then place the pyrite stone on top of the money.

Step 3: Program the Crystal

Place your hands above the pyrite crystal and repeat this prayer out loud or in your head:

> I call in the energy of the Universe to clear all unwanted energy and previous programming from this crystal. I command and program it now to work with my energy and harness the energy of the Universe around me to attract more money and prosperity into my life quickly and easily now.

Step 4: Call in the Higher Help

Light or turn on the candle, and say the following prayer out loud daily for nine days in a row:

> Dear Universe, I call in my angels, guides, loved ones who have passed on, and all those in my soul society, only those of the highest vibration, to be with me now as I am in need of more money quickly. [State what you are looking for, such as a specific amount and why, here.] I'm asking Saint Expedite and Goddess Lakshmi to please work your magic and help bring me this money as quickly as possible, if it be in my highest good and the highest good of all involved. Please send me the right people, opportunities, and ideas to create this money now, and help me

recognize the signs you send to guide me. I am so very grateful with all of my heart for all of your help on this matter. I am open to the unexpected and leave my financial worries in your hands now. Amen.

Say this prayer for nine days in a row. If you miss a day, start again at Day 1. If using a flameless candle, keep it lit daily until bedtime.

Ritual: The Wealth Bowl

Use this ritual to ignite the flow of money into your life, and if you would like to keep the flow going, repeat it periodically. I recommend doing it once a month to recharge the energy. I have my wealth bowl on my nightstand year-round, which is in the wealth corner of my bedroom, as well as the wealth corner of my house.

Items needed:

- One sage bundle or incense, palo santo wood, or frankincense incense to burn, or your favorite energy-clearing spray
- One $1, $5, $10, or $20 bill
- One of each of the following crystals (similar in size):
   - clear quartz
   - jade
   - amazonite
   - green aventurine
   - citrine

   You can exchange any of the above, except for the clear quartz, for pyrite, tiger's eye, peridot, or malachite
- A small bowl (any shape or size)

Step 1: Clear the Energy

Burn the sage, palo santo, or frankincense (or use your clearing spray) to clear the energy of the room, the bowl itself, and each individual crystal by passing them through the smoke or spraying them directly.

Step 2: Program the Crystals

Place all the crystals in front of you and put your hands over them, repeating this prayer out loud or in your head:

I call in the energy of the Universe to clear all unwanted energy and previous programming from these crystals. I command and program these crystals to hold the intention of bringing increased prosperity, wealth, and abundance into my life, as well as new opportunities to create these in all areas of my life, and I specifically program the clear quartz to amplify the energy of the other crystals around it to draw in even more abundance.

Step 3: The Setup

Place the money in the bowl and arrange the crystals on top of it with the clear quartz crystal in the middle and the others around it. The clear quartz is placed in the center because it amplifies the energy of the other stones. Next, place the bowl in the wealth corner of your home. If there are multiple floors of the home, you can place a wealth bowl on any and all floors. If for some reason this area of your home is unavailable, place it in the wealth corner of a meditation space, meditation altar, or desk in your home or office.

Step 4: Prayer

Stand in front of the bowl, and say the following prayer to call in higher help:

Dear Universe, I call in my angels, guides, loved ones who have passed on, and all those in my soul society, only those of the highest vibration, to be with me as I set this intention to draw more wealth and prosperity into all areas of my life. I specifically call on Goddess Abundantia and Goddess Lakshmi to help me manifest this and bring me any creative solutions to help me do so. Saint Expedite, you are known for providing quick results when it comes to material wealth, and I call upon you to help me manifest money as quickly as is in my highest good. Please send me signs, guidance, information, and ideas to help me, and please help me recognize them when they arrive. Thank you in advance for your help. Amen.

FOCUSED GRATITUDE FOR MONEY AND ABUNDANCE

Aside from prayer, consciously putting thoughts and emotions into the Universe is another way to ask for help creating more money, and one of the best ways to do this is to focus on what you already have rather than on what is still missing. You are already abundant. Even if it doesn't feel like it, there is evidence of abundance all around you, and these exercises help you become more conscious of it.

Exercise: Look for Abundance

You already have abundance in your life, and it's time to start consciously looking for and recognizing it. You don't believe me? Go open your refrigerator or freezer door and look at all the food inside. Do you have more than one condiment? I not only have ketchup, mayonnaise, and hot sauce, but I have more than one type of mustard in mine. Guess what that is? Abundance! Each item represents the money you had to purchase it, as well as what it's worth right now. Open your closet and look at your clothes. Do you have more than one pair of pants or shoes? I just have to look at the number of leggings I have (even just the black ones) to feel abundant! Pick any room in your house to see what you already have, whether it's the television in your bedroom, the throw on the living room couch, or the crystals you have collected. It all signifies money and abundance already present in your life.

Step 1: Set an Alarm
Set an alarm for three times a day on your mobile phone or watch—or "habit stack" this exercise with something you do three times a day, such as breakfast, lunch, and dinner. When the alarm goes off, go to Step 2.

Step 2: Stop and Look/Imagine

Take one to three minutes to look for and take note of the abundance around you. Do it in the room you are in at the moment, or go through the rooms of your house looking through the drawers, closets, and even your car. You can also bring to mind a space you are not currently in, and think of the objects and items there.

Step 3: Name Three Things

Take note of three things in the space that represent abundance, and feel the gratitude for having those things. Thank the Universe for the money it took to purchase them (or the person who gifted them to you, which also represents abundance). Say out loud or in your mind, "I'm so grateful for [fill in the blank]" or "I'm so very thankful for [fill in the blank]." Try to think of new things every time you do this exercise. For example:

- I'm so grateful for all the silverware I have in my kitchen.
- I'm so very thankful for all the candles I have throughout my house.
- I'm so grateful for all the throw blankets I own that make my house look beautiful and keep me warm when I'm relaxing at home.
- I'm so very thankful for the penny I found by my car today and its message of abundance coming my way.
- I'm so grateful for all the pairs of shoes I have in my closet.
- I'm so very thankful for the selenite crystal my sister gave me for my birthday.

Step 4: End with an Affirmation

After naming three things, close your eyes, put a smile on your face and your hands over your heart, and say out loud or silently to yourself, "I am so grateful with all my heart for the abundance all around me and the abundance I am creating that is on its way to me right now." Repeat this three times.

Exercise: Money Gratitude Jar

Keeping with the theme of focusing on the abundance already in your life, in this exercise you focus on your ability to purchase the things you need and want, within your budget, such as weekly groceries, gas for your car, or a new pair of shoes. Whether it's paying with cash, a debit card, or a credit card, it all represents abundance already present since the credit card companies allow you to borrow money and own items before you have to pay for them. That is abundance, too, as long as you don't carry a large debt.

Step 1: Create a Money Gratitude Jar

Find or make some type of container to be your money gratitude jar, ideally clear so you can see what is inside of it. Write these words on it (or create a label): "Proof of Abundance." Feel free to decorate it in any way that makes you happy.

Step 2: Add Your Receipts Each Day

As you go through your daily life, save all receipts for purchases, whether it's the post office, grocery store, drug store, department store, or dollar store. When you return home, take each receipt out, write on it, "Thank you, Universe, for the money," and then place it in the jar. Print out online receipts or write what you purchased and the amount on a piece of paper, and add them to the jar, too.

Step 3: Empty and Repeat

Once the jar is filled, go through the receipts one at a time and feel grateful for not only the fact that you have these items (or had them if it was food), but that you had money to purchase it all. Then start again!

Exercise: Thank You for the Savings

Another sign of abundance in your life is when you save money—and I don't just mean in your savings account or 401k. I'm also talking about money you save on something you need to or choose to purchase, or when someone gifts you something and you didn't have to spend your own money on it. That's right—the deal you got on frozen broccoli at the grocery store because it was $1 off is a sign of abundance and the Universe putting money back into your pocket. The coupon attached to your drug store receipt giving you $5 off your next purchase is also proof of abundance in your life. And the new pair of shoes your aunt bought you for your birthday represents abundance as well.

Any time you save money because something is on sale or you use a coupon for something you need or want is cause for celebration. Here is how to celebrate:

Stop and Express Gratitude in the Moment

Every time you add something to your online cart at a discount, find something on sale at the store, receive a coupon, use a coupon, or save money in some way, take thirty seconds to smile and say, "Thank you, Universe, for this abundance. I am so grateful. Keep it coming!" This immediately shifts your energy into gratitude for the money and abundance in your life right now, and asks the Universe for more of it.

Everything in this chapter is meant to assist you in shifting what you are saying to the Universe around money and abundance, consciously asking it for help, and harnessing its energy to create more of it in your life. In the next chapter, you will discover spiritual tools to do the same for physical health and healing.

Chapter 6

PHYSICAL HEALING

IF YOU ARE WORKING TOWARD healing something physical right now, you are not alone. Most people struggle with some type of physical condition, whether minor or major. Chronic conditions such as autoimmune disease, digestive issues, migraines, diabetes, chronic fatigue, fibromyalgia, Lyme disease, or high blood pressure seem like the new normal for so many, and what makes matters worse is people are often told by doctors that the condition they have can't be cured—it can only be managed. Upon hearing this, they take on this belief and settle in for a lifelong battle, making it that much harder to heal.

I was told this by a Harvard-trained allergy and immunology doctor, and I remember walking out of her office thinking, "Thanks, but no thanks. I'm not taking on that belief." And you shouldn't either. Healing comes in all forms. For some it's a complete absence of symptoms, and for others it's an improvement in those symptoms and overall quality of life. I am still on my healing journey, and while I am not 100 percent healed, I am in a much better place than I was for years. If I took on the belief that I just needed to manage my symptoms, I might never have pursued alternatives or allowed the Universe to lead me to new opportunities to heal. Don't judge yourself or your healing journey because it's different for everyone. But I hope you won't take on the belief that healing or improvement is not possible for you. There are so many stories of people healing when they didn't think it was possible and scientific studies showing the body's miraculous ability to heal itself. I refuse to believe it's not possible, and I hope you will, too.

Whether it's a sudden diagnosis, something you have been struggling with for years, or the sudden onset of pain, you have a vast amount of higher help available to assist you on your healing path, and when you take the time to call it in, miracles happen.

When calling in higher help for physical healing, I ask them to guide me to the right healers, doctors, resources, modalities, and solutions to assist me in the process. When you approach it this way, suddenly you're led to the right book, you hear about a new alternative therapy or modality, you discover the perfect doctor or other health practitioner to provide you with the support you need, or you cross paths with someone who healed from the same issue and leads you in the right direction for your own healing. That is the magic of asking the Universe for help instead of trying to figure it all out on your own. And this chapter helps you do it for your physical health.

HIGHER HELPERS FOR PHYSICAL HEALING

These higher helpers assist with physical healing. Some help with overall healing, while others specialize in specific ailments such as migraines, cancer, or menstrual issues.

Apollo

This Greek god is associated with both healing and medicine, and Apollo aids in all aspects of physical healing, including guiding you to the right healing modality for your symptoms.

Archangel Ariel

Known as the archangel of nature and the natural world, Archangel Ariel works with Archangel Raphael to provide healing to both humans and animals.

Archangel Faith

Along with her twin flame Archangel Michael, Archangel Faith is in charge of the development of the throat chakra and helps to heal and balance it, while also helping you to speak your truth and use your voice when needed. She also offers protection and strengthens and shields your aura.

Archangel Gabriel

Known as the angel of communication, Archangel Gabriel assists with anything related to children, including physical issues around conception, pregnancy, and childbirth.

Archangel Hope

The twin flame to Archangel Gabriel, Archangel Hope offers optimism and joy through life changes and hope that anything is possible, including healing.

Archangel Jophiel

Known as the angel of beauty, Archangel Jophiel helps you see the beauty in all things and to balance positive and negative emotions. She assists in quickly shifting your mindset from negative to positive around health, to hold more positive energy and see the blessings occurring.

Archangel Raphael

As his name means "God Heals," Archangel Raphael assists with healing physically, mentally, emotionally, and spiritually. He also directs you to the right doctors and healers, healing methods, modalities, and treatments, and helps healers in their practices.

Archangel Sandalphon

As the archangel of the natural world, or the Earth's guardian, Archangel Sandalphon is deeply connected to Earth energy and the physical world. He helps you connect to the healing powers of nature and stay grounded in the physical body so healing can take place.

Asklepios

This is the Greek god of medicine and doctors and the son of the Greek god Apollo, who is skilled in surgery, medicine, and all types of healing. Call on Asklepios before any surgery—not just to watch over the patient but also the doctors and nurses involved in and performing it as well. He also directs you to the right healing modalities or medicines to assist in healing.

Dom Ignacio

In his last life, this ascended master was a priest and founder of the Jesuit order. Also known as Saint Ignatius Loyola, Dom Ignacio helps with healing both the physical and etheric body, which is the first layer of the human energy field surrounding the physical body. He also works with doctors and healers to assist them when working with others.

Ganesha

The Hindu god known as the remover of obstacles, Ganesha removes those preventing or hindering physical healing.

Goddess Aja

A West African Earth goddess worshiped in parts of Nigeria and in the New World Yoruba tradition, Goddess Aja is known as the spirit or lady of the forest and is also known to cure the sick with herbs and plants. She is called on by herbal healers and those seeking natural healing remedies.

Goddess Frigg

This Norse goddess is associated with marriage and fertility. Goddess Frigg is called on by those who wish to get pregnant or are struggling with fertility issues.

Goddess Gula

This Babylonian goddess of health, healing, and well-being is also a patroness of doctors, the healing arts, and medical practices. Call on Goddess Gula to guide you in healing and finding the perfect doctor or healer to help with your issues. She is also called on by doctors and healers themselves to guide their work and practices.

Goddess Kali

This Hindu goddess aids those stuck in fear and attachment around health—especially when afraid to move out of your comfort zone, step into the unknown, or stand in your power. Goddess Kali assists in clearing and healing the solar plexus and in releasing addictions or unhealthy habits.

Goddess Ostara

The Germanic goddess of the dawn, also known as goddess of the spring, Goddess Ostara can be called on for those experiencing fertility issues or struggling to get pregnant.

Hildegard of Bingen

A 12th-century Christian mystic and herbalist, Hildegard of Bingen suffered from headaches that came along with her gift of visions. She practiced holistic healing using natural remedies and spiritual energy to cure illness and maintain good health. She helps with migraines and headaches, as well as finding natural or alternative remedies for ailments.

Holy Amethyst

One of the keepers of the violet flame, Holy Amethyst purifies and transmutes energy and helps you release negative thoughts and behavior patterns, including addictions. She also clears your aura and energy of lower frequencies hindering healing.

Jesus

As a master teacher of unconditional love, joy, and forgiveness, Jesus was also a master healer in life—even being called the "Divine Physician" by those in the early Catholic Church. Call on him to help with all aspects of healing.

Lord Dhanvantari

Known as a physician or doctor of celestial beings, Lord Dhanvantari is also the father of Ayurveda, a holistic healing system developed more than 3,000 years ago in India. Often referred to as the Hindu god of medicine, he assists with any health-related challenges, helps those practicing or studying Ayurveda, and guides you to the right treatments.

Louise Hay

Founder of the spiritual publishing company Hay House, as well as a teacher and author of many books on mind-body healing—including *Heal Your Body,* offering emotions and beliefs behind illness—Louise Hay healed from cancer. She offers guidance toward the right healing modalities, books, methods, and healers.

Mama Killa

Inca Goddess of the moon, marriage, and the female menstrual cycle, Mama Killa helps regulate the menstrual cycle, as well as with any other menstrual issues and imbalances.

Padre Pio

Born Francesco Forgione in Pietrelcina, Italy, in 1887, he became a priest of the Roman Catholic Church and Franciscan order in 1903 and was given the name Fra Pio or Padre Pio. A number of miraculous events occurred in his life, and he performed miraculous cures and healings. Known as a patron saint of stress relief and healing, Padre Pio helps with physical healing and provides relief from stress around your illness or healing journey.

Saint Agatha

The Catholic patron saint for breast cancer, rape victims, fire, nurses, and natural disasters, Saint Agatha is called on by those diagnosed with breast cancer or healing from a rape or natural disaster, as well as nurses in the wellness field working with others.

Saint Anne

As the mother of Mother Mary in the Catholic faith, Saint Anne is the patron saint of infertility, grandparents, and mothers. Call on her for help with fertility issues and when wishing to get pregnant.

Saint Dwynwen

This Welsh saint is known as the patron saint of lovers but is also the patron saint of sick animals. Saint Dwynwen helps with healing and guidance for pets or other animals in a person's life.

Saint Expedite

While Saint Expedite is called on for speedy intercession around money and abundance, he also does the same for health and healing and guides you to the right doctors, healers, and modalities in order to heal fully and completely.

Saint Francis of Assisi

As the patron saint of animals and the environment in the Catholic faith, Saint Francis of Assisi helps to heal animals and pets by sending healing energy and by guiding a person to the right solutions. He also assists an animal in transitioning to the other side in their physical death.

Saint Gerard

Often called "The Mother's Saint," Saint Gerard is the patron saint of unborn children and expectant mothers in the Catholic faith. He is called on for labor preparation, but also for any child who is sick, in distress, and in need of healing.

Saint Germaine

Not to be confused with Saint Germain, keeper of the Violet Flame, this Catholic saint is the patron saint of people who suffer from abuse or disabilities. Born with a disabled right arm and abused and neglected by her father and stepmother who forced her to live in the barn and starved her, Saint Germaine died at the age of twenty-two. She assists those healing from abuse, especially child abuse, and those suffering from physical disabilities not only to heal but to accept or overcome it.

Saint Jude

The Catholic patron saint of hopeless cases or impossible situations, Saint Jude may be called upon for intercession and help in any area of life, including physical healing—especially when feeling hopeless and helpless.

Saint Lidwina

For those suffering from chronic pain, call on this Dutch saint for help. Saint Lidwina was injured after falling down while ice skating. This incident left her bedridden and in excruciating pain for the rest of her life. She provides strength and healing, as well as guidance toward the right doctors, healers, and remedies.

Saint Maximilian Kolbe

A Polish Franciscan Friar, Saint Maximilian Kolbe is the patron saint of those chemically addicted to substances, as well as those suffering from eating disorders and other addiction issues. He was known for working with people struggling in these areas until his death and can be called on to help those struggling with the physical and emotional aspects of addiction.

Saint Peregrine

Known as the patron saint of cancer patients, Saint Peregrine was miraculously healed from cancer in his leg and provides assistance in healing from any type of cancer—including guidance to the right doctors, healers, and treatments.

Saint Philomena

This Catholic saint is the patron saint of infants, babies, and young children. Saint Philomena offers assistance in healing and intercedes on your behalf with other healing higher helpers.

Saint Theresa of Avila

As the patron saint of headache and migraine sufferers, Saint Theresa of Avila offers relief and guides you to the right doctors, healers, and modalities to help.

Serapis Bey

The ascended master Serapis Bey is often associated with healing the mental body, but doctors and healers who work with others call on him as well.

CRYSTALS TO ASSIST IN PHYSICAL HEALING

When it comes to physical healing, crystals can draw in energy from the Universe to shift the body, whether it's for overall healing or a specific symptom. Here is a list of crystals for overall healing as well as common issues.

Amber

This stone is fossilized resin from tree bark, and amber assists in alleviating and absorbing pain and negative energy, including headaches, joint pain, stiffness, and even teething in infants. It's also been said to boost immunity and help with fatigue, as well as aligning body, mind, and spirit to impact the body's natural healing abilities.

Amethyst

This purple quartz gemstone is often called a universal stone because it offers so many positive properties. When it comes to healing, amethyst is a high vibrational stone that assists with sleep issues—both falling and staying asleep—and is helpful for those looking to overcome addiction.

Bloodstone

This pain-relieving stone can be placed directly on an area of pain and carried with you to draw in healing energy for aches and pains.

Blue-Green Kyanite

Like selenite, blue-green kyanite does not collect or hold energy and does not need to be cleared. It cleanses the energy of other stones and comes in a variety of colors. Those crystals with a mix of both blue and green work to create balanced emotions and alignment (blue) and heal hormones and the endocrine system (green).

Citrine

This gemstone assists with overall gut health, including healing and balancing the stomach, gallbladder, and intestines. Citrine eases stomach pain and acid reflux and gives a boost to digestion.

Clear Quartz

Known as the master healer, clear quartz opens blocked chakras and realigns them, as well as amplifies the energy of any intention or other gemstone it is placed with or near.

Faden Quartz

Faden quartz is used to seal holes in the etheric body, which is the energy field outside of the physical body, and also assists with torn muscles and ligaments or broken bones.

Garnet

An invigorating and energizing stone, garnet has a cleansing effect on the body and chakras, flushing out toxins and balancing energy. It's also grounding and anchors you into the Earth's energy.

Golden Healer Quartz

This master-healing stone can clear and repair the etheric body, or energy field around the physical body, along with physical and emotional blocks. Golden healer quartz is an ideal stone for healers, energy workers, therapists, and all those who work to heal others, and while it is associated with the crown chakra, it assists in cleansing all the chakras.

Green Apophyllite

Like bloodstone, it can be used to ease pain (and even used in combination with bloodstone) and can also assist in getting a good night's sleep.

Lapis Lazuli

While soothing inflammation, lapis lazuli balances issues with the throat and thyroid, as well as respiratory symptoms. It also helps alleviate pain, particularly in the head and neck.

Libyan Desert Glass

Found near the Egyptian–Libyan border in the Sahara Desert, Libyan desert glass is said to be formed from a meteorite impacting and melting desert sand. It is helpful for the stomach and digestive system and for those suffering from ulcers, irritable bowel syndrome, acid reflux, nausea, and difficulties digesting food.

Malachite

As a healer of the Divine feminine, malachite balances the female-assigned reproductive system and eases pain during labor and delivery. It also balances mood swings and alleviates menstrual cramps.

Peridot

Peridot is used to provide relief from stomach pain, specifically the intestines and digestion, including chronic bowel problems, and offers balance and healing.

Prehnite

This gemstone is used to heal the healer. For those working to heal others, prehnite prevents the empathic absorption of energy and challenges from those being worked on and is beneficial to reiki practitioners, light-workers, and body workers.

Selenite

Like kyanite, selenite does not hold onto energy and cleanses the energy of your aura and that of other gemstones. It's also beneficial for issues with posture, as it opens the channel from the root chakra to the base of the skull, aligning the spine and helping with flexibility.

Septarian

Invite inner peace and connection to higher realms while balancing the emotions with septarian. It's also helpful for those struggling with overcoming addiction.

Shungite

Shungite is used to ground and shield you from electromagnetic field (EMF) emissions and has an overall grounding effect on the body.

Sugilite

Associated with the crown chakra, sugilite helps with headaches and muscle tension, as well as supports the overall immune system.

Super Seven

This crystal is made up of seven different minerals, including amethyst, clear quartz, and smoky quartz. As a full chakra activator, super seven is used to open, balance, and heal all the chakras in the body.

Turquoise

Another master-healer stone, turquoise benefits the entire body and opens all the chakras. It's associated particularly with the throat chakra and assists with any issues in that area, as well as ear and nose issues such as allergies, migraines, and respiratory issues.

PRAYERS FOR PHYSICAL HEALING

The nine prayers below can help call in higher help around healing for children, pets, addiction, fertility, chronic pain, and more.

Prayer: Healing for Children

Dear Universe, angels, guides, loved ones who have passed on, and all those in my soul society, only those of the highest vibration, I ask you to be with me now. I am calling in my higher help team and [name of child]'s higher help team to assist with healing them from [share symptoms/diagnosis].

I specifically call on Saint Philomena and Saint Gerard to please assist with the physical healing of [child's name], and please intercede on their behalf with other higher helpers who can assist with this as well.

I also collectively call on Archangel Raphael, Jesus, Dom Ignacio, and Padre Pio to help with all aspects of this healing, including guiding [me/us, child's name, or family's name] to the right doctors, healers, treatments, and modalities to provide relief and complete healing quickly and easily. I also ask Hildegard of Bingen and Goddess Aja to lead us toward any natural or alternative remedies that can provide healing, and Saint Expedite to intercede in this matter as quickly as possible, for the highest good of all involved.

Ganesha, I call on you to remove all obstacles, known or unknown, standing in the way of [child's name] healing fully and completely now, and I ask you to send the signs and synchronicities to guide [me/us, child's name, or family's name] on this path, and please help them be recognized and acted on when they arrive.

Thank you for all the guidance and healing you are sending now and will send in the future. Amen.

Prayer: Physical Healing

Dear Universe, angels, guides, loved ones who have passed on, and all those in my soul society, only those of the highest vibration, I ask you to be with me now. I am looking for guidance, assistance, and support on my current path to physically heal my body totally and completely, head to toe, specifically [share your symptoms/diagnosis and what you are seeking healing help with here].

I call in Archangel Raphael, Greek gods Apollo and Asklepios, Jesus, and Padre Pio to please help me to create miracles around my physical health. Padre Pio, please help relieve me of any stress I have around healing of my symptoms now. I also call on ascended master Dom Ignacio to help me not only heal my physical body but also to heal and clear anything in my etheric body.

Lord Dhanvantari, Hildegard of Bingen, and Goddess Aja, please guide me toward any holistic, natural, or alternative therapies that help me heal. Archangel Sandalphon, help me stay grounded in my body so that I am centered and balanced to assist in its healing.

[Add the following if you feel hopeless and helpless around your health.] I also call on the assistance of Saint Jude, who is the patron saint of hopeless cases. Please intercede on my behalf with other higher helpers so I may heal my body and return it to its perfect state of health. And please shift my energy around this, working with Archangel Hope, so I may feel more hopeful overall.

Archangel Jophiel, please assist me in seeing the beauty in all things around me, and help me shift my mindset from negative thoughts around my health to positive ones and to maintain those positive thoughts. I also call in Louise Hay to guide me to the resources, exercises, and practices that can assist me in healing myself completely as you healed yourself.

Lastly, I call in Saint Expedite for help finding healing solutions as quickly as possible in my highest good, and Ganesha to please remove any obstacles presently known or unknown to me, standing in the way of my creating the physical healing I desire.

Please guide me in the right direction toward healing now, including sending me the signs, synchronicities, ideas, opportunities, people, doctors, healers, treatments, and modalities that would be most beneficial, and please help me recognize them when they arrive. And Goddess Gula, I ask for you specifically to help guide me to the right doctors or healers who can help me now.

Thank you for the healing energy and guidance coming to me now. Amen.

Prayer: Healing Cancer

Dear Universe, angels, guides, loved ones who have passed on, and all those in my soul society, only those of the highest vibration, I ask you to be with me now.

I am asking for healing help around my diagnosis of [fill in the blank with type of] cancer. I specifically call on help and assistance from Saint Peregrine, who is the patron saint of cancer patients and who miraculously healed from leg cancer, along with Louise Hay, who healed from cervical cancer. Please assist me in healing quickly, easily, and completely, restoring me to perfect health.

[In the case of breast cancer] I call in Saint Agatha, who works specifically with those diagnosed with breast cancer, to help in this healing process.

I'm also asking for help from Archangel Raphael, Goddess Gula, Jesus, Padre Pio, Lord Dhanvantari, and Dom Ignacio. Please send healing energy, and also direct me to the right doctors, healers, treatments, and modalities that can help assist in total recovery.

Archangel Hope, please infuse me with the optimism needed on this healing journey, and Archangel Jophiel, please assist me in shifting my mindset from negative to positive around this diagnosis and my ability to heal completely, and help in maintaining those positive thoughts, as well.

And Ganesha, remover of all obstacles, I ask you to remove any and all obstacles standing in the way of total healing now, both known and unknown.

I am asking for guidance, signs, synchronicities, ideas, opportunities, and more to help on the path to total healing and recovery, and please help me recognize them and act on them when they arrive.

Thank you for your assistance in this time of great need. Amen.

Prayer: Healing Chronic Pain

Dear Universe, angels, guides, loved ones who have passed on, and all those in my soul society, only those of the highest vibration, I ask you to be with me now as I am struggling with chronic pain.

[Explain what you are dealing with specifically and what you would like help and guidance with here.]

Saint Lidwina, I ask you to send me healing energy now to alleviate and heal [fill in the blank with the pain and symptoms]. I also ask Saint Jude, patron saint of hopeless cases, to intercede with other higher helpers on my behalf to assist me in healing totally and completely from this pain.

Archangel Raphael, Greek gods Apollo and Asklepios, Jesus, Padre Pio, and Dom Ignacio, I ask that you also send me healing energy and guidance, and please work with Goddess Gula to point me in the direction of the right doctors, healers, treatments, and modalities to help me achieve this now.

Lastly, I call in Ganesha to please remove any obstacles, known or unknown, standing in my way of healing now.

I ask you all to send me the signs and synchronicities to guide me toward what is in my highest good so I may heal quickly and easily, and please help me recognize them and act on them when they arrive.

Thank you, thank you, thank you. Amen.

Prayer: Healing Headaches and Migraines

Dear Universe, angels, guides, loved ones who have passed on, and all those in my soul society, only those of the highest vibration, I ask you to be with me now.

I am seeking help in healing my headaches/migraines and their root cause fully and completely now. I call in Hildegard of Bingen to please help me uncover any holistic healing, natural remedies, or solutions that can assist me, and please work with Saint Theresa of Avila and Goddess Gula to not only heal me but guide me to the right doctors, healers, treatments, modalities, and resources to help me now.

[If your migraines are related to your menstrual cycle] I also call in Mama Killa to help me balance my cycle and hormones now to alleviate these headaches/migraines.

Please send me the signs and synchronicities to guide me forward toward anything that can assist me in healing fully and completely from these headaches/migraines now, and please help me recognize them when they arrive.

Thank you, thank you, thank you. Amen.

Prayer: Help for Healers

Dear Universe, angels, guides, loved ones who have passed on, and all those in my soul society, only those of the highest vibration, I ask you to be with me now as I work to heal others through [explain what you are doing to heal others, such as techniques and specialties].

I call in Archangel Michael to please protect me and my energy and surround me with white light to prevent me from taking on any energy that is not mine today, and please work with your twin flame, Archangel Faith, to offer protection and to strengthen and shield my aura. I also ask Archangel Sandalphon to help me ground my energy so I may stay centered, balanced, and present.

As I work to heal others, I am asking for support from Archangel Raphael, Dom Ignacio, Jesus, [for nurses: Saint Agatha,] and Goddess Gula. Please assist me in providing the knowledge, healing energy, ideas, and empathy to assist others today, so they may heal completely in mind, body, and spirit.

I also call in Ganesha to please remove any obstacles in my path and the paths of those I work with today, known or unknown, standing in the way of complete and total healing.

Thank you, thank you, thank you. Amen.

Prayer: Healing the Physical Aspect of Addiction

Dear Universe, angels, guides, loved ones who have passed on, and all those in my soul society, only those of the highest vibration, I ask you to be with me now as I struggle to overcome my addiction to [fill in the blank].

I call in guidance, assistance, and support from Saint Maximilian Kolbe to assist me in finding the strength to heal myself physically and emotionally. I also ask Holy Amethyst to help me release the negative thoughts and behavior patterns underlying this addiction, and please clear my aura and energy from lower frequencies.

I call in Archangel Raphael and Jesus to assist me in healing and to guide me to the right doctors, healers, treatments, modalities, and other people who can help. I also call on Saint Jude to be with me now in this time of need when I feel hopeless and helpless. Please intercede on my behalf with other higher helpers to assist me now. And Archangel Hope, please help me find hope within myself to move through this time with more grace and ease.

Lastly, I call on Ganesha to please remove any obstacles, known or unknown, preventing a complete recovery for me now. In gratitude for all of your help to aid me in overcoming this addiction completely and returning to perfect physical health. Amen.

Prayer: Healing for Surgery

Dear Universe, angels, guides, loved ones who have passed on, and all those in my soul society, only those of the highest vibration, I ask you to be with me now as I prepare for surgery for [fill in the blank].

I ask that Archangel Raphael be with me and the doctors, nurses, anesthesiologist, and anyone else involved in this surgery now to help it to go smoothly, fix the issues I have, and lead to a speedy, effortless, and complete recovery. Padre Pio, I ask for you to send the energy of miracles into surgery with me today and help me remain calm during the entire process. Archangel Jophiel, please help me shift my mindset from negative thoughts and fears connected to this surgery to positive ones and help me maintain this positive mindset throughout this process.

I'm also asking for help from Dom Ignacio and Greek god Asklepios on behalf of the medical team working with me today, that they may be on top of their game to perform this surgery, make the right decisions, and help me heal. Lastly, I call in Ganesha to please remove any obstacles, known or unknown, preventing a smooth and successful surgery in my highest good and the highest good of all involved.

Thank you, thank you, thank you. Amen.

Prayer: Pet and Animal Healing

Dear Universe, angels, guides, loved ones who have passed on, and all those in my soul society, only those of the highest vibration, I ask you to be with me and [animal name] now. I am looking for guidance and assistance to help and heal [animal name] from [fill in the blank] as quickly and easily as possible.

I specifically call in Archangel Ariel and Archangel Raphael to work together to provide healing energy and lead me to the right doctors, healers, treatments, and modalities that can help in this healing, and please work with Saint Francis of Assisi and Saint Dwynwen to assist with this, as well.

Ganesha, please remove any and all obstacles standing in the way of total and complete healing for [animal name] for their highest good and the highest good of all involved.

I ask that you please send me any signs, synchronicities, opportunities, ideas, and resources that can assist me now in helping [animal name], and please help me recognize and act on them when they arrive.

Thank you, thank you, thank you. Amen.

RITUALS FOR PHYSICAL HEALING

These rituals combine crystals, intention, and prayer to draw in the energy of healing as well as the guidance and direction to move forward toward the right opportunities and ideas that assist on a healing path.

Ritual: Rapid Guidance Healing

There are times in life when you just need fast answers and guidance and higher helpers to intercede on your behalf quickly. Whether you're struggling with symptoms and have no idea why or how to heal them, have tried different treatments and modalities and nothing seems to be working, or have received a sudden diagnosis and need support and direction on what to do next, this ritual helps.

It calls in Saint Expedite, who is known for speedy help for both abundance and health issues, and the angel of healing, Archangel Raphael—asking them to work together during this nine-day ritual.

If possible, perform this ritual in the health section of your home, which is the center, according to the Feng Shui Bagua (see chapter 2, page 51). All steps should be done on Day 1, and then repeat Steps 4 and 5 for eight more days in a row.

Items needed:

- One sage bundle/incense, palo santo wood, or frankincense incense to burn; or your favorite energy-clearing spray
- One white candle or a flameless candle
- Two turquoise gemstone crystals, one of which must be flat
- Two clear quartz crystals, one of which should be a double-terminated crystal point (points on both ends) so the energy flows in both directions.

As an alternative to the second set of crystals, which you will carry with you for nine days as explained below, you can also wear some form of jewelry, such as a bracelet or necklace, featuring the crystals.

Step 1: Clear the Energy

Burn the sage, palo santo, or frankincense (or use your clearing spray) to cleanse the energy of the room, as well as the energy of the turquoise and clear quartz crystals. Clear the crystals by passing them through the smoke or spritzing them directly with a cleansing spray.

Step 2: Program the Crystals

Place your hands above the crystals and repeat this prayer out loud or in your head:

> I call in the energy of the Universe to clear all unwanted energy and previous programming from these crystals. I command and program them now to work with my energy and harness the energy of the Universe around me to draw in guidance and direction on where to go and what to do next in order to heal, along with healing energy to assist my body in the healing process, as well as balancing and opening all my chakras now. Amen.

Step 3: The Setup

Place the candle on a table within the room that represents the health section of your home and in an area that won't be disturbed for the nine days of the ritual. In front of the candle, place the flat turquoise crystal and put the double-terminated clear quartz point on top of it to amplify its energy. Next to them, place the other turquoise and clear quartz crystal (or put on the jewelry if you are using that).

Step 4: Call in Higher Help

Light (or turn on) the candle and say the following prayer out loud or in your head:

> Dear Universe, I call in my angels, guides, loved ones who have passed on, and all those in my soul society, only those of the highest vibration, to be with me now as I am in need of speedy healing and guidance to help me on my path. [State what you are looking to heal here.] I'm asking Saint Expedite and Archangel Raphael to work with me now by bringing me answers and results in my time of need.
>
> I'm asking for healing energy to be sent my way, and for you to guide me to the right people, opportunities, treatments, healers, doctors, modalities, and resources that can help me now. I also ask for your help in recognizing the signs and answers you send my way. I am so very grateful with all of my heart for all of your help on this matter. I am open to the unexpected and leave my health and healing in your hands now, knowing the answers and guidance will come. Amen.

Step 5: Carry the Additional Crystals

Take the second set of crystals and carry it with you, or if you chose jewelry featuring the crystals, wear it, for the nine days of this ritual.

Step 6: Repeat for Nine Days

Perform Steps 4 and 5 for nine days in a row, and if you miss a day, start again with Day 1. If using a flameless candle, keep it lit daily until bedtime.

Ritual: Lord Dhanvantari Physical Healing Guidance

Adapt this ritual by using different stones depending on the type of physical healing needed. It uses clear quartz crystal points as master-healing stones and to amplify the energy of the other stones, directing the energy outward into the world and your life. While this ritual uses clear quartz, super seven, golden healer quartz, and turquoise, you can swap out the last two for a combination of any other crystals to work with your specific ailments or symptoms. For example, if you seek to overcome addiction, use a combination of amethyst and septarian; for chronic pain, use bloodstone and green apophyllite.

The crystals are laid out in a grid to form a merkaba (see figure 4). The merkaba is associated with ascension, but it also raises the vibration of the body to access the positive energy of the Universe. It has been called a vehicle for Divine light and stimulates the flow of energy throughout the body, while balancing both sides of the brain. The Hebrew word *merkaba* comes from three words: *mer* meaning light, *ka* meaning spirit, and *ba* referring to body. You can program it with an intention the same way crystals are programmed. You can either purchase a crystal grid in a merkaba, print an image, or draw it on a piece of paper for this ritual.

Like the previous ritual, perform it in the health section of your home, according to the Feng Shui Bagua (see chapter 2), if possible. All steps should be done on Day 1, and repeat Step 4 for eight more days in a row.

Items needed:

- One sage bundle/incense, palo santo wood, or frankincense incense to burn; or your favorite energy-clearing spray
- One merkaba (drawn, printed, or purchased)
- One super seven crystal, either a small sphere or tumbled
- Three small tumbled turquoise crystals
- Six small tumbled golden healer quartz crystals
- Six small clear quartz crystal points, with points on one end

Step 1: Clear the Energy

Burn the sage, palo santo, or frankincense (or use your clearing spray) to cleanse the energy of the room, as well as the energy of all the crystals and the grid of the merkaba. Simply pass all the items through the smoke or spray them directly with a cleansing spray.

Step 2: Program the Crystals

Place your hands above the crystals and repeat this prayer out loud or in your head:

> I call in the energy of the Universe to clear all unwanted energy and previous programming from these crystals and merkaba. I command and program them now to work with my energy and harness the energy of the Universe around me to draw in guidance and direction on where to go and what to do next in order to heal, along with drawing in healing energy to assist my physical body and balance and open all my chakras. I specifically command and program the clear quartz crystals to amplify the energy of the other stones here, amplifying my intention and the energy.

Step 3: The Setup

Place the merkaba grid on a table within the room that represents the health section of your home and in an area that won't be disturbed for the nine days of the ritual. In the center of the merkaba grid (A in figure 4) place the super seven crystal. On the three triangle points coming directly from the center (B), place the tumbled turquoise crystals. Moving outward again, on the next six points (C), place the tumbled golden healer quartz. Finally, on the outer six points, place the clear quartz crystals (D) with the points facing outward.

Step 4: Call in the Higher Help

Sitting in front of the crystal grid, call in Lord Dhanvantari, known as the Divine physician and Hindu god of medicine, to help you access the signs, synchronicities, guidance, and answers you need on your path to

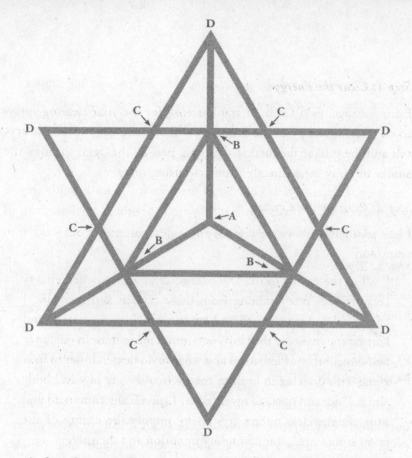

A - Super Seven   B - Turquoise   C - Golden Healer   D - Clear Quartz Point

Figure 4. Merkaba.

physical healing. First, say the short prayer below, and then chant the Dhanvantari Mantra 108 times. This is one of the mantras for healing that calls in Lord Dhanvantari for assistance. Feel free to use a strand of 108 mala beads to track your mantras. The number 108 has deep meaning in a variety of philosophies and religions, and in Hindu tradition, 108 is the number of creation and represents the Universe.

The prayer:

Lord Dhanvantari, I call upon you now as the Divine physician and god of medicine to assist me on my healing path as I ask for direction and guidance in healing [fill in the blank]. Please send me healing energy, as well as the signs, synchronicities, and ideas to guide me toward the perfect doctors, healers, and modalities that can assist me on this path now, so I may heal fully and completely. Thank you, thank you, thank you. Amen.

The Sanskrit Hindu Mantra: *Om Shree Dhanvantre Namaha*

This translates to "Oh Lord Shri Dhanvantari, I bow humbly to you with prayers." Use this mantra to maintain health, as well as clear all forms of mental and physical disorders.

Step 5: Repeat

Perform Step 4 for nine days in a row, and if you miss a day, start over from Day 1.

FOCUSED GRATITUDE TO ALIGN YOUR ENERGY FOR HEALING

When you are physically sick, especially where there is pain or other uncomfortable symptoms involved, it's often difficult to focus on anything else. For those who have suffered with a condition or disease for a long time, it often feels even more impossible to see yourself as healthy and healed. But in this situation, it's more important than ever to shift your focus to thoughts that feel better because it shifts your mood and vibration and allows the body to release stress and move out of the sympathetic nervous system of fight and flight, and into the parasympathetic nervous system, which is when the body's self-healing mechanisms kick in.

Exercise: Health and Healing Gratitude

I recommend adding this exercise to your daily routine twice a day to shift your energy and focus and send signals out to the Universe that you are ready to create a different physical state in your body.

Step 1: Set an Alarm

Set an alarm on your mobile phone or watch to go off two times a day, or habit-stack this with your morning and evening routine. You are going to use these times to look for what is going right, specifically related to your health and overall wellness. If you are struggling to come up with something, look to the past and be grateful for a time when you did feel well, bringing it into your mind with as much vivid detail as possible.

Step 2: List Three Things

Each time the alarm goes off, think of three things you are grateful for related to your health and wellness, put a smile on your face, and *feel* the gratitude. Here are some examples:

- I'm so grateful my doctor spends time answering my questions.
- I'm so thankful I woke up feeling a little less tired today.
- I'm grateful my eyesight is so good, and I don't need glasses.
- I'm so thankful my body is telling me to rest right now, and I'm honoring that.
- I'm so grateful I didn't have [fill in the blank with symptom] today.

Step 3: End with an Affirmation

After naming three things, close your eyes, take a deep breath in and out, and with a smile on your face say: "I am so grateful the Universe is partnering with me to create health and wellness in my life right now! I can move forward into health with ease now." Repeat this three times.

Exercise: Grateful for the Healing Visualization

Your mind is a very powerful resource, and it has a direct connection to the Universe and its all-loving, all-knowing, creative energy. In this exercise you are going to harness that energy to visualize yourself as fully healed, while feeling the overwhelming gratitude for it.

Not only does this boost your mood and vibration around your health, but neuroscience shows the brain does not distinguish what is real from what is imagined. In his bestselling book, *How Your Mind Can Heal Your Body,* Dr. David Hamilton[1] shares this result and how visualizing something creates physical changes in the brain. He cited studies on athletes and those recovering from a stroke who visualized, or imagined, their muscles moving and how this alone contributed to "significant improvements in their muscles."[2] This exercise uses that mind-body connection to help you with your mood and overall healing.

This exercise should be done one or two times a day for three to five minutes each time.

Step 1: Relax and Smile

Once or twice a day, get into a comfortable position either in a chair or lying down, relax, and put a smile on your face.

Step 2: Imagine Yourself Healed

Imagine yourself waving a magic wand into the air (yes, like Cinderella's fairy godmother) and see yourself entering a scene where you are completely healed and happy. What are you able to do in this scenario that you could not do before? Picture yourself doing it, and feel the enormous gratitude for being happy and healed and able to do whatever you desire. For example, if you have food allergies, picture yourself eating the foods you can't now, digesting them with ease and with no negative reaction in your body. If you have chronic pain, picture yourself exercising or running on the beach and feeling complete bliss and happiness with no pain whatsoever.

The first time you do this, try to come up with at least three different scenarios in which you see yourself healed and doing what you are unable to do now. Or, go back to a time in the past when you could do these things and picture that in vivid detail. Then, when you go back to this exercise again, you can easily flip through the different scenes in your mind, or focus on the one that feels the best to you during the three-to five-minute period. It's important to imagine it *and* feel that gratitude for having already achieved it.

If for some reason your mind wanders into a negative place while doing this exercise, simply take a deep breath in and out, say to yourself, "Release, Release, Release," and go back into the feel-good visualization.

Step 3: Affirm Your Health

At the end of the visualization, repeat this affirmation three times: "I am creating complete health, wellness, and balance in my mind and body, head to toe, right now. And so it is."

In the next chapter, we move into tools for help with emotional healing, which you can also combine with those in this chapter when working on both areas of healing.

Chapter 7

EMOTIONAL HEALING

IF YOU ARE EXPERIENCING ANYTHING less than joy, ease, and happiness—whether it's a lifelong struggle with anxiety or depression, or the acute grief of losing a loved one or the ending of a relationship—you are not alone. Nearly 20 percent of adults in the United States—almost 50 million—experienced mental illness in 2022, according to Mental Health America.[1] Mental illnesses are referred to as disorders affecting behavior, mood, or thinking and are attributed to biological factors, traumatic life experiences, or genetics, according to the Substance Abuse and Mental Health Services Administration, which is part of the U.S. Department of Health and Human Services.[2] Both depression and anxiety fall under this umbrella, affecting people all over the world, including children and teens.

This chapter focuses on the spiritual tools to ask the Universe for help in healing and balancing emotionally, no matter what issue you are facing now, so you move forward into more joy, happiness, peace, and love.

HIGHER HELPERS FOR EMOTIONAL HEALING

Here is a list of higher helpers to assist with a variety of emotional struggles, including heartbreak, the grief of losing a loved one, addiction, anxiety, and depression.

Archangel Azrael

Known as the angel of death, Archangel Azrael helps loved ones cross over to the other side and aids in healing a grieving heart from the loss of a loved one, as well as anxiety, exchanging these emotions for a sense of calm and peace within.

Archangel Chamuel

Not only does he assist in healing broken bonds or misunderstandings in relationships, but Archangel Chamuel also provides a sense of peace to those who suffer from anxiety.

Archangel Charity

As the twin flame of Archangel Chamuel, Archangel Charity's work is centered around love—both of others and oneself. As she embodies Divine love, she assists with healing the heart chakra and helping a person cultivate self-love.

Archangel Haniel

Known as the angel of joy and Divine communication, Archangel Haniel assists in staying centered no matter what is going on around you, connecting you to the energy of vitality and passion. She also uses her blue orb of healing light to move through any heavy energy and emotions, cleansing and transmuting these lower-energy vibrations and worry into love.

Archangel Jeremiel

He has been called the angel of change, the angel of forgiveness, the angel of hope, and the angel of Divine visions. Archangel Jeremiel assists in the soul's transition to the other side and is called on to help you see the patterns in life that led to your current emotional state to gain perspective and insight—and also to see blessings in past experiences. He also helps with forgiveness and understanding, both of oneself and others.

Archangel Jophiel

Known as the angel of beauty, Archangel Jophiel balances negative and positive emotions and quickly shifts your mindset from negative to positive—helping you hold more positive thoughts throughout the day—and also to find the beauty and joy around you, even in the midst of struggle.

Archangel Metatron

Often associated with spiritual connection and ascension, Archangel Metatron clears and cleanses your energy to release what no longer serves you and your highest good and to balance the aura.

Archangel Zadkiel

As the angel of mercy, Archangel Zadkiel assists with forgiveness of oneself and others and helps you find freedom from emotional pain. As the ruler of the violet ray, he uses the violet flame to transmute any negative emotions toward yourself or others into pure love, light, and positivity.

Buddha

Siddhartha Gautama, known to the world as Buddha, is called on by those looking to find and maintain emotional balance and peace in the midst of chaos and difficulties. Known as the awakened or enlightened one, he taught others how to achieve this state of inner peace and helps to overcome unhealthy attachments to people or things that no longer serve you.

Ganesha

The Hindu god Ganesha is the remover of obstacles. Call on him to remove any obstacle standing in the way of emotional balance and healing.

Goddess Aurora

This Roman goddess, whose name Aurora means sunrise or dawn, leads you to better and brighter days and also helps you see things more clearly. She symbolizes new beginnings and encourages people to try something new and start fresh, whether it's a job, relationship, or place to live.

Goddess Frigg

This Germanic goddess of marriage, motherhood, and fertility is called on by those who wish to get pregnant, but also by mothers who are grieving the death of a child, as she is said to have lost her own son.

Goddess Kali

Goddess Kali is a Hindu goddess you can call on when stuck in fear and attachment and afraid to move out of a comfort zone or step into the unknown. She is known for turning darkness to light and helps people struggling to release addictions or other unhealthy habits. Also known as a goddess of endings and new beginnings, she provides strength to face unavoidable confrontation.

Goddess Ma'at

An Egyptian goddess of truth, balance, and justice, Goddess Ma'at may be called upon to find harmony, balance, and order when life is chaotic and disordered.

Holy Amethyst

As the twin flame of Archangel Zadkiel, Holy Amethyst is one of the archangels of the seventh ray and violet flame, and she uses it to transmute negative energies or situations no longer serving you. She helps release pain and negativity and helps those looking to heal addictions.

Jesus

As a master healer during his physical lifetime, you can call on Jesus for both physical and emotional healing, whether it's releasing grief, sorrow, anxiety, depression, anger, worry, or fear.

Louise Hay

The bestselling author of many books on healing and self-love, Louise Hay taught the power of affirmations, mirror work, self-love, and more. Ask for her help and direction to shift emotionally and open up to more self-love and healing, as well as for guidance toward any resources and people who can assist in this.

Mother Mary

Known in Christianity as the mother of Jesus, Mother Mary brings a nurturing, loving, accepting, and compassionate energy to all who need her. She also helps parents grieving the loss of a child.

Padre Pio

While this Italian saint can help with all aspects of healing, Padre Pio is also a patron saint of stress relief. Call on him for relief from anxiety, fear, worry, and stress.

Quan Yin

A Bodhisattva, which means one who is awakened or enlightened in the Buddhist culture—also known as Kwan Yin or Guanyin in East Asian culture—Quan Yin is a master of unconditional love, compassion, and mercy and comforts you when in need, helps you forgive, and aids in releasing emotional baggage.

Saint Dwynwen

This Welsh saint is the patron saint of lovers, the equivalent of the Roman Saint Valentine. Call on Saint Dwynwen to help find true love, improve a romantic relationship, or when suffering from a broken heart and in need of healing.

Saint Dymphna

An Irish Saint who suffered from nervous and mental afflictions during her life, Saint Dymphna is the patron saint of depression and mental illness, including anxiety. Call on her for help with all mental illness and emotional imbalance struggles.

Saint Germain

Keeper of the violet flame, an extension of God's heart energy, Saint Germain helps transform negative energy into love and light and assists in overcoming anything that is creating emotional discord in a person's life.

Saint John of God

Born in Portugal in 1495, Saint John of God is the patron saint of people with mental and physical illnesses and helps those suffering from any mental affliction, including anxiety and depression.

Saint John the Baptist

Known as a saint in the Catholic Church, as well as an ascended master, Saint John the Baptist may be called upon for help achieving emotional and mental balance. He can align your mind with the Divine mind and help you find balance on all levels—physical, emotional, and mental.

Saint Jude

The patron saint of hopeless cases or impossible situations, Saint Jude helps with anything in life, especially when you are feeling emotionally hopeless and helpless. He intercedes on your behalf with higher helpers to move forward into hope, peace, and healing.

Saint Maximilian Kolbe

The Catholic patron saint of addictions, Saint Maximilian Kolbe was known for working with people struggling in this area during his lifetime. Call on him for direction, guidance, and healing when struggling with any type of addiction or addictive behavior.

Vishnu

The Hindu god Vishnu helps you when you're in need of calm energy and patience in the face of fear and worries. He works to stop fear from overpowering you and disturbing your peace.

CRYSTALS FOR EMOTIONAL HEALING

These crystals are used when you seek to draw in emotional healing and balance for a variety of issues, including clearing emotional blocks, healing a grieving heart, or overcoming anxiety, depression, and stress.

Angelite

Calming to the emotional, mental, and etheric body, angelite soothes overwhelming emotions, brings in calming vibrations, and connects you to the angelic realm and its messages.

Apache Tear

A strong emotional healer, Apache tear is an obsidian stone that brings comfort in times of grief and sorrow and absorbs grief for deep emotional healing.

Aquamarine

This light-blue stone helps in times of grief and releases attachments to another person's physical presence. Aquamarine also balances emotion and heals emotional trauma. Aligning with both the heart and throat chakras, it is helpful during emotional conversations, allowing you to speak your truth with love and compassion.

Blue Kyanite

A throat chakra stone, blue kyanite assists with fear around speaking your truth and expressing yourself.

Celestite

A calming and balancing stone, celestite provides clarity and peace to any environment it's placed in, connects you with the angelic realm, and alleviates fear and worry.

Chrysoprase

Chrysoprase calms the energy of your fears, phobias, and nightmares and works with your subconscious mind to draw out the source of irrational fears and restore peace and balance.

Clear Quartz

Clear quartz is a master healer stone that is universal and amplifies any intention it is programmed with, and it also amplifies the energy of any stone it is placed near or on.

Danburite

This heart chakra stone eases emotional pain and increases acceptance of both yourself and others. When carried with you, danburite eases stress and calms difficult situations.

Dioptase

A heart-healing stone, dioptase aids in letting go of the past and opening up to compassion and forgiveness. Often referred to as a stone of forgiveness, it assists in letting go of past wrongs and anger.

Golden Healer Quartz

This master healing stone clears and repairs the etheric body, or aura/energy field around the physical body, and clears both physical and emotional blocks. As a crown chakra stone, golden healer quartz also promotes peace and soothes the mind.

Green Aventurine

The soothing energy of green aventurine, a heart chakra stone, is ideal for those suffering heartache as it helps to process and release old emotional wounds. It also balances the emotional body to create harmony within.

Hematite

Often referred to as a stone for the mind, hematite alleviates anxiety and stress. As a root chakra stone, it promotes a feeling of grounding, safety, and security and assists with concentration and focus.

Hematoid Quartz

Containing the properties of both quartz and hematite, hematoid quartz is ideal for those who suffer from low self-esteem. It assists with emotional balance, optimism, and courage and helps you feel grounded, balanced, and focused. It also attunes the entire chakra system from the crown to the root.

Howlite

Struggling with anxiety, stress, and worry? Howlite is the gemstone to reduce all of these emotions, including anger and panic. It is a calming stone and is helpful for those who suffer from insomnia due to an overactive mind.

Kunzite

Effective at clearing emotional blocks, this heart chakra stone brings the energy of unconditional love, self-compassion, and emotional balance. Kunzite is also a calming stone to reduce stress and anxiety and assists in releasing negativity and past emotional trauma.

Larimar

Stimulating the heart, throat, third-eye, and crown chakras, this calming stone resembles the ocean with its soft shades of blue, and larimar washes away anxious energy to encourage peace, clarity, and stillness.

Lepidolite

Containing the mineral lithium, lepidolite has a calming effect on the mind and body and is helpful to those with anxiety and depression. It relaxes a stressed and frayed nervous system, an overworked mind, and tension in the body.

Lithium Quartz

A clear quartz crystal with minor inclusions of lithium, it assists in finding emotional peace, stress relief, and relaxation. Said to balance the brain and emotions, lithium quartz helps those with anxiety, panic attacks, and depression, as it soothes the nervous system and alleviates worry and fear.

Malachite

This stone releases old traumas and wounds or energy patterns stored in the mind and body, and malachite heals the heart in times of heartbreak and loss.

Moonstone

Use moonstone to soothe and balance emotions and stress and calm the nervous system when emotionally triggered.

Peacock Ore

A stone of happiness and joy, peacock ore helps you move in a positive direction as it radiates the energy of optimism and assists you in finding joy in each moment.

Pink Opal

Connected to the heart chakra, pink opal heals emotions and opens the heart to love. It also cultivates self-compassion and compassion toward others and restores balance from grief and loss by emanating vibes of peace and tranquility. It's also helpful to dissipate stress, worry, and anxiety.

Pink Tourmaline

A heart chakra stone with the properties of love and compassion, pink tourmaline is helpful when trying to heal emotional wounds, including those from childhood, and can release emotional pain. It also stimulates feelings of love, joy, happiness, and peace.

Rainbow Fluorite

Find freedom from overthinking, overanalyzing, and overload in the mind with rainbow fluorite, which also brings clarity to the mind, stabilizes emotions, and balances the brain and the energy body.

Rhodochrosite

A crystal for self-forgiveness, rhodochrosite helps release self-judgment, self-criticism, guilt, and shame and assists with overall emotional balance. It opens the heart, alleviates depression, cultivates a positive outlook, and is helpful to those healing from abuse or a broken heart.

Rose Quartz

This heart chakra stone heals the heart from pain, disappointment, and trauma and releases emotional blockages. As a stone of universal love, rose quartz also cultivates more self-love and balance and harmonizes the body, mind, and spirit.

Selenite

Selenite is a calming stone that creates a sense of peace within you, clears energy and emotions from your aura, and assists with meditation.

Smoky Quartz

As a grounding and relaxing stone, smoky quartz increases one's ability to handle stress and calms the nervous system. It's also helpful for those struggling with fear, anxiety, and depression and aids in dispelling nightmares.

Snowflake Obsidian

Referred to as a stone of purity, snowflake obsidian balances the body, mind, and spirit and assists you in staying centered and stable no matter what is going on around you. It's a grounding stone with a calming and soothing energy.

Sugilite

This nurturing stone strengthens and soothes the nervous system, and sugilite also releases worry and stress.

Tangerine Quartz

A stone that stimulates happiness, joy, and passion, tangerine quartz inspires enthusiasm and energizes you, as well as improves your physical, emotional, mental, and spiritual health by creating harmony and balance.

PRAYERS FOR EMOTIONAL HEALING

For those times when you need emotional healing and guidance to move forward into joy, happiness, and peace in this area of life, I've included six prayers that can be used for a variety of issues, including healing heartbreak, releasing emotional baggage, and overcoming anxiety and depression.

Prayer: Healing Heartbreak

Dear Universe, I call in my angels, guides, loved ones who have passed on, and all those in my soul society, only those of the highest vibration, to be with me now as I seek to heal my heart from [fill in the blank].

I am asking for help in releasing the pain and sorrow I am carrying with me, and in replacing it with contentment and the ability to feel joy and happiness with ease again.

I call in help from Archangel Charity and Saint Dwynwen, and ask you to envelop me in the energy of Divine love and assist me in healing my heart during this difficult time. Goddess Aurora, I ask for your help in seeing my current situation more clearly, as well as assisting me with a new beginning filled with more joy in my life.

Archangel Haniel, please use your orb of blue healing light to dive into any heavy or negative emotions I am carrying within me now and transform them to love and peace, and Saint Germain, please use the violet flame to transform my heartbreak, hurt, and grief into love and light.

I also call on Archangel Jeremiel and Archangel Zadkiel to help me find forgiveness for [name person or situation causing heartbreak], which triggered this heartbreak and pain, so I may find freedom from it. Archangel Jophiel, please help me shift my mindset from negative to positive in all areas of my life and assist me in holding more positive thoughts throughout the day today.

Finally, I call in Ganesha to remove any obstacles, known or unknown, standing in the way of my emotional healing and freedom from this pain, grief, and sorrow. I ask that you all send me the signs and synchronicities to let me know you are around me, so I know I am not alone in this grief, and please also send them to show me the way out of it and into healing. I am open and ready to receive them now and ask you to help me recognize them when they arrive and act on them when needed.

Thank you for your support, guidance, and love during this difficult time in my life. Amen.

Prayer: Healing from the Loss of a Loved One

Dear Universe, I call in my angels, guides, loved ones who have passed on, and all those in my soul society, only those of the highest vibration, to be with me now.

I am seeking help, support, and guidance to heal my heart from the devastating loss of [fill in the blank]. While I know and believe [fill in the blank] is still with me, I am very much missing their physical presence around me.

Archangel Azrael and Archangel Charity, please help me heal my grieving heart after this loss so I may find a sense of peace and calm during this difficult time and discover how to move forward in the midst of this loss.

I also call in Archangel Haniel to use your orb of blue healing light and clear any heavy emotions I'm carrying with me now, transforming them into love and peace, and Saint Germain please use the violet flame to transform my grief into peace and love.

[If the loss of a child] I call in Goddess Frigg and Mother Mary to help me grieve the loss of my child as I've never felt pain like this before and need your support and assistance to move through this now.

Goddess Aurora, I call on you to guide me forward toward brighter days so that I may heal and move forward with my life, and Ganesha, please remove any obstacles standing in my way of doing this with ease, grace, support, and love.

I ask that all my higher helpers send me the signs, synchronicities, resources, opportunities, and people that can help me do this now, and please help me recognize and take action on them when they arrive.

Thank you so much for your support, guidance, and love during this difficult time in my life. Amen.

Prayer: Healing Anxiety and Fear

Dear Universe, I call in my angels, guides, loved ones who have passed on, and all those in my soul society, only those of the highest vibration, to be with me now, as I call on your guidance and assistance in releasing and healing the anxiety and fear I am carrying now.

I specifically call on Buddha to help me with emotional balance and peace no matter what is going on around me, and to assist me in finding ways to cultivate that inner peace. Padre Pio, please help me to find freedom from stress, anxiety, fear, and worry, and work with Saint Dymphna and Saint John of God to send me to the right healing modalities, resources, healers, and more to help me do so. And please help me recognize the guidance when it arrives.

Archangel Haniel, I ask you to help me stay centered and balanced no matter what is going on in my life, and use your orb of blue healing light to transform any heavy or negative emotions within me now into a higher vibration of love and peace. Please also work with Saint Germain and the violet flame to clear this anxiety and any emotions or energy triggering it now.

Vishnu, I ask for your assistance in finding freedom from worry and ushering in a sense of peace and calm, and Archangel Jophiel, please shift my mindset from negative to positive in all areas of my life, especially the thoughts contributing to anxiety and fear, and assist me in holding more positive thoughts throughout the day.

Lastly, I call in Saint Jude to intercede on my behalf with other higher helpers so I may find total freedom from the anxiety and fear that plague me now, and Ganesha, to remove any and all obstacles blocking my path to peace.

I am open to all of the signs and synchronicities you send to guide me now into a better place with more ease, peace, and joy. Thank you in advance for all of your assistance in this urgent matter. Amen.

Prayer: Healing Depression and Sadness

Dear Universe, I call in my angels, guides, loved ones who have passed on, and all those in my soul society, only those of the highest vibration, to be with me now, as I struggle to lift this cloud of depression and sadness from my heart, mind, and soul.

I specifically call on the help of Saint Dymphna, patron saint of depression and mental illness, and Saint John of God, patron saint of those who are mentally and physically ill, along with Saint Jude to assist and guide me now as I seek relief from the hopeless and emotional state I am currently stuck in.

Archangel Charity, please envelop me in your energy of Divine love so I may heal my heart during this difficult time, and Archangel Jophiel, please help me shift my mindset from negative to positive in all areas of my life so I may notice the good and the joy around me, and help me to hold more positive thoughts throughout the day.

I also ask Archangel Haniel to use your orb of blue healing light to transmute any heavy or negative emotions I am carrying with me now into the positive vibrations of love and peace, and Saint Germain, please use the violet flame to do the same.

I'm also calling in Goddess Aurora to help me see things in my life more clearly and truthfully, and facilitate a new beginning where I can notice, find, and feel joy in my life with more ease. Finally, Ganesha, I ask you to remove any and all obstacles in my path right now blocking me from feeling more joy or finding the answers I seek to do so.

I ask all my higher helpers to send me the signs and synchronicities to guide me to the right healers, resources, modalities, opportunities, and people that can help, and please assist me in recognizing them and acting on them when they arrive.

Thank you in advance for all of your help and guidance in the past and for what I know will be coming in the future. Amen.

Prayer: Overcoming Addictive Behaviors

Dear Universe, I call in my angels, guides, loved ones who have passed on, and all those in my soul society, only those of the highest vibration, to be with me now, and I ask for help in releasing my addiction to [fill in the blank].

I specifically call in Goddess Kali, Holy Amethyst, Saint Maximilian Kolbe, and Buddha to help release my struggle with this and replace it with healthier ways of coping with my life, uncertainty, and stress and to help me connect with inner peace and wholeness now.

I'm also calling in Goddess Aurora to help me see things more clearly and truthfully to aid in this recovery and to facilitate a new beginning where I can notice, find, and feel more joy in my life to help me overcome this addiction. Finally, Ganesha, I ask for you to remove any and all obstacles in my path right now to overcoming this addiction and moving forward in my life without it.

Please send me all the signs, synchronicities, resources, opportunities, and people who can assist me with this now, and please help me recognize them when they arrive. I also ask for the strength I need to act on them when they arrive to help myself let go and heal.

Thank you, thank you, thank you. Amen.

Prayer: Self-Love and Acceptance

Dear Universe, I call in my angels, guides, loved ones who have passed on, and all those in my soul society, only those of the highest vibration, to be with me now. I'm asking for help in letting go of any self-sabotaging behaviors and thoughts so I may move toward unconditional love and acceptance of myself as I am now, a soul who is already whole, complete, and perfect as I was created.

I specifically call in Archangel Charity to envelop me in the energy of Divine love and to heal my heart in whatever way necessary for me to fall in love with myself unconditionally. Archangel Jeremiel and Archangel Zadkiel, please help me forgive myself for how I've treated myself in the past, for allowing things I should not have allowed in my life, and any other areas I am currently beating myself up around. I also ask Archangel Jeremiel to assist me in seeing any patterns that led me to where I am now and to find the blessings in my past experiences rather than focusing on the negative.

Archangel Jophiel, I ask for your help in shifting my mindset from negative to positive around myself, my body, my mind, my abilities, and my life and to assist me in holding more positive thoughts throughout the day around this.

I also call in Louise Hay, who taught so many people how to tap into self-love while in this physical world, to help me not only tap into this for myself, but to send me the people, resources, and opportunities that can help me. Quan Yin, master of unconditional love, please assist me in cultivating this for myself and in finding more compassion for myself. And Ganesha, I ask you to please remove any and all obstacles blocking my path to total and complete acceptance and love for myself.

I am ready to love and accept myself, and thank you in advance for any guidance you may send to help me achieve this now. I am open to all the signs and synchronicities you will send to guide me forward, and I ask you to help me notice them and act on them when they arrive.

Thank you, thank you, thank you. Amen.

RITUALS FOR EMOTIONAL HEALING

Here are two rituals to help balance emotions and heal the heart. They combine intention, crystals, and prayer to help you heal and call in higher help to assist.

Ritual: Infinite Harmony and Balance

This ritual is a combination of prayer and crystals to call in higher help and harness the energy of the Universe, but it takes it one step further by placing the crystals on your physical body. It also incorporates the healing and emotionally balancing power of meditation.

In choosing crystals, I recommend always placing selenite above your head to clear and open your crown chakra and smoky quartz at the base of your feet to ground and calm the nervous system. However, for the crystal to place over your heart, choose from the list of crystals on pages 155–160 based on what you are trying to achieve emotionally. If there is more than one that fits the description, choose the one that resonates the most with you.

For example, if you are trying to cultivate more self-love and self-acceptance, you could use rose quartz, rhodochrosite, or kunzite. If you are looking to calm your nervous system and balance anxiety, you might choose howlite, larimar, or celestite.

Items needed:

- One sage bundle/incense, palo santo wood, or frankincense incense to burn; or your favorite energy-clearing spray
- One selenite crystal (any shape or size)
- One heart-healing chakra crystal (any shape or size)
- One smoky quartz crystal (any shape or size)

Step 1: Clear the Energy

Burn the sage, palo santo, or frankincense (or use your clearing spray) to cleanse the energy of the room, as well as the heart chakra stone you chose and the smoky quartz. The selenite does not hold energy and does not need to be cleansed. Simply pass the crystals through the smoke or spray them directly with a cleansing spray.

Be sure to clear your own energy as well, using the smoke, spray, or selenite crystal. To use the selenite, hold it approximately three to six inches away from your body, use a combing motion around your legs, arms, torso, and head, and say out loud, "Clearing any negative energy or energy that does not belong to me. Replacing it with love and light. And so it is."

Step 2: Program the Crystals

Place your hands above all three crystals and repeat this prayer out loud or in your head:

I call the energy of the Universe to clear all unwanted energy and previous programming from these crystals. I command and program them now to work with my energy and harness the energy of the Universe around me to draw in guidance and direction on where to go and what to do next in order to heal. I also command them to balance my emotions and help me heal from [fill in the blank]. I specifically program the selenite to clear any negative energy and emotions from my body and help balance my energy from my crown chakra to the root chakra; the [insert heart-healing stone and what you intend it to do here], and the smoky quartz to ground my energy into my body so I may feel centered and balanced.

Step 3: Call in Higher Help

NOTE: For this prayer, feel free to call in specific higher helpers who specialize in what you are trying to heal emotionally from in the "specific intentions" section below.

Repeat the following prayer either out loud or in your head:

Dear Universe, I call in my angels, guides, loved ones who have passed on, and all those in my soul society, only those of the highest vibration, to be with me now as I seek emotional healing. I call in the spirit of Buddha, Archangel Azrael, and Archangel Haniel to please help me remain calm, balanced, and centered no matter what is going on around me. Buddha and Archangel Metatron, please help me let go of any attachments and energy that no longer serve me and are no longer healthy for my mind and body. I also ask Archangel Haniel to use your blue orb of healing light and to work with Holy Amethyst and Saint Germain with the violet flame to remove any heavy emotions and negative energies I am carrying and transmute them into love.

Archangel Charity, please heal my heart from any pain or grief I'm feeling, and Archangel Jeremiel, Archangel Zadkiel, and Quan Yin, please help me open my heart to forgiveness and compassion both for myself and others.
[Add your special intentions and call in other specialized help here.]

Lastly, I call in Ganesha to please remove any obstacles standing in the way or blocking my path to healing, balancing my emotions, and finding joy. Thank you, thank you, thank you. Amen.

Step 4: The Setup

This ritual essentially creates a crystal grid using your body and laid out in the shape of the infinity symbol to open the flow of any stuck energy and emotions.

1. Lay down flat with enough space above your head and below your feet for crystals.

2. Place the selenite crystal a couple of inches above your head.

3. Place the smoky quartz crystal a couple of inches below your feet.

4. Place the heart-healing crystal on top of the middle of your chest.

Step 5: Meditation Mantra

Take three deep breaths in through the nose and out through the mouth. For ten minutes or more (feel free to set a timer), repeat the following mantra while imagining the energy flowing in a figure eight over your body: "Release, release. All is well. I am safe." Repeat this ritual for nine days in a row.

Ritual: Heart-Healing Crystal

Heartbreak is a real thing. There is even a medical diagnosis called broken heart syndrome, also known as stress cardiomyopathy, where stress and stress hormones quickly weaken the heart and can feel like a heart attack. Whether suffering from an ongoing battle with anxiety and depression, the ending of a relationship, the death of a loved one, or a betrayal by someone you care about, the result is the same: a heart (and heart chakra) in need of healing.

This ritual can be done once every seven days as needed. It uses the power of prayer and the energy of crystals to call in solutions, as well as heal and balance the heart chakra.

Items needed:

- One sage bundle/incense, piece of palo santo wood, or frankincense incense to burn; or your favorite energy-clearing spray
- One selenite wand (optional)
- One crystal pendant or necklace (choose any heart-healing crystal or a combination of them from pages 155–160)
- One crystal bracelet featuring any heart-healing crystal or combination of them from pages 155–160 (optional)

Step 1: Clear the Energy

Burn the sage, palo santo, or frankincense (or use your clearing spray) to cleanse the necklace or pendant (and bracelet if using one) by passing it through the smoke, or spray it directly with a cleansing spray.

Be sure to clear your own energy as well using the smoke, spray, or, optionally, a selenite crystal wand. To use the selenite, hold it approximately three to six inches away from your body, use a combing motion around your legs, arms, torso, and head, and say out loud: "Clearing any negative energy or energy that does not belong to me. Replacing it with love and light. And so it is."

Step 2: Program the Crystals

Place your hands above the jewelry and repeat this prayer out loud or in your head:

I call in the energy of the Universe to clear all unwanted energy and previous programming from this crystal. I command and program it now to heal and balance my heart and heart chakra from [fill in the blank] and to assist me in releasing any negative or stuck emotions and opening my heart to more joy and love.

Step 3: Call in Higher Help

With your hand still above the crystal(s), repeat the following either out loud or in your head:

Dear Universe, I call in my angels, guides, loved ones who have passed on, and all those in my soul society, only those of the highest vibration, to be with me right now. I am seeking help in healing my heart and my heart chakra, releasing negativity and negative emotions, and opening up to love in all forms.

Archangel Charity and Saint Dwynwen, I ask you to help me feel Divine love and assist in healing my heart chakra, as well as creating more self-love. Archangel Jeremiel and Archangel Zadkiel, please help me forgive myself and others so my heart can open and mend.

I also ask Archangel Haniel to use your orb of blue healing light to clear any heavy or negative emotions from my heart chakra now and transmute them into love, and please work with Archangel Metatron, Saint Germain, and Jesus to clear any energy and emotions from my heart no longer serving me.

[If grieving the loss of a loved one] Archangel Azrael, assist in healing my heart from the loss of [fill in the blank].

Lastly, I call in Ganesha to please remove any obstacles blocking my heart from healing and opening to love now.

Please send me the healing, signs, synchronicities, and more to guide me forward now, and please help me recognize and act on them when they arrive. Thank you, thank you, thank you. Amen.

Step 4: Wear the Crystals

Place the necklace (and bracelet if using one) on your body, and wear it for the next seven days. If you prefer not to sleep or shower with it on, you can remove it and then put it back on as soon as you're done showering or sleeping. Repeat this ritual every seven days as needed.

FOCUSED GRATITUDE FOR EMOTIONAL HEALING

When feeling anxious, depressed, heartbroken, or stuck in grief, it is often difficult to find and reach for gratitude. However, it's so important to reach for a more positive feeling to shift your energy into a higher vibrational state so you can start to see changes, notice the guidance coming in, and change what flows into your life. These two exercises assist with this and can be done separately or together for a more powerful impact.

Exercise: Mine the Past for Joy Gratitude

In this exercise, you focus gratitude on the past—specifically looking back to situations and people that brought you joy, bringing them to mind with as much detail as possible, while feeling gratitude in your heart. You can go back to any time in the past, whether it's a week ago or twenty years back. The goal is to find things that occurred prior to feeling unhappy and unhopeful so you can bring that feeling of gratitude into the present.

If you are healing emotionally from a specific circumstance or in a certain area of your life, feel free to focus the gratitude in that area. For example, if you ended a relationship with a significant other, focus your gratitude on all relationships throughout your life. If you are trying to heal from anxiety, go back to your childhood and feel grateful for specific times or events when you felt carefree and relaxed.

I recommend adding this exercise into your daily routine at least three times a day to shift your energy and focus and to send signals out to the Universe that you are ready to create and sustain a more positive and uplifting emotional state.

Step 1: Set an Alarm
Set an alarm on your mobile phone or watch for three times each day. You can also habit-stack this exercise with an established routine, such as breakfast, lunch, and dinner.

Step 2: List Three Things
Think back to a time in your past when you were happy. Bring the scene to mind, imagining it with as much vivid detail as possible, and feel the gratitude in your heart. Who is with you? What is happening? Why are

you so happy? What can you be grateful for about this? Focus on the positive emotions you felt during that time or event, and feel them as if you are living it right now with a smile on your face.

Specifically, think of three times, circumstances, or people to be grateful for from the past—either around the specific area you are healing or in general. And feel free to repeat these each time you do this exercise if they continue to feel good.

For example:

- I'm so grateful for the Disney vacation my parents gave me when I was ten years old. I had so much fun on the rides, taking pictures with the characters, and eating ice cream.
- I'm so grateful for the summers I spent swimming in my best friend's pool and relaxing in the sun when I was in high school.
- I'm grateful with all my heart for all the holiday presents I received every year from my parents, and how excited I would get when opening them.
- I'm so grateful for the time I slept over at my best friend's house, when we ate snacks and watched movies all night long.
- I'm so very grateful for the teacher who helped me with extra tutoring in sixth grade so I could get better test scores.

Step 3: End with an Affirmation

Close your eyes, take a deep breath in and out, and with a smile on your face say:

I am so grateful to the Universe for all the happy, carefree, and loving times in my life, and I am so grateful the Universe is partnering with me to create more of them in my life right now.

Repeat this three times.

Exercise: Find Good on the Hour Gratitude

When on a journey to heal emotionally in some way, there can be many ups and downs in your emotions and overall vibration throughout the day. This exercise helps to lift your mood and shift your energy back into a positive state so that you break up the negative feelings and emotions and replace them with positive ones. It also trains your brain to look for the good throughout the day so you are more likely to notice it in the future.

Step 1: Set an Alarm

Set an alarm on your mobile phone or watch for the top of every hour starting when you wake up in the morning and continuing until you go to sleep each night. You can also download a mindfulness-bell app to go off each hour.

Step 2: Look for the Good

When the alarm goes off, stop and think of at least one good thing that happened in the past hour. If you really can't find anything from the past hour, you can go to a past event, but try for something as close to the present as possible. For example:

- I'm so grateful I slept well last night (or I didn't wake up as many times as I usually do).
- I'm so grateful for the food I had for breakfast and the money to buy it.
- I'm so grateful I got a parking space at the doctor's office so close to the door.
- I'm so very grateful my friend called to invite me out to lunch this weekend.
- I'm so grateful I didn't have any anxiety in the past hour.

Step 3: Ending Affirmation

Close your eyes, take a deep breath in and out, and with a smile on your face say: "I am so thankful the Universe is continually providing me with things to be grateful for and that I can easily recognize them when they occur." Repeat this three times.

No matter what emotional turmoil you may be working through, this chapter offers you solutions to guide you to a better place. In the next chapter, we dive into relationships. Whether you're looking for a new one or repairing an existing one, there are tools to help.

Chapter 8

RELATIONSHIPS

ALL RELATIONSHIPS ARE VEHICLES FOR growth—the ones that bring us joy and the ones that bring us pain. They all serve a purpose, and in many cases are preplanned before our souls even incarnate into a physical body. Each soul makes the choice to come into this physical world and chooses its parents, the lessons it will learn, and the people who will help and hurt it along the way. Yes, you have free will and can go in whatever direction you choose once here, but there is always a plan and purpose underlying it all.

Many people think of purpose as a career or job, and that definitely plays a role in your overall purpose. Part of my purpose is to teach others how to tap into the Divine higher helpline and communicate with the Universe for guidance and direction to create a life they love. You may be a stay-at-home mom, nurse, doctor, teacher, accountant, or airplane pilot. Whatever role you play is part of your purpose. But the greater plan—a true purpose we all share—is to grow and evolve as a spiritual being. You do this by learning how to love, forgive, and heal yourself physically, emotionally, and spiritually, and the chaos, adversity, and pain you encounter along the way helps you do that. What better way to learn this than through relationships with others who are on the same journey?

Your parents, siblings, teachers, friends, schoolyard bullies, neighbors, coworkers, bosses, and romantic partners all play a role in helping you work toward that purpose of growth, and this chapter gives you tools to navigate the joys and heartbreaks that come with all relationships—and, of course, to partner with the Universe to create positive change, heal your heart, and find more happiness and love.

HIGHER HELPERS FOR RELATIONSHIPS

Whether looking for a new love relationship or a friendship, seeking to repair a relationship, or healing a broken heart, there are higher helpers standing by to assist. Below is a list of higher helpers for relationships.

Archangel Aurora

In relationships, Archangel Aurora heals and balances the solar plexus chakra, especially when you've given your power to another. She can help you take your power back, develop the personal power within to stand up for yourself, and create healthy boundaries with others.

Archangel Chamuel

Archangel Chamuel aids in finding new love relationships and supportive friendships and assists in repairing relationships and misunderstandings between people.

Archangel Charity

As the twin flame to Archangel Chamuel, Archangel Charity also helps you find new love and new friendships, as well as heal relationships and mend broken bonds. She also helps heal the heart chakra and assists in cultivating self-love.

Archangel Christine

Call on Archangel Christine to open the crown chakra and allow higher wisdom into your consciousness around relationships and decisions regarding them. She also helps you stay present in the moment and release any judgment against yourself or another.

Archangel Faith

As the twin flame to Archangel Michael, Archangel Faith aids in developing and awakening inner faith, as well as restoring it when lost. She also assists in building self-confidence and trusting and believing in yourself, others, and the Universe as a whole. Call on her to heal and balance the throat chakra and assist with speaking your truth.

Archangel Gabriel

The messenger of God, Archangel Gabriel assists in all forms of communication and overcoming fear and procrastination related to it. Ask for his help in speaking honestly, clearly, and with Divine love.

Archangel Haniel

Call on Archangel Haniel for help creating new beginnings and positive change and noticing the signs and synchronicities sent to guide you to a new love or friendship. She also helps you stay centered and balanced no matter what is going on in a relationship and uses her blue orb of healing light to transmute negativity and worry dragging your energy down.

Archangel Jeremiel

As the angel of visions and dreams, Archangel Jeremiel helps you see through the eyes of another to gain a new perspective—showing you the effect you have on another for more clarity and compassion.

Archangel Jophiel

As the archangel of beauty, Archangel Jophiel quickly shifts your mindset from negative to positive and helps you hold more positive thoughts. She also heals misunderstandings between people.

Archangel Metatron

In relationships, Archangel Metatron helps you to clear your energy and release what no longer serves you and your highest good. Call on him at the end of a relationship or when cutting any negative cords or bonds with another person.

Archangel Raguel

The archangel of harmony and justice, Archangel Raguel heals arguments and brings harmony to any relationship challenge, as well as assists in creating new, positive, and harmonious friendships.

Archangel Raphael

The archangel to call on for any time of healing, Archangel Raphael heals broken bonds, heartache and offers healing when cutting cords between you and another person.

Archangel Raziel

Call on Archangel Raziel to heal from painful memories or past traumas in relationships and acquire knowledge from past lives—especially vows made in another life affecting your current life, such as a vow of loyalty. He breaks or dissolves these vows and any karmic contracts negatively impacting current relationships.

Archangel Zadkiel

The angel of freedom, benevolence, and mercy, Archangel Zadkiel boosts self-esteem and assists you in letting go of what no longer serves you, including a relationship. Ask for his help with forgiveness, letting go of resentment, anger, and other negative emotions toward another, as well as toxic relationships.

Eros

The Greek god of love and sex, Eros opens and heals the heart chakra and ignites the flames of passion in a relationship, as well as aids in finding a new, passionate, and loving relationship.

Ganesha

The Hindu god Ganesha is the remover of obstacles and works to remove any obstacles standing in the way of repairing a relationship, preventing you from moving out of a toxic relationship, or blocking you from finding a new relationship.

Goddess Aphrodite

The Greek Goddess Aphrodite guides you in all aspects of romance and love—whether you're looking to attract a new relationship partner or increase the passion in a current relationship.

Goddess Hera

As the Greek goddess of marriage, Goddess Hera assists with infidelity or jealousy in a marriage and provides the strength and determination needed to stand up for yourself. She also helps you stay committed when you are ready to give up and brings about justice for any type of betrayal.

Goddess Parvati

As the Hindu goddess of fertility, love, and devotion, Goddess Parvati brings more joy, peace, or understanding into your romantic relationship and assists any time love goes awry. She helps to understand the value of patience and devotion without sacrificing your own needs, dignity, and power.

Goddess Sophia

Call on the Greek Goddess Sophia to bring wisdom, knowledge, and clarity into any difficult situation, to separate truth from delusion, and to illuminate a path forward to guide your relationship to a better place.

Goddess Venus

This Roman goddess of love, sex, fertility, and beauty is the counterpart to the Greek goddess Aphrodite. Goddess Venus ignites passion in your relationship and helps attract a new love relationship.

Jesus

During his lifetime, Jesus demonstrated forgiveness and called on God to forgive others for wrongdoing toward him, including his death. Ask him for help with forgiveness when feeling angry, hurt, or betrayed.

Lady Nada

A member of the Council of Light, Lady Nada was a high priestess in Atlantis and is one of the leaders of the Karmic Board—a group of spiritual beings who implement cause and effect. She clears karmic blockages if you are struggling to find a romantic partner or to get close to and bond with others.

Quan Yin

A bodhisattva, which means one who is awakened or enlightened in the Buddhist culture—also known as Kwan Yin or Guanyin in East Asian culture—Quan Yin is a master of unconditional love, compassion, and mercy. She helps release guilt and self-judgment, while also opening your heart to forgiveness toward someone who has done something to hurt or betray a relationship.

Saint Anthony of Padua

Because he is known as the patron saint of lost causes, most people pray to Saint Anthony when they have lost an item. However, when you feel a relationship is a lost cause, he intercedes either to help improve it or to find the way out of it and into a healthier relationship.

Saint Dwynwen

This Welsh saint is the patron saint of lovers and is the equivalent of the Roman Saint Valentine. Saint Dwynwen helps find true love, improve a romantic relationship, or heal a broken heart.

Saint Germain

This ascended master is the keeper of the violet flame, which is an extension of God's heart energy. Saint Germain uses this to transmute negative energy and anything creating discord into a vibration of love.

Saint John

One of Jesus's twelve apostles, Saint John is the patron saint of love, loyalty, and friendships. He helps find loyal and like-minded friendships, as well as improves existing ones.

Saint Valentine

The patron saint of love, engaged couples, and happy marriages, Saint Valentine is the reason Valentine's Day is celebrated on February 14. As a Catholic priest in ancient Rome, he was sent to jail for performing weddings for couples when new marriages were outlawed. He helps you find and experience true love, assists with a wedding, and creates a happy marriage.

Serapis Bey

As an ascended master, he heals the mental body and helps you on your path to ascension and spiritual enlightenment. In relationships, he helps maintain and repair connections with the other people and creates more harmony when faced with conflict.

White Tara

A key figure in the Tibetan branch of Buddhism, White Tara is a bodhisattva known for compassion, and she expands the heart chakra toward understanding. She also helps you attain the far sight and clear vision needed to see the truth in any situation.

CRYSTALS FOR RELATIONSHIPS

There are so many crystals to assist us with relationships. There are those to help attract love, heal the heart, enhance communication, strengthen bonds, and ignite passion. Here is a list of stones to assist in all aspects and intentions in this life area.

Apache Tear

This emotionally healing stone is useful in situations when forgiveness is needed and in navigating grief and loss. Apache tear also offers powerful psychic protection and stability when dealing with demanding or controlling people.

Aquamarine

Aquamarine is a light blue stone that aids in times of grief, releases attachments to another person's physical presence, balances emotions, and heals emotional trauma. Aligning with both the heart and throat chakras, it is used when having emotional conversations, allowing you to speak your truth with love and compassion.

Blue Lace Agate

Use blue lace agate to neutralize anger and other intense emotions, while calming the mind around relationship struggles. It also enhances peace, love, and happiness and facilitates communication and compassion.

Carnelian

This sacral chakra stone supports sexual energy in a relationship and is called a seduction stone. Carnelian gets you in touch with your own sensuality and improves vitality.

Danburite

A stone of harmony, marriage, and beneficial relationships, danburite is used to attract strong, healthy relationships in all areas of life. Twin danburite crystals formed by two stones growing together are particularly useful in healing relationship struggles.

Dioptase

A heart-healing stone, often referred to as a stone of forgiveness, dioptase helps you let go of the past, including anger and perceived wrongdoing, and opens you to compassion and forgiveness.

Emerald

A heart chakra stone associated with love and fidelity, emerald is the crystal of Goddess Venus and is used to attract new love or friendships. It also improves relationships already established and has been called a stone of successful love, opening the heart and enhancing unconditional love.

Fire Agate

Fire agate is associated with the lower chakras and ignites passion between two people in a relationship, promoting sexual intimacy and connection with one another.

Green Apatite

Green Apatite opens the heart chakra to aid in healing from a traumatic experience or situation in a relationship and enhances compassion, empathy, and unconditional love.

Green Aventurine

An excellent heart chakra healing stone for long-term relationships, green aventurine offers positive energy and rekindles love. It also soothes anger and arguments and creates more harmony and happiness in a relationship.

Lapis Lazuli

A stone of truth and friendship, lapis lazuli not only creates strong bonds and increases harmony in love relationships and friendships, but also, as a throat chakra stone, enhances communication to aid you in expressing your feelings and emotions honestly and clearly.

Orange Selenite

Resonating with the sacral chakra, orange selenite boosts passion, desire, and sexual energy in a romantic relationship.

Peridot

Peridot is a green heart chakra stone that stabilizes your mood and assists with letting go of jealousy, resentment, grudges, and emotional baggage dragging your energy down in a relationship.

Pink Topaz

Pink topaz opens the heart to healing and love so it can attract a genuine love connection and match. It also supports loving relationships and restores hope and love in a relationship.

Prasiolite

Also known as green amethyst or green quartz, prasiolite helps two people understand one another better, to see the other's point of view more clearly. As a heart chakra stone, it clears disharmony and opens one up to love and compassion. It unifies the heart and mind and opens and heals the heart chakra, assisting in creating positive relationships with others.

Rhodochrosite

This stone connects you with the Divine love of the Universe, opening your heart to self-love and acceptance, as well as acceptance of others. Rhodochrosite balances out giving and receiving and heals emotional wounds and past trauma. It also energetically removes walls built around your heart from past hurts.

Rhodonite

Another heart chakra stone, rhodonite encourages mutual understanding and the ability to compromise in a relationship and aids those in disarray, allowing for the creation of more harmony and happiness. It also facilitates forgiveness and compassion and has been called the "rescue stone," unearthing unconditional love.

Rose Quartz

A stone of unconditional love, self-love, and harmony, rose quartz opens the heart and assists in attracting a romantic soulmate. It restores trust, harmony, and peace in any relationship.

Ruby

If you are looking to deepen a romantic relationship and create a closer bond, ruby intensifies emotions and stimulates passion, sensuality, energy, and enthusiasm.

Sardonyx

Sardonyx, made up of both onyx and carnelian crystals, assists in mending broken bonds or arguments in marriage, as well as struggles between a parent and a child, and facilitates happiness.

Sugilite

A great stone to turn to when you have negative attachments or cords to be cut in relationships. Sugilite's purifying energy releases attachments and past trauma and brings a sense of calm and emotional healing.

Unakite Jasper

Often called the stone for couples, unakite jasper contains both pink and green colors connected to the heart chakra and removes stuck or blocked energy in this area, including old resentments and anger. It promotes rebirth, balances the emotional body, and provides balance in a relationship, as well as helping to release unhealthy or toxic habits causing issues.

PRAYERS FOR RELATIONSHIP HELP AND GUIDANCE

There are many types of relationships, and experiences within them, that you may struggle with or desire to change in some way. Here are seven prayers to tackle some of the most common themes that fall under relationships.

Prayer: Attracting New Love

Dear Universe, I call in my angels, guides, loved ones who have passed on, and all those in my soul society, only those of the highest vibration, to be with me now.

I am asking for help in attracting new romantic love into my life. I would like assistance in opening my heart and healing any wounds preventing my next romantic soulmate from entering my life now.

I specifically call on Archangel Chamuel, Archangel Charity, Archangel Haniel, Goddess Aphrodite, Goddess Venus, Saint Dwynwen, and Saint Valentine to work together as a team and guide me toward a new loving partner in my life and to help facilitate this meeting now.

Archangel Charity and Greek god Eros, I ask you to work with me and heal my heart so I am ready and open to my new love when they arrive, and Archangel Raziel, please help me heal from any painful memories preventing me from attracting this person easily and effortlessly when the time is right. Also, please help me remove any vows made in past lives still having a negative impact on my finding my soulmate now. And Lady Nada, I ask you to clear any karmic blockages preventing me from attracting new love.

I also call on Archangel Faith to help me believe in myself and boost my confidence so I attract someone wonderful, kind, loving, and respectful of me, who thinks I am amazing and loves me unconditionally. And Archangel Jophiel, please help me hold positive thoughts around finding new love as I await this person's arrival, especially when I fall into a negative mindset.

I ask all of my higher helpers, especially Archangel Haniel, to aid me in this new beginning and to send me the signs, synchronicities, ideas, opportunities, and people to lead me to this person now, and please help me recognize the signs and the person when they arrive. Lastly, I call in Ganesha to please remove any and all obstacles in the way of my attracting this person into my life now.

In gratitude for all of your help, now and in the future. Thank you, thank you, thank you. Amen.

Prayer: Calling in Like-Minded Friendships

Dear Universe, I call in my angels, guides, loved ones who have passed on, and all those in my soul society, only those of the highest vibration, to be with me now.

I am asking for help bringing new, like-minded, supportive, loyal, and loving friends into my life, and I ask Archangel Chamuel, Archangel Charity, Archangel Raguel, and Saint John to assist me on this quest now.

I also call on Archangel Jophiel for help with my mindset, shifting me from negative to positive thoughts around my ability to meet new friends, and please help me maintain these positive thoughts. Lastly, I call in Hindu god Ganesha, to please remove any and all obstacles that may be in the way of my attracting new friendships into my life now.

In creating this new beginning in my life, Archangel Haniel, I ask for your assistance, and please work with the other higher helpers to direct me toward these new friendships through signs, synchronicities, ideas, opportunities, and people. And please help me recognize the signs and the friends when they arrive. I am ready and open to receive now.

Thank you for all your help in this matter. Amen.

Prayer: Find Forgiveness

Dear Universe, I call in my angels, guides, loved ones who have passed on and all those in my soul society, only those of the highest vibration to be with me now, as I am struggling to forgive [name] for [fill in the blank].

I know forgiveness is needed, not just for [name's] benefit, but for my own peace, happiness, and health, and I am ready and open to receive help in doing this now.

Archangel Christine, please assist me in obtaining guidance from higher realms and releasing any judgment toward myself or [name], and Archangel Zadkiel, help me let go of any resentment, anger, or other negative emotions I am holding toward [name], which I know are only hurting me.

Archangel Raziel, I ask for your assistance in healing from any painful memories or traumas connected to [name] or any other relationship in the past still negatively impacting my life, and please dissolve any vows from a former life negatively impacting this situation as well. I also ask Archangel Charity and Greek god Eros to heal my heart from any pain I am holding onto connected to [name] and our relationship so I can feel more free and at ease.

Archangel Jeremiel, I ask for help in seeing through [name's] eyes so I may understand their actions and point of view—as well as my own actions if needed—to gain more clarity and compassion around this situation. And Goddess Sophia, please help me separate truth from illusion, while illuminating the path forward to a better place.

Jesus, I ask for your help in forgiving [name] not only to free them but to free myself as well, and I call on Quan Yin to lend her wisdom and energy to me so I may find more compassion and forgiveness. Ganesha, please remove any and all obstacles in my way from forgiving [name] now.

I ask that all my higher helpers send me the guidance, answers, signs, and more to help me move through this with ease and grace, and please help me recognize them and act on them when they arrive.

In gratitude for your assistance in this situation, and for the healing I know is on its way. Thank you, thank you, thank you. Amen.

Prayer: Healing from Betrayal

Dear Universe, I call in my angels, guides, loved ones who have passed on, and all those in my soul society, only those of the highest vibration, to be with me now as I struggle with the shock and pain of betrayal from [fill in the blank].

I am longing to heal and move past this to free myself from this energy dragging me down and blocking movement forward in life, as I feel so lost and hurt right now. I specifically call in Archangel Charity, Archangel Raphael, the Greek god Eros, and Saint Dwynwen to help me heal my heart and to send me all the resources, people, and more that can help me do so.

I also ask Archangel Aurora to assist me in taking power back I knowingly or unknowingly gave to [name] and help me create any healthy boundaries needed to heal and move forward. Archangel Raziel, I call on you to help me move past any pain or trauma I'm carrying from this situation or from my overall relationship with [name], as well as anything triggered from my past in this life or another. And please help dissolve any vows connected to [name] holding me back from moving forward and healing.

I am also asking for help in letting go of any anger, resentment, or other negative emotions toward [name] bringing my energy and vibration down, and I ask for Archangel Zadkiel's help with this. I also ask Archangel Christine for help releasing any judgment toward myself or [name].

Jesus, Quan Yin, and White Tara, please help me find the strength within myself to forgive [name] and release this pain to free myself and move on from this betrayal. And Ganesha, please remove any obstacles in my path to healing and forgiveness now.

I ask all my higher helpers to send me any signs, synchronicities, guidance, ideas, and resources to move through this time and truly heal my heart and soul. I thank you in advance for your help. Amen.

Prayer: Improve Communication

Dear Universe, I call in my angels, guides, loved ones who have passed on, and all those in my soul society, only those of the highest vibration, to be with me now, as I am looking to improve communication between myself and [name] to better understand one another through the eyes of love moving forward.

I ask Archangel Faith to balance both [name]'s and my throat chakras so we can speak our truth in a loving manner and from a place of confidence. Archangel Gabriel, I ask you to guide our conversations so we truly listen to one another with an open heart, and provide us with wisdom and strength to speak honestly, clearly, and lovingly without fear or hesitation.

Archangel Jeremiel, please work with us both to come from a place of compassion and view each discussion and situation from one another's viewpoint to facilitate greater understanding and compassion for one another. And Ganesha, I ask you to remove any obstacles blocking our path to open, healthy, and healing conversations now.

Please guide our words and our hearts, and please send me the signs to point me in the direction of any people or resources that can help improve communication between us as well—and help me recognize and act on them when they arrive.

Thank you, thank you, thank you. Amen.

Prayer: Relationship Repair

Dear Universe, I call in my angels, guides, loved ones who have passed on, and all those in my soul society, only those of the highest vibration, to be with me now as I am looking for guidance and assistance in my relationship with [name].

[Explain the situation and what you specifically want help with here.]

I call in Archangel Chamuel, Archangel Charity, Archangel Jophiel, Archangel Raguel, [and Goddess Parvati for love relationships] to repair any misunderstandings and broken bonds between myself and [name] now so we can move to a place of more harmony, peace, respect, love, and understanding.

Archangel Raziel and Archangel Raphael, I call on you to heal any past pain or trauma from both of our hearts, dissolving any vows either of us made in a past life, or karmic contracts between us, negatively impacting us and our relationship now. I also call on Saint Germain to use the violet flame and transmute any energy creating disharmony between us into the higher vibration of love.

I am seeking guidance and insight from the higher realms and ask Archangel Christine to help open my crown chakra to receive this now and to help me release any judgment toward myself or [name]. And Archangel Zadkiel, please help us both release any anger and resentment we may be holding toward one another now. I also call on Jesus, Quan Yin, and White Tara to work together in helping us find more compassion and forgiveness for any perceived wrongs on either side.

Archangel Faith, please help me restore my faith in the ability to repair this relationship and assist me in speaking my truth when necessary in a loving and respectful way. And Archangel Gabriel, please help with overall communication between us so we can speak honestly, clearly, and lovingly without fear. I also call on Archangel Jeremiel and Goddess Sophia to help both of us see one another's viewpoints.

[If you feel you have given your power to another or need better boundaries] Archangel Aurora, I ask for your help in taking my power back and standing in my power when it comes to my relationship with [name], and please help me create healthy boundaries to move forward into a more positive light.

[If a romantic relationship or marriage, include this section] Goddess Aphrodite and Goddess Venus, I ask for your help in increasing the passion in my relationship with [name].

Lastly, I call in Ganesha to clear and remove any obstacles that continue to trip us up in this relationship now. I ask all of my higher helpers to send me the guidance, signs, and synchronicities to help me move forward and repair this relationship now, and please help me recognize and act on them when they arrive.

I ask all of this knowing that if what is in my highest good and the highest good of [name] is to end this relationship now, that I be guided to understand and accept this, and heal from this, as well.

Thank you, thank you, thank you. Amen.

Prayer: Taking My Power Back

Dear Universe, I call in my angels, guides, loved ones who have passed on, and all those in my soul society, only those of the highest vibration, to be with me now as I ask for assistance in taking my power back and standing confidently in that power in my relationship with [name].

I am ready to heal my solar plexus and release anything blocking it or me from standing in my power, creating healthy boundaries and saying no when needed, and I ask for Archangel Aurora's help with this now. Please offer me the strength I need to do so. I also ask for Goddess Parvati's help in balancing my ability to give and receive in this relationship, so I no longer sacrifice my needs, dignity, or power moving forward.

I also call on Archangel Christine to help me release any judgment toward myself or [name] around this issue and Archangel Raziel to heal from any past pain or trauma preventing me from easily standing in and owning my power, as well as standing up for myself and creating healthy boundaries. I also ask that you remove or dissolve any vows or karmic contracts from another life that are negatively impacting this area now. And Jesus, Quan Yin, and White Tara, please help me find compassion for myself and [name] so I can forgive and move into a new, healthy, and empowered energy now.

Additionally, I ask for the help of Archangel Faith and Archangel Gabriel so I may speak my truth from a place of confidence when needed and in a clear, honest, and loving manner without fear or hesitation. And I ask Ganesha to remove any obstacles preventing me from powerfully owning who I am and my truth now.

I ask all my higher helpers to send me the strength and energy I need to accomplish this now and to please direct me through signs, synchronicities, and ideas to anything and anyone who can help me.

Thank you, thank you, thank you. Amen.

RITUALS FOR RELATIONSHIPS

There are three rituals combining intention, crystals, prayers and more to assist in the area of relationships below, including one to fix a relationship, draw a new one in, and break and heal a toxic bond.

Ritual: Relationship Repair

If you need to repair or heal a relationship between you and another person, this ritual draws in and activates harmonious energy and calls in higher helpers to assist. The shape of the crystal grid used is called the vesica piscis, which is a geometric shape featuring two circles intertwined. In both Greek and Roman mythologies, this shape resonates with the goddesses Venus and Aphrodite, which makes it perfect for relationship work. The seed of life, a universal symbol of creation, is made from several vesica piscis laid together, as is the flower of life, which represents the entire creation process.

The gemstones in this ritual are for overall relationship healing and harmony. However, feel free to change the two main crystals to better align with the specific issues and intentions you are working on. For example, if you are looking to ignite passion and sexual energy between you and a partner, you might choose fire agate and carnelian. To create more forgiveness and release past hurt, dioptase and rhodonite are ideal, and for better communication, combine sodalite and blue kyanite.

I recommend doing this ritual in the relationship section of your home according to the Feng Shui Bagua (see chapter 2), which is the far right when walking in the front door, and placing it in an area where it won't be disturbed.

Items needed:

- One sage bundle/incense, piece of palo santo wood, or frankincense incense to burn; or your favorite energy-clearing spray
- One vesica piscis (drawn, printed, or purchased)
- Eight emeralds, small tumbled stones (or a relationship stone of your choosing)
- Eight rose quartz crystals, small tumbled stones (or a relationship stone of your choosing)
- One green aventurine stone (preferably flat to place the clear quartz on top)
- One clear quartz crystal (either tumbled or double terminated with points on both ends)

Step 1: Clear the Energy

Burn the sage, palo santo, or frankincense (or use your clearing spray) to cleanse the energy of the room as well as the energy of all the crystals and the vesica piscis grid. Simply pass all the items through the smoke or spray them directly with the cleansing spray.

Step 2: Program the Crystals

Place your hands above the crystals and repeat this prayer out loud or in your head:

I call in the energy of the Universe to clear all unwanted energy and previous programming from these crystals and grid. I command and program them now to work with my energy and the energy

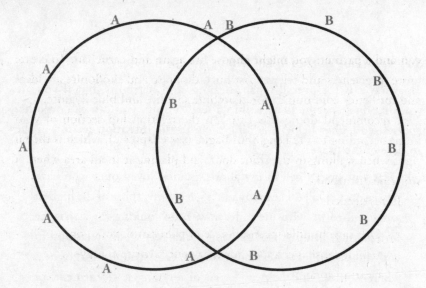

A - Stone 1   B - Stone 2

Figure 5. Vesica Piscis grid.

of [fill in the blank] and to harness the energy of the Universe around me to create more harmony, balance, peace, and healing in our relationship now. And I command the clear quartz crystal to amplify the energy of these other stones and project it into the Universe to draw in the energy to repair and renew this relationship.

Step 3: The Setup

Looking at the vesica piscis grid, start with the left circle (see figure 5) and place the eight emeralds (or other stone of your choosing) around it to complete the circle. Moving to the right side, do the same with the rose quartz (or other stone of your choosing) around this circle. In the center, there is an almond shape where the two circles meet. Place the green aventurine crystal here with the clear quartz crystal on top of it. If using a double terminated crystal, place the points horizontal so they are facing each side of the two circles.

Step 4: Calling in the Higher Help

This prayer is for overall repair, healing, and harmony, but if you are working on a specific issue within a relationship, you can call on other specialized higher helpers, adding them to the intention section in the middle of the prayer.

Dear Universe, I call in my angels, guides, loved ones who have passed on, and all those in my soul society, only those of the highest vibration, to be with me right now. I am looking for assistance in repairing, healing, and shifting the energy in my relationship with [name]. Please heal both of our hearts, ignite forgiveness where needed, and help us let go of any anger, resentment, or hurt toward one another now.

I specifically call on Archangel Chamuel, Archangel Charity, Archangel Raguel, and Serapis Bey to help create more harmony, peace, and understanding between [name] and me and assist us both in moving past this current conflict or misunderstanding.

Goddess Sophia, I ask you to bring wisdom and knowledge to us both so we can see our parts in this and face the truth to move this relationship to a better place, and please work with White Tara to assist in this as well. I also ask Saint Germain to use the violet flame and transmute any discord, disharmony, or negative feelings between us now, replacing them with the vibration of love. [Add other higher helpers for your specific issues here.]

Finally, I call in Ganesha to remove any obstacles standing in the way of repairing this relationship and strengthening the bond between [name] and me now if it is in our highest good.

I ask that you send any signs, synchronicities, ideas, and opportunities to heal this relationship, and please help me recognize them when they arrive so I may act on them. And if this relationship is meant to end, please send me the signs and synchronicities to recognize and accept this as well.

In gratitude for your help and assistance with this matter. Thank you, thank you, thank you. Amen.

Repeat this ritual every thirty days, as needed.

Ritual: Attract New Love

Many years ago, I read the book *The Soulmate Secret*, by Arielle Ford, which teaches how to manifest love in your life. Shortly after turning thirty-seven, I adapted an exercise from the book and created a ritual for myself to do on the night of a new moon. Eight months later, I met my husband.

I've shared this ritual with many people who have had similar results, some faster than eight months and some that took longer. Know that Divine timing is always at play, and you must place your trust in the Universe to bring you the right person at the right time. Also, I recommend performing this ritual outdoors on the evening of a new moon, which happens once every month.

Items needed:

- One piece of paper
- One pen
- One sage bundle/incense, piece of palo santo wood, or frankincense incense to burn; or your favorite energy-clearing spray
- One rose quartz crystal (any shape or size, but I like using a heart-shaped one for this)
- One candle (red, if you have it)
- One ceramic bowl or fire-proof bucket
- One lighter or matches
- One glass of water

Step 1: Cleanse and Program Your Crystal

Burn the sage, palo santo, or frankincense (or use your clearing spray) to cleanse the rose quartz crystal. Simply pass it through the smoke or spray it directly with a cleansing spray.

After cleansing, place your hands over the crystal and say the following:

"I call in the energy of the Universe to clear all unwanted energy and previous programming from this crystal. I command and program it now to open my heart to love, help cultivate unconditional self-love, and to draw to me a new romantic love that is also unconditional and in my highest good."

Step 2: Make a Love List

Light the candle and sit down with the pen and paper, and place the rose quartz crystal next to where you are writing or in your lap. Close your eyes and take two deep, centering breaths. Now write down on the paper all the qualities you would like to have in a romantic partner. Be sure to list more than physical characteristics; focus on the things that are important to you. For example, they must love dogs (or cats in my case) and have a family who loves and accepts you as their own, loves to cook, understands your need for time alone, enjoys hiking, loves you unconditionally, likes to surprise you with flowers, is financially secure, and is open to your spiritual beliefs. I learned this part from Ford's book, along with the next step.

Step 3: Make a Copy of the List

After you write the list, make a second copy of it to save somewhere. After you meet your new partner, it's fun to go back to the list to see how much fits them. When I went back to mine, my husband fit almost every item I listed.

Step 4: Release It to the Universe

Now it's time to release the list to the Universe and allow it to start working with you to bring the two of you together at the right place and time.

Take your bowl or bucket (I used the stoneware insert of my slow cooker) outdoors along with your list, matches, and water. You are going to burn the list in the bowl or bucket and use the water to put it out if it doesn't go out on its own. But before burning the list, hold the rose quartz over your heart and say this prayer out loud:

Dear Universe, I call in my angels, guides, loved ones who have passed on, and all those in my soul society, only those of the highest vibration, to be with me now and assist me in drawing a new romantic partner into my life. I release this list and the intentions within it to you, asking that I attract someone who is in my highest good.

Archangel Chamuel and Archangel Charity, I call on you to help me find this person. Greek god Eros, I call on you to open my heart and heal any wounds that might block or prevent this person from entering my life. And Ganesha, I ask you to remove any obstacles standing in the way of this now.

Please send me the signs, synchronicities, opportunities, and people to assist me with this, and please help me recognize both the signs and the person when they arrive in my life.

Thank you, thank you, thank you. Amen.

Now you can burn the list and release it to the Universe, knowing love is on its way.

Step 5: Keep the Rose Quartz by Your Bed

After the ritual, place the rose quartz beside your bed on a nightstand or table, and cleanse and reprogram it every so often to keep the energy flowing.

Ritual: Break Toxic Bonds

Any relationship with another person creates an energetic connection, or energetic cord, tying you together. These cords exist even if the relationship is over and the person is no longer in your life, and that means energy can still flow back and forth between the two of you.

When a relationship is negative, toxic, hurtful, abusive, or draining, it's important to stop the flow of negative energy between you and the other person. If the person is no longer in your life, this ritual cuts the ties between you for good. However, this ritual is also for someone who remains in your life, but from whom you wish to break the toxic bond of negativity. This ritual clears and releases the negative energy and bonds to promote healing. Though the other person won't consciously know you did this, on a subconscious or soul level, they feel a shift. You may even notice a change with them if you are still in contact.

Items needed:

- One selenite wand, any size

Step 1: Lie Down

Lie down in a comfortable position and place the selenite wand over your solar plexus chakra (belly button area).

Step 2: Visualize

This visualization is adapted from a cord-cutting meditation created by energy therapist Amy B. Scher.[1] The purpose of this ritual is to remove any negative or toxic energy flowing between you and another person. During this visualization, you will call on your higher self or soul to connect and interact with the other person's higher self or soul.

Close your eyes. Start with a breathing exercise called box breathing. Breathe in through your nose for a count of four, hold it for a count of four, then breathe out through your nose for a count of four, and hold it for a count of four. Do this for three complete cycles.

Now bring to mind the person from whom you wish to break the negative bond, and picture them standing in front of you. Imagine a cord connected from your solar plexus (belly button area) to their solar plexus, and take note what it looks like to you. Is it gray, black, cloudy, or darkened in some way? This is the negative energy and attachments we are going to clear now.

Call on your higher self or soul to speak now. Imagine looking yourself in the eye, and start sharing everything that is upsetting you, or has ever upset you, about the other person, how they have treated you and your overall relationship.

Continue this for as long as necessary for you to feel complete, remembering to breathe.

Now you are going to allow this person's higher self to respond to you. Let the answers flow into your mind and remember this is their higher self or soul, not the human being speaking. Don't question or force the information to come through. Simply allow it to unfold before you. If you feel stuck at any point, simply return to your breath, breathing in through your nose and out through your mouth, and ask them to continue.

Listen until you feel the information is complete.

Now call in Archangel Raphael, asking him to send healing energy to both of you, and Archangel Metatron to help you release what no longer serves you in this relationship—including any negative energy, thoughts, or emotions. Allow them to do this now.

Call in Archangel Raziel to help you heal from any painful memories or past traumas connected to this person and to release any vows keeping you tied to this relationship in any way. Allow him to do this now.

Then, pick up the selenite wand lying on your solar plexus, and, keeping your eyes closed, take a deep breath in through your nose, let it out through your mouth, and wave the selenite wand horizontally and then vertically across the middle of your body to cut the cord of negativity flowing between the two of you. State out loud or silently to the Universe: "I release and purify any negative energy no longer serving me in this relationship, and I dissolve it into pure love and light. I connect to my own higher self and my own energy now, and so it is." Then place the selenite wand back on your solar plexus.

Take another deep breath in through your nose and let it out through your mouth.

You are protected. You are safe.

The image of the other person slowly starts to disappear, and you feel centered and balanced. When you are ready, open your eyes.

Step 3: Repeat Two More Times

I recommend doing this exercise three times in total, with two days between each session.

FOCUSED GRATITUDE TO ALIGN YOUR ENERGY

As in any area of life, gratitude can fuel change in relationships. The following exercises will help you use focused gratitude to either mend a broken bond with someone or create a new connection.

Exercise: Relationship Repair Gratitude

Turn to this exercise any time a relationship is struggling in some way. Whether you are in a fight with someone, not on speaking terms, or just struggling to connect or find peace, this exercise can shift the energy between you and another person to create more harmony and diffuse negativity. The best part is, the other person doesn't have to know you're doing it, but on an energetic and soul level, they feel a shift. And you will, too!

It's important to note that in some cases, a relationship may have run its course. The lessons may have been learned and completed, and the relationship as you know it may never be the same or may come to an end. Leave that to the Universe and what is in the highest good, and use this exercise with the intention of healing yourself so you move into a place of peace and acceptance.

I recommend using this exercise at least two times per day until you either see a shift in the relationship or find yourself feeling more at peace and content with the person—even if you never speak again.

Step 1: Picture the Person
Find a photo—digital or physical—of the person who is the focus of this exercise. You can also imagine the person standing in front of you if you don't have a photo.

Step 2: Express Gratitude

Look at the picture, or imagine the person in front of you, and state out loud three things you are grateful for about them, past or present. Try to think of different things each time you do the exercise.

For example:

- Thank you so much [name] for the time you surprised me with flowers.
- [Name], thank you so much for going to the doctor with me when I was sick.
- I am so grateful to you [name] for talking to me that time I was upset about [fill in the blank].
- [Name], I am so very grateful for the time you picked me up from work so I didn't have to drive in the snow.

Step 3: Send Them Loving Kindness

The traditional Buddhist practice known as Loving Kindness, or Metta, is thought to have originated in India prior to the time of Buddha. The practice has been shown to cultivate compassion, acceptance, and love for oneself and others as it intentionally sends positivity and kindness to oneself and others. It can be challenging to send someone loving kindness when you are angry or hurt, and if that is the case, I recommend imagining this person as a child rather than the adult who hurt you.

Look at the picture, or bring their image to mind, and recite the following phrases:

Just like me, you want to be happy.

Just like me, you want to be free from pain.

Just like me, you have felt sadness and sorrow in your mind and heart.

Just like me, you can be angry and act out.

Just like me, you love and want to be loved.

Again, look at the picture, or bring their image to mind, and recite the following, pausing after each statement to send the energy from your heart to their heart. You can even imagine a green, healing energy leaving your heart and entering theirs.

May you be happy.

May you be healthy.

May you be at ease.

May you be and feel safe.

May you love and be loved.

Step 4: Send Yourself Loving Kindness
Place your hands over your heart and send the same loving kindness to yourself. Recite the following:

May I be happy.

May I be healthy.

May I be at ease.

May I be and feel safe.

May I love and be loved.

Exercise: Find New Love Gratitude

When looking to find a new love or romantic partner to share life with, we often focus more on the fact that the person isn't with us yet, rather than the excitement of what life will be like when they arrive. There is impatience, longing, and sadness when your mind focuses on what you don't have, but you can't create new love when focused on the emptiness you feel right now. That is where this exercise comes in!

This exercise helps you cultivate excitement and joy around the new relationship being cocreated with the Universe, and I recommend practicing it at least three times a day, as well as any time you find yourself feeling sad or lonely while waiting for your new love to arrive.

Step 1: Imagine Life with Your Love

Three times a day, stop and think of one thing you do daily or weekly, such as making breakfast, commuting to work, watching your favorite television shows, reading in bed, or grocery shopping. Then imagine doing this activity with your new love already part of your life. Imagine what that looks like and feels like for you. Even imagine it while you are actually doing the activity.

For example:

- Picture yourself making breakfast for the both of you— or this person cooking you breakfast! Imagine chatting with this person while you do this and what it will feel like to be with them in the morning.
- While commuting to work, imagine getting a text from this person saying, "I love you and I miss you already," and feel what that feels like and how you respond back.
- When you are reading in bed, imagine your new love reading next to you because they are a book lover too!
- Picture yourself grocery shopping with your new love, and feel the happiness of being with them during this activity.

Step 2: Imagine Something You Will Do Together

Think of a hobby, or something you love to do, that you want your new love to enjoy or experience with you. It could be a yoga class, going out to dinner, seeing a new movie, hiking a new trail, or vacationing in Italy. Then imagine yourself doing it with your new love and how you feel having them by your side. See yourself on the airplane together or driving to a restaurant on a date night. Feel the gratitude in your heart for these moments and for the Universe bringing the two of you together.

Step 3: End with an Affirmation

Feel the gratitude for this person being in your life. Put a big smile on your face and say out loud or silently to yourself and the Universe, "I am joyfully creating this unconditionally loving relationship in my life right now."

BONUS: As you move through your entire day, think about how it will change when your new love is in your life, imagining them already with you.

The next chapter focuses on career and purpose. If you are looking to embark on a whole new career, find a new employment opportunity, get a promotion, start or grow a business, or find your passion and purpose, there are spiritual tools to help.

Chapter 9

CAREER AND PURPOSE

THE AVERAGE PERSON SPENDS ONE-THIRD of their life at work, and unfortunately far too many of them work simply to earn a paycheck rather than engage in something they love to do while getting paid for it. There are also far too many who are unhappy with their current job or employer even if they love what they do, so they choose to stay out of fear—fear of change, fear that they won't be able to pay their bills if they make a change, or fear that a new job or employer will put them in a worse situation. Instead of taking the leap, they stay in situations that make them miserable, and over time it begins to eat away at their joy, robs them of peace, and blocks them from doing something they love or are meant to do in this life.

Does that sound like you? It was certainly me when I was working full-time as a magazine editor in New York City but longing to focus only on my own business. I shared that story in the introduction, and how the Universe helped me get out in a surprising way, and the same can happen for you. The business idea you have, your longing to change careers, or the feeling of loving what you do but not loving the company or person you work for are signs there are other options out there for you. It is possible to make a change, and when you have the Universe guiding you, it's always easier to achieve it. You might not see the road ahead right now, but there is a road. And when you ask for the help, the path will light up before you. This chapter is dedicated to helping that path light up.

Additionally, for those of you looking for growth and expansion in a current career, or in your own business, the same tools can be used. Any time I am stuck in my business, need a solution, am looking for new ideas and inspiration, or want to make a change, I use the tools in this chapter. My higher helpers have never let me down, and yours won't either.

HIGHER HELPERS FOR CAREER AND PURPOSE

No matter what solution or change you seek around career and purpose, there are higher helpers to assist you. Call on them for new business ideas, more confidence, career growth, and to uncover the best path to pursue to bring you the most joy.

Albert Einstein

A physicist who won the Nobel Prize for physics, Albert Einstein made many discoveries and revolutionized scientific thought during his lifetime. He is called on by entrepreneurs or anyone looking to solve problems, create new products, or come up with novel business ideas.

Andrew Carnegie

Andrew Carnegie was a leader in the expansion of the steel industry and became one of the richest Americans in history. Call on him to generate new ideas, for help making business decisions, especially as an entrepreneur, to assist with keeping thoughts aligned with prosperity and success, and direct a person to resources that can help.

Archangel Aurora

As the twin flame to Archangel Uriel, she facilitates a new beginning or rebirth, as well as ignites passion in career or purpose. Archangel Aurora governs the solar plexus chakra and is called on for help standing in your power and owning who you are and what you desire, while maintaining peace within.

Archangel Chamuel

Often associated with finding love and new relationships, Archangel Chamuel can also be called upon to find your life purpose, a new career path, or a new job.

Archangel Gabriel

As the angel of communication, Archangel Gabriel assists with all aspects of communication, specifically writers, teachers, and artists who want to convey their messages clearly and with love. He also helps you overcome fear and procrastination when it comes to communication.

Archangel Haniel

Call on Archangel Haniel to assist in creating new beginnings around career or life purpose and to align with signs and synchronicities, helping to recognize the guidance sent.

Archangel Hope

The twin flame of Archangel Gabriel, she is called on to tap into creative ideas or inspiration around work. Archangel Hope helps you give birth to new ideas, heighten creativity, and hold the vibrations of hope and optimism to bring desires into form in the physical world.

Archangel Jophiel

Known as the angel of beauty, Archangel Jophiel helps balance negative and positive emotions and assists you in quickly shifting from a negative mindset to a positive one. She also helps you hold more positive thoughts and find the beauty and joy around you even in the midst of struggle.

Benjamin Franklin

A founding father of the United States who helped draft and sign the Declaration of Independence, he was also a scientist, inventor, writer, printer, and publisher. Benjamin Franklin is called on to generate new ideas for success and to solve problems. He assists writers, those involved with politics, and any entrepreneur looking to grow their business.

Bob Proctor

Bestselling author and teacher on the law of attraction, manifestation, and success, he also built a successful business called the Proctor Gallagher Institute, which offers courses and mentoring for those building a business and looking to increase wealth. Bob Proctor is called on by entrepreneurs looking to start or grow a business, as well as anyone looking to increase their wealth and shift their mindset to a more positive one in this area.

Charles F. Haanel

New Thought teacher, successful businessman, and author of *The Master Key System* (published in 1912), Charles F. Haanel taught on a variety of metaphysical subjects including the law of attraction, the power of the mind, and achieving success and prosperity. Call on him if you are looking for help with manifestation, maintaining a positive mindset, abundance, and career success.

Djwal Khul

An ascended master who was a follower of Buddha and known as a Tibetan Buddhist master during his lifetime, Djwal Khul, also known as Djwahl Khul, Djwal Kul, the Master D. K., or simply DK, helps those on a search for a deeper purpose in life to find and follow their dharma, or soul path, in this lifetime.

Dr. Wayne Dyer

A bestselling author and spiritual teacher, he taught about manifestation and self-actualization and was also a successful author—at one time selling books out of the trunk of his car. Anyone pursuing a career in a spiritual field, pursuing a career as a writer, or marketing themselves and a business can call on Dr. Wayne Dyer for guidance and support.

Elizabeth Arden

Born Florence Nightingale Graham, she was an innovator and entrepreneur in the cosmetic industry, opening her first salon in 1910 on Fifth Avenue in New York. After a trip to Paris, Elizabeth Arden was the first person to introduce eye makeup to the U.S. market, and by 1929 owned 150 salons in both the United States and Europe. Entrepreneurs call on her for help with business ideas, perseverance, and assistance in making key business decisions.

Florence Scovel Shinn

An American artist and metaphysical teacher, Florence Scovel Shinn wrote a number of books on prosperity, success, and the use of affirmations for the mind including *The Game of Life and How to Play It* and *Your Word Is Your Wand*. Call on her for help with money and abundance, success, and shifting your mindset to the positive.

Ganesha

A Hindu god known as the remover of obstacles, Ganesha assists with the removal and clearing of any obstacles blocking movement forward around career or purpose.

Geneviève Behrend

A New Thought and mental science teacher, she authored a number of books, including *Your Invisible Power* and *Attaining Your Heart's Desire*. Geneviève Behrend lectured about the power of the mind and the use of visualization for success and founded New Thought schools in New York and Los Angeles. Call on her for help in shifting your mindset and energy to stay in alignment with what you want to create around career and business.

Goddess Athena

Call on this Greek goddess to help with any intellectual pursuits, whether taking a test, learning a new skill, or making an important career decision. Goddess Athena also assists women who seek equality in the workplace and helps you stand up for yourself and have confidence in your skills and abilities.

Goddess Brigid

An Irish deity of spring, fertility, fire, and water, Goddess Brigid sparks imagination, inspiration, creativity, and a new flow of ideas in career and business, and assists anyone feeling blocked creatively to get ideas flowing again. She also helps with clarity, courage, and confidence in your abilities and talents.

Goddess Demeter

This Greek goddess of the harvest, grains, and fertility of the Earth, Goddess Demeter nurtures efforts in growing a business or new project, providing perseverance to help achieve goals.

Goddess Ostara

This Germanic goddess of the dawn and spring helps create new beginnings and birth new ideas. Goddess Ostara is ideal to call on at the start of a new venture, as she provides inspiration and guidance, as well as boosts self-confidence.

Goddess Saraswati

The Hindu goddess of knowledge, wisdom, and education, Goddess Saraswati provides guidance in any intellectual pursuit and is also a patroness of artistic people. Call on her to dissolve creative blocks or help with a new creative project. She is also the goddess of music and provides support to musicians and those who work with music.

Madam C. J. Walker (Sara Breedlove)

The first self-made female millionaire in the United States, according to the *Guinness Book of World Records,* Madam C. J. Walker was an entrepreneur, activist, and philanthropist. She developed a line of cosmetics and hair-care products specifically for Black women. She is called on by entrepreneurs looking to create new products or services and for perseverance.

Napoleon Hill

Author of the book *Think and Grow Rich,* teacher of the law of attraction and manifestation, and mentored by Andrew Carnegie, Napoleon Hill spent years interviewing businessmen to uncover common principles for success. Call on him for help with shifting your mindset from negative to positive and specifically creating a mindset of growth and success.

Steve Jobs

The obvious person to call on for any issues with technology, specifically Apple devices, Steve Jobs was the cofounder, chairman, and CEO of Apple. As such, he is called on by entrepreneurs and those running companies to help facilitate new ideas, inspiration, and growth.

W. Clement Stone

He built a successful insurance company and also practiced and taught the law of attraction and manifestation, writing books on the subject, including *The Success System That Never Fails.* Call on W. Clement Stone for all business pursuits, sales, and shifting your mindset to focus on success.

CRYSTALS FOR CAREER AND PURPOSE

Here is a list of crystals that help with confidence, communication, problem-solving, creativity, and purpose.

Brown Aragonite

Brown aragonite helps with multitasking and problem-solving, helping you get to the root of an issue to find a solution and break through creative blocks.

Carnelian

A great stone for success at work, carnelian boosts motivation, creativity, confidence, and leadership. When kept in an office, it boosts productivity and assists with finding a new job, promotion, or career growth.

Citrine

While it's often thought of as a stone of abundance, citrine also amps up confidence and productivity, helps draw attention to your work, and increases professional success.

Clear Quartz

This master healer stone is universal and amplifies any intention it is programmed with, and clear quartz also amplifies the energy of any stone it is placed near or on.

Falcon's Eye (also known as Hawk's Eye and Blue Tiger's Eye)

As a stone of protection and strength, falcon's eye provides clarity and helps you find direction and purpose in life and career to get clear on the message and work you want to bring into the world. It also helps release fear and blocks to success.

Fire Agate

This highly creative stone ignites passion and joyful energy to follow your dreams and bliss and find the right career or job. Fire agate sparks your desire to take action and is helpful to anyone in a creative field, such as artists, writers, and performers, as it encourages creative expression and clears creative blocks. It's also a protective and grounding stone.

Fluorite

A perfect stone for seeking clarity and focus, as well as emotional balance, Fluorite helps when making important decisions in career or business.

Green Tourmaline

Use green tourmaline to attract both success and abundance in career and business ventures. It's also ideal for looking to turn a passion into a successful career or business.

Kambaba Jasper (or Crocodile Jasper)

This gemstone enhances prosperity and flow of money, improves an established career, and deflects unwanted or unnecessary changes in business to bring in new beginnings and the energy of expansion. Kambaba jasper is ideal to use when starting a new project with the intent of creating profit.

Lapis Lazuli

Place lapis lazuli in your home or office to welcome prosperity, abundance, fortune, and good luck, and when looking to create business success and career advancement.

Mookaite Jasper

This stone increases self-confidence and self-worth and assists in realizing your full potential, while activating the solar plexus chakra to step into and own your power. Mookaite jasper is a grounding stone and helpful in overcoming procrastination, while encouraging motivation toward goals.

Moss Agate

Another stone associated with wealth, abundance, growth, expansion, and new beginnings, moss agate is ideal for entrepreneurs and those looking to bring in new business.

Polychrome Jasper

This gemstone connects with your imagination and creative channels and assists with problem-solving or finding creative solutions and ideas. Polychrome jasper is helpful to those looking for a new job, a change in career, or growing a company. It's also a powerful manifestation stone, associated with passion and movement.

Pyrite

Although this stone is known as a money magnet, pyrite also helps attract career opportunities and the right resources and people needed for growth and success.

Rhyolite

Whether looking to uncover purpose or transition to a new career, rhyolite encourages you to go after your dreams, ignites creativity, and helps uncover and recognize higher potential.

Stilbite

The name of this gemstone comes from the Greek word meaning "to shine," and that is what it helps you do. Stilbite boosts self-confidence and peace of mind and frees you from the judgment of others, helping to increase awareness of love and joy. It's also helpful for entrepreneurs looking to build an effective and strong team.

Sunstone

This stone of leadership helps you find and embrace your personal power, overcome self-doubt, and advocate for yourself when it comes to a job promotion or career growth. Sunstone is associated with overall career success and is linked to joy, good luck, prosperity, and fortune. It balances masculine and feminine energies, encourages optimism, and is helpful when weighing options and making important career decisions.

Tiger's Eye

Often referred to as the stone of courage, tiger's eye boosts confidence and strength and as a root and sacral chakra stone is very grounding and protective. It helps build a strong foundation in a business or career and provides clarity by activating the intellect and sharpening mental powers.

PRAYERS FOR HELP WITH CAREER AND PURPOSE

Whether looking for a new job, to change a career, or find purpose, these seven prayers help you call in a specialized team of higher helpers to assist.

Prayer: Find My Purpose

> Dear Universe, I call in my angels, guides, loved ones who have passed on, and all those in my soul society, only those of the highest vibration, to be with me now, as I am looking to connect with my true purpose and the work I am meant to do in this lifetime.
>
> I specifically call in Archangel Chamuel, Djwal Khul, and Goddess Ostara to direct me on this quest and ask Archangel Aurora and Archangel Haniel to assist me in creating this new beginning and rebirth in my life, igniting my passion toward my purpose now and in the future. Also, please help me to step into my power and own who I am and what I desire around it without fear or worry. And Ganesha, please remove anything blocking me from finding and following my purpose now.
>
> Please send me signs, synchronicities, and ideas to not only uncover my purpose but to follow it, and please help me recognize and act on them when they arrive.
>
> In gratitude for all of your help in this matter. Amen.

Prayer: Growing My Business

> Dear Universe, I call in my angels, guides, loved ones who have passed on, and all those in my soul society, only those of the highest vibration, to be with me now. I am looking to grow my business, specifically [add any intentions you have here].
>
> To assist me with this, I call on Albert Einstein, Andrew Carnegie, Archangel Hope, Benjamin Franklin, Bob Proctor, Elizabeth Arden, Goddess Brigid, Goddess Ostara, Goddess Saraswati, Madam C. J. Walker, Steve Jobs, and W. Clement

Stone to work as a collective group using your skills and wisdom to help me, particularly when it comes to discovering new ideas and solutions to meet my customers' needs and grow my business in size and profit, and to make the best decisions to do so.

Greek Goddess Demeter, I ask for your assistance in helping me find the perseverance within to achieve my goals no matter what obstacles I may face on this path, and Goddess Athena, Goddess Brigid, and Goddess Ostara, please help boost my confidence in my skills and abilities, as well as the confidence I need to make the right decisions to lead to business growth.

Andrew Carnegie, Archangel Hope, Archangel Jophiel, Bob Proctor, Charles F. Haanel, Florence Scovel Shinn, Geneviève Behrend, Napoleon Hill, and Dr. Wayne Dyer, please help me with my mindset so I may stay positive while holding the vibration of hope and optimism around my business. I also ask you to direct me to any resources that may help me do this, as well. And Ganesha, I ask you to work with me and remove anything blocking me and my business from success and growth now.

Please send me the signs, synchronicities, people, and ideas that can help me achieve this and more, and please help me recognize them and act on them when they arrive.

In gratitude for all of your help and insight now and in the future. Amen.

Prayer: Increasing Confidence in Business

Dear Universe, I call in my angels, guides, loved ones who have passed on, and all those in my soul society, only those of the highest vibration, to be with me now.

I am asking for help in believing in myself and my abilities when it comes to career and business, and in finding the confidence within to do my work and make the best decisions moving forward.

I call on Andrew Carnegie, Archangel Hope, Archangel Jophiel, Bob Proctor, Charles F. Haanel, Florence Scovel Shinn, Geneviève Behrend, Napoleon Hill, and Dr. Wayne Dyer to help me keep my thoughts aligned with success, to view myself in a positive light, and to direct me to any and all resources that can help.

Archangel Aurora, Goddess Athena, Goddess Brigid, and Goddess Ostara, I ask you to work together and assist me in having the confidence I need to step into my power, own who I am and what I desire connected to my career, and have more confidence in my skills and abilities. Also, Archangel Gabriel, please help me to overcome fear or procrastination when it comes to speaking up for myself and communicating my needs and desires within my career and business.

I also call on bestselling author and spiritual teacher Louise Hay, who taught self-love and healing, to guide me on my path to increasing my own self-love and to find ways to heal anything standing in the way of my confidence and my ability to believe in and love myself no matter what.

I ask you all to guide me with signs, synchronicities, ideas, opportunities, and people to assist me in this now, and please help me recognize and act on them when they arrive. Thank you in advance for all of your help. Amen.

Prayer: Job Growth and Promotion

Dear Universe, I call in my angels, guides, loved ones who have passed on, and all those in my soul society, only those of the highest vibration, to be with me now, as I am seeking growth in my career either through a promotion or some other way that is in my highest good.

To help me with this, I call on Andrew Carnegie, Archangel Hope, Archangel Jophiel, Bob Proctor, Charles F. Haanel, Florence Scovel Shinn, Geneviève Behrend, Napoleon Hill, and Dr. Wayne Dyer to assist me in keeping my thoughts aligned with success and prosperity and to send me any resources that can help me do this.

Archangel Aurora, Archangel Haniel, Goddess Athena, Goddess Brigid, and Goddess Ostara, I ask for your help in stepping into my power and owning who I am and what I desire connected to my career, and to help me create more confidence in my skills and abilities. Archangel Gabriel, please assist me in overcoming any and all fear or procrastination holding me back now from speaking up for myself and communicating my needs and desires. And Ganesha, please remove any and all obstacles blocking my path now from achieving this growth and success.

Please guide me and send me the signs, synchronicities, ideas, people, and opportunities I need to achieve this or something better now, and please help me recognize them and act on them when they arrive. I thank you for all of your assistance and guidance on this matter now. Amen.

Prayer: New Employment

Dear Universe, I call in my angels, guides, loved ones who have passed on, and all those in my soul society, only those of the highest vibration, to be with me now, as I seek a new job in the field of [fill in the blank] that pays me [fill in the blank] or more per [year or month] and that brings me happiness, joy, and fulfillment each day.

I call on Archangel Chamuel to direct me toward this new job and Andrew Carnegie, Archangel Hope, Archangel Jophiel, Bob Proctor, Charles F. Haanel, Florence Scovel Shinn, Geneviève Behrend, Napoleon Hill, and Dr. Wayne Dyer to help me keep my thoughts aligned with success and prosperity and send me any resources that can help me do this.

Archangel Aurora and Archangel Haniel, please work together to facilitate this new beginning and rebirth in my life and assist me in stepping into and owning my power around my career—especially on job interviews. I also ask Archangel Gabriel to help me communicate clearly and intelligently in any job interview to highlight my abilities and portray myself in a good light to potential employers. And Goddess Athena, please assist me in making the right decision on which job to take while helping me have confidence in my skills and abilities in the work I do, as well as confidence in my ability to find a new job I love.

Finally, Ganesha, I ask you to please remove any and all obstacles blocking my finding and obtaining this new job now with ease and grace.

Please send me the signs, synchronicities, ideas, people, and opportunities to help me achieve this now. In gratitude for all of your guidance and assistance now. Amen.

Prayer: New Career

Dear Universe, I call in my angels, guides, loved ones who have passed on, and all those in my soul society, only those of the highest vibration, to be with me now as I look to shift gears into a new career. [Explain what you are looking to do here, if you know.]

I am looking to make [dollar amount] or more per year doing work that lights me up, ignites my passion, and makes me feel happy and fulfilled every day, and I ask Archangel Chamuel to direct me toward the perfect opportunity now.

Archangel Aurora and Archangel Haniel, please assist in creating this new beginning and rebirth in my life and career, and Goddess Athena, guide me to any new skills to assist me now. I also call in Goddess Brigid and Goddess Ostara to boost my confidence in myself and my abilities to create a new career opportunity now.

I also ask for assistance with my mindset—specifically to keep a positive mindset throughout this process and one aligned with success and prosperity—and I ask Andrew Carnegie, Archangel Hope, Archangel Jophiel, Bob Proctor, Charles F. Haanel, Florence

Scovel Shinn, Geneviève Behrend, Napoleon Hill, and Dr. Wayne Dyer to assist with this and to send me any resources that can help. Ganesha, I call on you to please remove any obstacles blocking my path to finding a new career that is both prosperous and fulfilling and that makes me truly happy each day.

I ask you to send me the signs, synchronicities, ideas, people, and opportunities to lead me forward faster now, and please help me to recognize and act on them when they arrive. Thank you for all of your help in this quest. Amen.

Prayer: Starting a Business

Dear Universe, I call in my angels, guides, loved ones who have passed on, and all those in my soul society, only those of the highest vibration, to be with me now as I begin a new venture starting a business. [State what business you are starting here.]

I am asking for my thoughts and decisions to be guided so I may create a successful and profitable business while serving others in the process. I specifically ask Albert Einstein, Andrew Carnegie, Benjamin Franklin, Bob Proctor, Elizabeth Arden, Madam C. J. Walker, and Steve Jobs to collectively use your skills in business and invention to guide me toward new ideas and solutions to meet my customers' needs and grow my business now and in the future. Goddess Demeter, I also ask for your help in persevering with my goals to start and grow this business even when obstacles appear in my path.

As I embark on this new venture, I call in assistance from Archangel Aurora and Archangel Haniel to help me create this new beginning and rebirth in my life, and Goddess Athena to direct me toward any new skills I can acquire for success. I also ask Goddess Brigid and Goddess Ostara to assist me in boosting confidence in my skills and abilities when it comes to this business and operating it successfully now and in the future.

Additionally, I call on Andrew Carnegie, Archangel Hope, Bob Proctor, Charles F. Haanel, Florence Scovel Shinn, Geneviève Behrend, Napoleon Hill, and Dr. Wayne Dyer for help with my mindset to keep my thoughts aligned with success and prosperity and to send me any resources that can help me do this. Finally, Ganesha, please remove any obstacles blocking my path to a successful business venture now.

Please send me the signs, synchronicities, ideas, resources, people, and opportunities to assist me with my new business now, and please help me recognize and act on them when they arrive.

In deep gratitude for all of your assistance in this process now and in the future. Amen.

RITUALS FOR CAREER AND PURPOSE

These four rituals are used to draw in new opportunities, growth, and ideas.

Ritual: Career and Business Growth

Looking for a promotion, career growth, or to expand your business? This ritual can help, and includes modifications for entrepreneurs versus those employed by someone else. While the setup for this ritual only needs to be done once, the prayer to call in higher help should be done for forty days in a row without skipping a day. Why forty days? Research shows it takes forty days to change a behavior or create a shift in the subconscious mind, and it's also a number referenced in many spiritual traditions and religions as the ideal time period to create a positive transformation, move through challenges, and grow on a spiritual level. For example, in the Catholic religion, the season of Lent lasts forty days and represents the length of time Jesus spent fasting and praying in the desert before he dedicated himself to teaching and helping others.

Items needed:

- One sage bundle/incense, palo santo wood, or frankincense incense to burn; or an energy-clearing spray

- Paper and pen
- [For entrepreneurs and business owners] One moss agate stone (any shape or size)
- [For non-entrepreneur career growth] One pyrite stone (any shape or size)
- Eight small clear quartz crystal points (point on one end)
- Your business card or the name of your business/job title written on a piece of paper

Step 1: Clear the Energy

In the career section of your home according to the Feng Shui Bagua (see chapter 2), which is near the front door, clear the energy using the sage, palo santo, or frankincense (or clearing spray). Also clear the energy of the crystals by passing them through the smoke or spraying them directly.

Step 2: Program the Crystals

Place your hands above the crystals you are using and repeat this prayer out loud or silently in your head:

> I call in the energy of the Universe to clear all unwanted energy and previous programming from these crystals. I command and program them now to work with my energy and harness the energy of the Universe around me to promote growth and expansion in all areas of my career or business—both my reach and responsibilities as well as financially. And I program the clear quartz crystals specifically to amplify the energy of the effects of the [fill in the blank].

Step 3: The Setup

Take the pen and paper, and write down the growth you desire as if it already happened. For example, if you want to grow your own business by a certain amount of money each month or year or by a certain amount of clients, write, "My business brings in X amount of money per month/year or more, easily, effortlessly, and consistently," or "My business has X amount of clients per month, easily, effortlessly, and consistently." If you are looking to grow your career, you can write down a specific title you want to be promoted to, responsibilities you would like to grow into, and even a specific salary. For example, "I am a vice president of sales in charge of X and making X amount per year or more now," or "At my job, I am in charge of X/running the X department, and making X amount per year or more now."

Then write the words, "This or something better."

Fold the paper in half, place your business card or the name of your business or title written on another piece of paper on top, and place the moss agate or the pyrite on top of that in the center. Next, surround the center stone with the eight clear quartz points, with the points facing outward from the center stone.

Step 4: Call in Higher Help

Stand in front of the crystal grid and say either the "Growing My Business Prayer" if you are looking to see growth in your own business or the "Job Growth and Promotion Prayer" if you work for someone else, both found earlier in this chapter.

Step 5: Repeat

Leave the crystal grid in place and repeat the prayer for forty days or until you reach the desired result. If you miss a day, start again at Day 1.

Ritual: New Job or Career

When it comes to career, I come across two types of clients or students—those who are unhappy with their current employer or boss and want a new job in their chosen profession, and those who currently work only to pay the bills but don't feel passionate about or fulfilled by what they do. Whichever category you fall under, my guess is you are looking for a change, and this ritual activates help from the Universe to achieve it.

Unlike the Career and Business Growth Ritual, which is more of an ongoing process in need of continuous energy movement and mindset shifts, this ritual is about activating the energy and the help and then letting it work for you to start creating new opportunities and ideas.

Instead of forty days, you only say the prayer for nine—the traditional novena I spoke about in chapter 2. The Seed of Life pattern for the crystal grid is used because this sacred geometry is a universal symbol for creation (see figure 6).

Items needed:

- One sage bundle/incense, palo santo wood, or frankincense incense; or your favorite energy-clearing spray
- Paper and pen
- A crystal grid or printed image of the Seed of Life pattern
- One green aventurine stone (any size or shape)
- Six clear quartz crystal points, with a single point on one end
- Six polychrome jasper tumbled stones

Step 1: Clear the Energy

In the career section of your home according to the Feng Shui Bagua (see chapter 2, page 51), which is near the front door, clear the energy of the area with your choice of cleansing tool. Also clear the energy of the crystals and the grid by passing them through the smoke or spraying them directly with a clearing spray.

Step 2: Program the Crystals

Place your hands above the crystals and repeat this intention out loud or silently in your head:

> I call in the energy of the Universe to clear all unwanted energy and previous programming from these crystals. I command and program them now to work with my energy and harness the energy of the Universe around me to create a new job or career opportunity for me and draw the perfect people and opportunities to me to help me do so. And I program the clear quartz crystals to amplify the energy of the other crystals and my intention into the Universe.

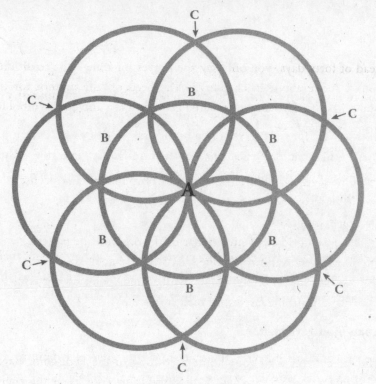

Figure 6. Seed of Life.

Step 3: The Setup

On the piece of paper, write what your ideal job or career would be, and if you don't know exactly, write out how you want to feel doing it. For example, "I am working as a college professor teaching graphic design and making X amount of money or more per year, working only two days per week," or "I am working in a new job or career that I am passionate about and can't wait to wake up to every day."

After this, write the words, "This or something better."

Place the paper down, and place the Seed of Life image on top of it. Next, arrange the crystals as shown in figure 6, with the green aventurine in the center of the grid (A), followed by the clear quartz points (B), and then the polychrome jasper (C).

Step 4: Call in Higher Help

Stand in front of the crystal grid and recite either the "New Employment Prayer" if seeking a new job in your current profession or the "New Career Prayer" for starting over in a brand-new line of work, both found earlier in this chapter. Repeat the prayer for nine days in a row without missing a day, at the same time of day if you can. If you miss a day, start over with Day 1.

Step 5: Repeat as Needed

After the nine days, you can let the crystal grid sit and harness the energy created for an additional nine days. Then repeat the entire ritual as often as needed until you find the new job or career you desire.

Ritual: Find My Purpose

When it comes to purpose, there are many different viewpoints. Each one of us is here for the purpose of soul growth and evolution and to learn various lessons, including how to love and forgive. But we also have a purpose that allows us to contribute in some way to the world and others around us, and this is where career and purpose come together. This ritual helps you uncover your passion and the ways you can use it to contribute to the world while bringing yourself joy in the process.

Items needed:

- One sage bundle/incense, palo santo wood, or frankincense incense to burn; or your favorite energy-clearing spray
- A purple candle (or a flameless candle)
- One falcon's eye (blue tiger's eye) or rhyolite gemstone (your choice)
- Eight clear quartz crystals, each with one point

Step 1: Clear the Energy

In the career section of your home according to the Feng Shui Bagua (see chapter 2), which is near the front door, clear the energy of the room. Also clear the energy of the crystals by passing them through the smoke or spraying them directly with a clearing spray.

Step 2: Program the Crystals

Place your hands above the crystals and repeat this intention out loud or silently in your head:

> I call in the energy of the Universe to clear all unwanted energy and previous programming from these crystals. I command and program them now to work with my energy and harness the energy of the Universe around me to help me uncover and follow my purpose and what I am meant to do here while in this lifetime that will serve others and bring me joy.

Step 3: The Setup

Light (or turn on) the candle and place the falcon's eye or rhyolite crystal in front of it. Then place the eight quartz crystal points around it with the points facing outward from the center stone. If using a flameless candle, you may leave it on all day, turning it off at bedtime.

Step 4: Call in Higher Help

Stand in front of the crystal grid and say the "Find My Purpose Prayer." Repeat lighting the candle and saying the prayer for nine days in a row without missing a day, at the same time of day if you can. If you miss a day, start over with Day 1.

Step 5: Repeat as Needed

After nine days, let the crystals sit and harness the energy you created for an additional nine days, and then repeat the entire ritual again until you see movement forward on your purpose.

Ritual: Boost My Confidence

Confidence in who you are, what you desire, and your ability to create and sustain it is key to moving forward and growing in your career, whether headed into a job interview, starting a brand-new position, or operating your own business. This ritual helps you release what is holding you back and boosts your confidence in yourself, your desires, and your abilities.

Items needed:

- One sage bundle/incense, palo santo wood, or frankincense incense to burn; or your favorite energy-clearing spray
- Pen and paper
- One small fire-proof bowl or metal bucket
- One lighter or matches
- Water to put out flames if needed
- One tiger's eye pendant, necklace, or bracelet (or a combination)

Step 1: Clear the Energy

Choose a spot outdoors to do this ritual, and cleanse the energy of the area, as well as the tiger's eye jewelry and the container you chose, with the sage, palo santo, or frankincense; or the clearing spray.

Step 2: Release Your Blocks to Confidence

Take your pen and paper and write down the energy you would like to release that is currently blocking you from feeling confident in your career. This can include the name of an old employer or boss, comments made from relatives or loved ones, a specific circumstance or event that occurred to negatively impact your confidence, and a list of emotions that you want to release around it. For example:

- [Name], my old/current boss
- My mother telling me I am not good at X
- Fear of failure holding me back

- Criticism I've received in the past from X and X about X
- The time I did X wrong
- Helpless
- Hopeless
- Worthless
- Unsafe
- Insecure

Make your list and then write the words:

I now fully and completely release all of this old energy, as well as any beliefs, emotions, experiences, memories, or fears in my subconscious mind currently blocking me from stepping into my power, owning who I am and what I desire, and feeling fully confident and capable in my abilities and skills. I also release anything blocking me from believing I can and deserve to create what I desire or something better now.

Hold the paper against your solar plexus chakra—just above your belly button—and close your eyes. Imagine a white light coming up from the bottom of your feet, up into your legs and torso, down both arms, and then up through your neck and head until it spills out of the crown of your head and all around your body. Take a few deep breaths and repeat, "Release, release, release," for sixty seconds.

Now open your eyes, take the matches or lighter, and holding the paper over the bowl or bucket, light that paper and drop it into the bowl or bucket, saying out loud:

I release this to the Universe and ask it to be replaced with acceptance, love, confidence, and empowerment within me.

Step 3: Program the Tiger's Eye Jewelry

Place your hands above the tiger's eye jewelry and repeat this intention out loud or silently in your head:

I call in the energy of the Universe to clear all unwanted energy and previous programming from these crystals. I command and program them now to work with my energy and harness the energy of the Universe around me to help me embody confidence and courage within in all areas of my life, including my career, and to move forward in a place of knowing and trust to create all that I desire and more.

Step 4: Wear the Jewelry

Place the jewelry onto your body and wear it until you can see and feel a change within yourself and intuitively feel the work has been completed. I recommend at least forty days, periodically cleansing and reprogramming the crystal jewelry every seven days. Feel free to remove the jewelry to shower, take a bath, or sleep.

FOCUSED GRATITUDE FOR CAREER AND PURPOSE

Here are two gratitude exercises for finding a new job, for guidance around a total career change, or for entrepreneurs seeking business growth.

Exercise: New Job or Career Gratitude

If you are unhappy with your current job or career, looking for a promotion, or are unemployed and searching for your next opportunity, this exercise helps. In order to create a new opportunity in your career, you must shift your focus from being unhappy to being grateful for what is going right. For example, you may feel grateful for the paycheck you have now, the vacation time, the ability to work from home, or your coworker helping with a task. If you are unemployed, this might be feeling grateful for the jobs you are applying for, the interviews you get (even if you don't get the job), the friend helping you with your resume, and even the downtime you have while looking for a job.

Step 1: Look for the Good

At least one time per day, think of three things you are grateful for around your job or career. Put a smile on your face as you say them, and feel the gratitude in your heart for the amazing future you are creating. If you are unemployed, focus on the job-hunting process or the perks of having time off while looking for a new opportunity. For example:

- I'm so grateful for the steady paycheck I get every two weeks to pay my bills.
- I'm so thankful my meeting went well today.
- I'm so grateful I can work from home every Friday.
- I'm so thankful my boss let me leave early today for an appointment.
- I'm so grateful I found a new job to apply for today.
- I'm so thankful for the extra time I have to relax and recharge as I create a new job opportunity now.

Step 2: End with an Affirmation

Keeping the smile on your face, say out loud or silently to yourself and the Universe: "I am so grateful for the new career path I am creating in my life right now." Repeat this five times.

BONUS: Any time you hear about someone else being happy in their job, getting a promotion, landing a dream job, or otherwise succeeding in their career, thank the Universe for sending you the sign of reassurance that *your* career success is on the way.

Exercise: Grow My Business Gratitude

Whether starting a new business or working to grow and expand one already established, this exercise shifts your mindset to focus on growth, gratitude, and positivity.

Step 1: Look for Signs of Growth

At least once per day, list and feel the gratitude for any signs of growth you've seen in your business that day. For example:

- I'm so grateful for the two new customers/clients I got today.
- I'm so very thankful for the X amount of sales that came in this week.
- I'm so very grateful for the help X is providing me to take my business to the next level.
- I'm so grateful for the new resource I found.

Step 2: State What You Want to Create

The first time you do this exercise, make a list of the growth goals you have for your business. Then, twice a day read the list out loud. Bestselling author of the book *Conscious Creation,* Dee Wallace recommends stating commands to the Universe from your "love place" to open your heart and connect you to the creative vibration of love. To do this, think of someone who opens your heart, such as your child, significant other, or pet. Then, with a smile on your face, you state what you are creating. For example:

- I am lovingly and joyfully creating money everywhere in my life right now—people love to give me money.
- I am creating [fill in the blank with the amount of money you desire] easily and effortlessly right now.
- I am creating X amount of customers every week/month right now.
- I am creating speaking engagements in X industry paying me thousands of dollars right now.

Step 3: End with Gratitude

State to the Universe, "Thank you, thank you, thank you for cocreating this or something better with me in my life right now."

The next chapter is filled with resources to help anyone struggling with fertility, pregnancy, or parenting. There are tools to help with the intention of becoming pregnant—or bringing a child into one's life in another way—moving through pregnancy and birth with ease, and accessing guidance around any struggles while parenting a child.

Chapter 10

FERTILITY, PREGNANCY, AND PARENTING

THERE IS NO HARDER JOB in the world than parenting. It's 24 hours a day, 7 days a week, and 365 days a year. It doesn't matter if you are trying to get pregnant, waiting for the child's arrival, or parenting a baby, toddler, tween, teen, or adult; there is almost always worry and stress involved. Whether you are a biological parent, grandparent, stepparent, adoptive parent, or guardian, you want what is best for your child. You want to guide them toward success, help them avoid suffering, and take on their pain when they do. After all, you are responsible for another human being, and it's your job to make sure they survive and thrive.

But did you know that while you are doing the work to help your child learn, grow, and evolve, they are doing the same for you? They are teaching you unconditional love, patience, joy, and so much more, and are helping you evolve on your spiritual path. Every single person in your life plays a role in your growth, and that includes your child. And just like every other area of your life, there are higher helpers and spiritual tools to help both you and your child along the way. This chapter shares them specifically around conception, pregnancy, birth, and struggles with parenting.

HIGHER HELPERS FOR PARENTING

As a parent—or soon-to-be parent—you have access to a higher team of specialized advisors to assist you, whether it's in fertility, pregnancy and birth, the adoption process, or navigating the decisions, worry, and stress that come with parenting. There are also those to call on for your child when they are struggling in some area, including managing sensitivity, finding new friends, or excelling in school.

Archangel Chamuel

As the archangel who helps you find purpose, a love relationship, or a new job, Archangel Chamuel is also called on to help find supportive friendships. Parents call on him on behalf of their child to help with socializing and attracting healthy and supportive friends.

Archangel Charity

As the twin flame to Archangel Chamuel, Archangel Charity can assist a child in creating healthy and happy friendships, as well as healing any arguments or misunderstandings with friends.

Archangel Gabriel

Not only is Archangel Gabriel the angel of communication, but his job is to also watch over children and assist parents with any issues related to children—including conception, pregnancy, and childbirth. He is also called on to help children who are very sensitive or empathic.

Archangel Hope

As Archangel Gabriel's twin flame, she helps both parents and children hold a positive and hopeful outlook when needed. Archangel Hope also does this for anything related to conception, pregnancy, and childbirth—including help adjusting to pregnancy.

Archangel Jophiel

Known as the angel of beauty, she helps balance negative and positive emotions and to quickly shift from a negative mindset to a positive mindset around conception, pregnancy, childbirth, and parenting. Archangel Jophiel also helps you hold positive thoughts and find the beauty and joy around you even in the midst of struggle.

Archangel Metatron

As a teacher of all things esoteric and metaphysical, Archangel Metatron assists with acclimating to spiritual growth and ascension changes and helps a sensitive or empathic child adjust to socialization in any area of life, including school. Parents also ask him to provide an understanding around their child's behavior.

Archangel Michael

This archangel helps with protection in all areas of life and is called on to protect a parent or child's energy, especially for those who identify as empathic and sensitive. Archangel Michael is also called on for physical protection and to alleviate fear in a parent or child.

Archangel Raguel

As the archangel of harmony, Archangel Raguel helps overcome conflict or repair a relationship between a parent and child and is called on by a parent on behalf of their child who is struggling in another relationship or friendship. He also helps right an injustice or provides aid when a child is being mistreated in any way.

Archangel Raphael

Parents call on this angel of healing for any type of physical or emotional healing on behalf of themselves or their child, whether acute or ongoing. Archangel Raphael also directs parents to the right doctors, modalities, healers, and more.

Archangel Uriel

Considered the angel of wisdom, Archangel Uriel helps with all forms of intellectual pursuits and helps children with schoolwork, studying, or tests. Call on him to help a child improve grades or to guide them through an upcoming test in school.

Ganesha

This Hindu god is known as the remover of obstacles, and Ganesha is called on to remove any obstacles blocking a child's success and happiness, as well as anything blocking a parent from helping their child or finding success around conception, adoption, pregnancy, or childbirth.

Goddess Aphrodite

As the Greek goddess of love and fertility, Goddess Aphrodite helps anyone wanting to conceive, or struggling to conceive, a child.

Goddess Danu

As a Celtic mother goddess, she can assist in all aspects of parenting, lending wisdom, guidance, and protection to any parent who calls on her. Goddess Danu also assists with issues around fertility, conception, or the adoption of a child.

Goddess Diana

This Roman goddess (counterpart to the Greek Goddess Artemis) is a protector of childbirth and can be called on for protection, guidance, and ease during this time. Goddess Diana also assists during pregnancy and helps all mothers care for their children without limiting her own freedom.

Goddess Frigg

The Germanic goddess of marriage, motherhood, and fertility, Goddess Frigg helps women who wish to get pregnant, as well as mothers grieving the loss of a child, as she lost her son.

Goddess Hera

The Greek goddess of women, marriage, and childbirth, Goddess Hera offers protection and ease during childbirth.

Goddess Isis

Also known as ascended master Isis, she is the Egyptian goddess of motherhood and fertility. Goddess Isis assists with fertility and conception of a child, as well as with the process of adoption, and offers strength and power to parents so they can make the best decisions.

Goddess Ostara

Call on Goddess Ostara, the Germanic goddess of the dawn and spring, for new beginnings around fertility and conception—as well as the adoption of a child.

Goddess Parvati

As the mother of Hindu god Ganesha, Goddess Parvati is the Hindu goddess of fertility, love, and devotion. She assists with conception and provides protection for pregnant people. As a mother, she provides parents with strength when needed and guidance to navigate any aspect of parenting.

Goddess Rhea

Greek goddess of fertility and motherhood, Goddess Rhea assists those looking for guidance in all aspects of parenting from conception, pregnancy, adoption, and childbirth. She also works with parents in need of guidance when making decisions and navigating any issues around parenting.

Lady Nada

This ascended master works to heal inner-child wounds and also works with children, especially those in emotional pain. Lady Nada also assists those struggling with monthly cycles, reproductive organs, or other fertility issues.

Mother Mary

Known in the Catholic faith as the mother of Jesus, Mother Mary brings a nurturing, loving, accepting, and compassionate energy to all parents looking for her help and guidance. She is called on by parents for direction, help in making decisions, finding balance, and making self-care a priority.

Padre Pio

In the Catholic faith, Padre Pio is referred to as the patron saint of stress relief, but he is also a patron saint of adolescents—those between the ages of ten and nineteen. He offers help to relieve stress related to parenting and is called on to aid adolescents in any area of life.

Saint Anne

As the mother of Mother Mary and the grandmother of Jesus in the Catholic religion, Saint Anne assists with conception, infertility, and people experiencing difficult pregnancies.

Saint Gerard

Recognized as "The Mother's Saint" and the patron saint of unborn children and expectant mothers, Saint Gerard assists those trying to conceive or adopt a child, as well as mothers in need of guidance for parenting. He is also called on to watch over a child's health during pregnancy and childbirth, or any time a child is in danger or sick.

Saint Joseph

Known in the Catholic faith as Jesus's father, Saint Joseph is the patron saint of fathers and families (as well as workers) and is called on by fathers looking for guidance and support with anything related to parenting.

Saint Jude

As the Catholic patron saint of hopeless cases or impossible situations, parents call on Saint Jude for any issue where they feel hopeless and helpless. Whether trying to conceive or adopt a child, dealing with the loss of a child, or struggling with any aspect of parenting, he can intervene with other higher helpers to provide guidance, comfort, and solutions.

Saint Nicholas

As the patron saint of children in the Catholic faith, Saint Nicholas led to the tradition of Santa Claus and gift-giving at Christmas. Call on him to guide and protect children.

Saint Philomena

As the patron saint of infants, babies, and youth in the Catholic faith, Saint Philomena aids in all aspects of parenting, including conception and with unborn children. She also helps with healing children.

CRYSTALS FOR PARENTING

These are specific crystals that assist with fertility, pregnancy, childbirth, alleviating stress and worry, and even providing a boost of energy when needed.

Clear Quartz

The master healer, clear quartz is used as an all-purpose healing stone, and you can program it with any intention. It also works to amplify the energy of other stones placed with it.

Emerald

This stone is often used to increase fertility and provide support during pregnancy and childbirth. As a heart chakra stone, emerald is helpful in calming emotions and creating balance.

Fluorite

Often referred to as a multitasking stone, fluorite helps busy parents improve concentration and focus and promotes clear thinking to make decisions. It also calms anxiety and stress.

Lepidolite

Containing the mineral lithium, lepidolite has a calming effect on the mind and body and is helpful for dealing with anxiety and depression. It relaxes a stressed and frayed nervous system, an overworked mind, and tension in the body, which makes it an ideal stone to use during labor as well as for everyday parenting concerns and stress.

Malachite

As a healer of the Divine feminine, malachite is helpful for the female-assigned reproductive system and is called the "midwife's stone" because it stimulates contractions during birth, while easing pain during labor and delivery.

Moonstone

Balancing to the hormones and the emotions, moonstone is beneficial for fertility, pregnancy, and childbirth. It also assists a parent in staying calm and balanced during difficult times and situations with their child.

Pink Agate

As a heart chakra crystal, pink agate helps create a loving bond between parent and child and boosts unconditional love and compassion.

Pink Chalcedony

This stone is often recommended for breastfeeding parents to help increase milk supply and to nurture the bond between a mother and child. Pink chalcedony is also helpful in relieving stress and worry about pregnancy or a newborn baby.

Pink Opal

This heart chakra stone supports balance in emotions and assists with tapping into empathy, compassion, and understanding. Pink opal helps dispel nightmares and can be placed under the pillow or bed of a child suffering from this.

Red Jasper

As a grounding stone red jasper provides an energy boost when needed, activating the root chakra to counteract feeling tired and exhausted.

Rose Quartz

Rose quartz is used by pregnant parents for protection of themselves and their fetus during pregnancy and childbirth. It's also used to increase fertility and can be combined with moonstone for this purpose.

Sardonyx

Sardonyx is made up of both onyx and carnelian crystals and assists in mending broken bonds, arguments, or struggles between a parent and a child to facilitate more happiness and harmony.

Shiva Lingam

Shiva lingam activates the lower chakras and is often used to increase fertility by opening and balancing these chakras to aid in conception.

Unakite

Unakite is called a "stone of pregnancy" because it promotes a healthy pregnancy and delivery, supports the growth of the baby, and creates a strong bond and connection between a biological parent and child.

PRAYERS FOR HELP WITH PARENTING

These seven prayers help in all aspects of parenting, including conceiving a child, having a healthy pregnancy and easy childbirth, and seeking guidance as a parent for oneself or on behalf of a child.

Prayer: Academic Help for My Child

Dear Universe, I call in my angels, guides, loved ones who have passed on, and all those in my soul society, only those of the highest vibration, to be with me now, as I am asking for help regarding my child [name of child] and their work at school, including studying, test taking, and grades. I am also asking for guidance on what I can do to assist them in improving this area.

Specifically, I would like help with [explain the current situation here, including where your child is struggling and what result you are looking for now].

To assist my child and me with this, I call on Archangel Uriel to guide my child with schoolwork, studying, and test taking so they can improve their academic situation, and Archangel Raphael to heal anything that may be getting in the way of their success now—and please send me the ideas that can assist with this.

Lady Nada and Saint Philomena, I ask you to help them move through any negative emotions being triggered by this struggle now, and I ask Padre Pio to look after [name of child] and assist them to speed up positive results and reduce any stress this may be causing both of us.

Archangel Gabriel, please help with any communication issues affecting their schoolwork or grades now, and Archangel Hope and Goddess Danu, please provide me with any ideas on how I may help them with this as well.

Archangel Michael, please protect my child and their energy while in school to minimize distractions and energetic interferences negatively impacting them and their academic studies, and Ganesha, please remove any obstacles, known or unknown, negatively impacting my child and their ability to do well in school now.

Please send me the signs, synchronicities, ideas, people, modalities, and more that can help me guide my child, and help me recognize and act on them when they arrive.

In gratitude for your assistance in this matter now and in the future. Amen.

Prayer: Calm, Happy, and Healthy Pregnancy

Dear Universe, I call in my angels, guides, loved ones who have passed on, and all those in my soul society, only those of the highest vibration, to be with me now as I am seeking support and guidance for a calm, happy, and healthy pregnancy.

I ask Archangel Michael to surround both me and my unborn child with your protective light and protect us from any energy that does not belong to us or is not beneficial to us today. Archangel Raphael, please watch over the health of me and my baby, guiding me to the right doctors, healers, and modalities that will help make this pregnancy healthier, easier, and happier.

Archangel Gabriel, Archangel Hope, Goddess Diana, Goddess Parvati, Goddess Rhea, Saint Gerard, and Saint Anne, I call on you all to watch over and protect me and my energy during this pregnancy and to assist me in easily adjusting and flowing through the changes my mind and body are going through during this time. And I also ask Archangel Jophiel to keep my thoughts and mindset positive during this pregnancy, focused solely on the beauty and good around me on this journey.

Lastly, I ask Ganesha to walk beside me and remove any obstacles preventing me from having a calm, happy, and healthy pregnancy now.

I ask that all of my higher helpers guide and direct me through signs and synchronicities toward anything that may help me and my child in a positive way during this pregnancy, and please help me recognize and act on them when they arrive.

In gratitude for your love and assistance during this important time in my life. Amen.

Prayer: Child Protection

Dear Universe, I call in my angels, guides, loved ones who have passed on, and all those in my soul society, only those of the highest vibration, as well as those of my child [name of child] to be with me now as I ask for protection for them physically, emotionally, and energetically.

Archangel Michael, I ask you to surround [name of child] with your protective light and love and prevent them from taking on or being affected by any energy around that does not belong to them. I also ask you to protect them from any physical harm, and I call on Saint Nicholas, the patron saint of children, to watch over and protect my child now. [For adolescents age 10 to 19] Padre Pio, please watch over and protect my child and keep them from harm or stress.

[If struggling with bullying or emotional difficulties] Lady Nada, I know you work with children to heal their emotional pain, and I ask you to partner with Archangel Raphael to help heal my child now from [fill in the blank].

[For sensitive and empathic children] Archangel Gabriel and Archangel Metatron, [name of child] is highly sensitive and empathic, and I ask you both to also watch over them so they stay grounded and balanced no matter what is going on around them.

Thank you so much for your help, love, and protection now. Amen.

Prayer: Easy, Healthy, and Joyful Childbirth

Dear Universe, I call in my angels, guides, loved ones who have passed on, and all those in my soul society, only those of the highest vibration, to be with me now as I am seeking support and guidance for an easy, healthy, and joyful childbirth.

I specifically ask Archangel Michael to protect the energy of my child and me from taking on or absorbing any energy that does not belong to us or is not beneficial to us during labor and delivery, and Archangel Raphael, please send me the perfect doctors, nurses, and other staff to ensure a smooth process, and watch over my health and the health of my child during this time, as well.

I'm also asking Archangel Gabriel, Archangel Hope, Goddess Diana, Goddess Hera, Goddess Rhea, and Saint Gerard to watch over and protect me and my energy while giving birth, to help facilitate an easy and positive experience, and to keep me as calm and centered as possible.

Archangel Jophiel, I ask for your help to keep my thoughts and mindset positive during the birthing process no matter what is going on around me, and Ganesha, please work to remove any obstacles preventing this labor and childbirth from being calm, healthy, and happy for me and my baby.

Thank you, thank you, thank you for your help during this important time in my life. Amen.

Prayer: Fertility and Conception

Dear Universe, I call in my angels, guides, loved ones who have passed on, and all those in my soul society, only those of the highest vibration, to be with me now, as I am asking for help and guidance to conceive a child [or bring a child into my life through some other means] if it is in my highest good and the highest good of the child.

I call in Archangel Raphael to help me heal anything that could make it difficult to become pregnant and to guide me to the right doctors, healers, and modalities to do so more easily. I also ask Archangel Gabriel and Archangel Hope to watch over me and assist me through the process of conceiving this child and bringing them into the world.

Goddess Aphrodite, Goddess Danu, Goddess Ostara, Goddess Frigg, Goddess Parvati, Goddess Isis, Goddess Rhea, Saint Gerard, Saint Philomena, and Saint Anne, I ask for your assistance with all matters of fertility and conception and to help me let go and surrender to allow this to happen easily, if it is meant to be in this lifetime.

I am also asking Archangel Jophiel to help me keep my mindset positive and quickly shift any negative thoughts back to positive, around getting pregnant, and Padre Pio, please help me stay free of stress and worry so my body can relax and allow this conception more easily.

Finally, Ganesha, please remove any obstacles standing in the way of my bringing a child into this world. I am open and ready to receive any signs and synchronicities that can lead me forward to success in this area now, and I ask that you please help me recognize and act on them when they arrive.

I am so very grateful for all of your help and guidance now. Amen.

Prayer: Find Positive Friendships for Children

Dear Universe, I call in my angels, guides, loved ones who have passed on, and all those in my soul society, only those of the highest of vibration, as well as those of [name of child], to be with me now. I am asking for help and support for them regarding friendships, specifically [explain the situation your child is facing here, whether it's trouble with unhealthy friends, trouble making new friends, etc.].

I specifically call on Archangel Chamuel and Archangel Charity to guide my child in establishing and growing supportive and healthy friendships with others who will have a positive influence on their life now and in the future. Regarding any emotional healing that may be needed, I call on Archangel Raphael, Lady Nada, and Saint Philomena to assist now.

[For sensitive children] I also ask Archangel Metatron and Archangel Gabriel to watch over and help them create and sustain these friendships despite their empathic nature and sensitivity.

[For adolescents age 10 to 19] Padre Pio, please watch over and protect my child and keep them from harm or stress when it comes to friends in their life.

And Ganesha, please remove any obstacles in their path now to finding and maintaining happy and healthy friendships that will have a positive impact on them.

As a parent, I ask you to send me any signs, synchronicities, or ideas to assist me in helping [name of child] in this area of their life and to help me recognize and act on them when they arrive.

Thank you, thank you, thank you. Amen.

Prayer: Parenting Guidance

Dear Universe, I call in my angels, guides, loved ones who have passed on, and all those in my soul society, only those of the highest vibration, to be with me now as I'm asking for support, help, and guidance for my child [name of child] with [explain the situation here].

I ask Archangel Gabriel, Archangel Hope, Goddess Danu, Goddess Rhea, Mother Mary, Saint Gerard, Saint Joseph, and Saint Philomena to guide me now so I may understand what I can do or say to help my child with this situation for their highest good and the most positive outcome possible. I also ask Archangel Metatron to help me understand my child's behavior or point of view so that I may better assist them now.

I call on Goddess Parvati and Goddess Isis to provide me with both strength and guidance around this situation, and I ask Padre Pio to support me as well during this stressful time so that I may release any stress and worry that could be blocking me from seeing solutions.

[If this is an ongoing situation and you feel hopeless] Saint Jude, patron saint of hopeless cases, I ask you to assist in this and intercede on my behalf with other higher helpers regarding this situation, and please work with Archangel Hope to assist me in finding the strength and hope I need to move through this.

Ganesha, please remove any obstacles blocking me from finding a solution and moving forward in this area now. I ask all my higher helpers to send me the signs and synchronicities to guide me forward now, and please help me recognize and act on them when they arrive.

Thank you so much for your assistance now and in the future. Amen.

RITUALS FOR HELP WITH PARENTING

There are two rituals below—one for fertility and conception, and the other to obtain guidance on any aspect of parenting.

Ritual: Fertility and Conception

Wanting to start or expand a family is an exciting time, but for those struggling to do so, it can also be heartbreaking. The purpose of this ritual is to harness the energy of the Universe to create new life and also open oneself up to guidance and answers around doing so. As I explained in chapter 4, we don't always create exactly what we desire, in the way we think or in the timeline we believe it should happen. For example, you may wish to become pregnant and give birth to a child, but the Universe may be aware of a child waiting for you that will be born through another person—whether that is a surrogate or through adoption. This ritual, along with all rituals, must be done with surrender and the understanding that the outcome will be in your highest good. No matter what, it will open you up to guidance and help create what is meant for you in this life.

As per the Feng Shui Bagua in chapter 2, on page 51, I recommend setting up and performing this ritual in the family section of your home. When walking through the front door, this section is found in the middle of the left side of the home. It uses the Egg of Life sacred geometry pattern as a grid to set up the crystals, which is part of the Seed of Life and Flower of Life sacred geometry patterns and represents new life, rebirth, and fertility (see figure 7).

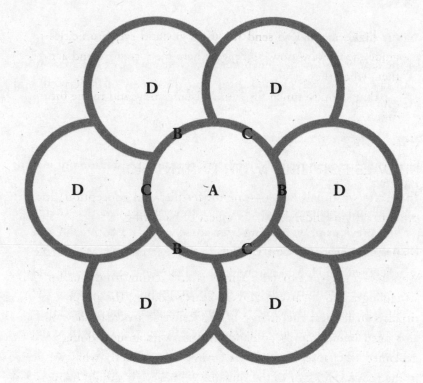

Figure 7. Egg of Life.
A - Shiva Lingam   B - Moonstone   C - Rose Quartz   D - Clear Quartz Point

Items needed:

- One sage bundle/incense, palo santo wood, or frankincense
  incense to burn; or your favorite energy-clearing spray
- One crystal grid or printed image of the Egg of Life pattern
- One Shiva lingam stone (any size or shape)
- Three small tumbled moonstone crystals
- Three small tumbled rose quartz crystals
- Five small clear quartz crystals, single points

Step 1: Clear the Energy

In the family section of your home, clear the energy of the space using your favorite clearing method. Also clear the energy of the crystals and the grid.

Step 2: Program the Crystals

Place your hands above the crystals and repeat this intention out loud or silently in your head:

> I call in the energy of the Universe to clear all unwanted energy and previous programming from these crystals. I command and program them now to work with my energy and harness the energy of the Universe around me to help me create new life and conceive a child in whatever way is in my highest good and the highest good of the child. I program the clear quartz crystals to amplify the energy and effects of the other crystals as well as my intention.

Step 3: The Setup

Place the Egg of Life grid in an area where it will not be disturbed because you will leave it there for twenty-eight days and might repeat the ritual. This is the average length of a menstrual cycle. In the center circle of the grid, place the Shiva lingam (A). Next, place the moonstone and rose quartz crystals in the center connection for each exterior circle, alternating each one as you go (B and C). Last, place one clear quartz point, with the point facing outward, in the center of each outside circle (D).

Step 4: Call in Higher Help

Stand in front of the crystal grid and repeat the "Fertility and Conception Prayer" found earlier in this chapter (which I recommend saying daily, even once the ritual is complete). Then leave the crystal grid undisturbed to do its work for twenty-eight days, and be open to any ideas, information, or opportunities that might pop up to help you move forward.

Step 5: Repeat

Repeat the entire ritual every twenty-eight days as needed, beginning with Step 1.

Ritual: Parental Guidance

There are an unlimited number of situations and circumstances that require guidance when raising children, and no matter what situation you are facing, this ritual allows you to call in the guidance and direction you seek.

As per the Feng Shui Bagua found in chapter 2, page 51, I recommend setting up and performing this ritual in the family section of your home. When walking through the front door, this section is found in the middle of the left side of the home.

Items needed:

- One sage bundle/incense, palo santo wood, or frankincense incense to burn; or your favorite energy-clearing spray
- Paper and pen
- One photo of your child (or one of you and your child together)
- One tumbled, flat, blue-green kyanite stone
- One double-faceted quartz crystal point (points on both ends)

Step 1: Clear the Energy

Clear the energy of the space using your favorite clearing method, as well as the crystals you are using.

Step 2: Program the Crystals

Place your hands above the crystals and repeat this intention out loud or silently in your head:

I call in the energy of the Universe to clear all unwanted energy and previous programming from these crystals. I command and program them now to work with my energy and harness the energy of the Universe around me to bring in the guidance, ideas, and solutions from higher dimensions, and to open me up to the signs and synchronicities pointing me forward toward the highest good for me and [name of child].

Step 3: The Setup

On the piece of paper, write what you would like help or guidance with now. For example, "I would like guidance and assistance in helping my child [name of child] heal from his anxiety" or "I would like guidance and assistance in helping my child, [name of child] improve her grades in school." Then write the words, "What can I do to help my child with this situation? What is the best way for me to handle this for a positive outcome? Please show me the way to a solution."

Place the photo of your child (or you and your child) where it won't be disturbed. Fold the paper with your intention and place it on top of the photo. Next, place the blue-green kyanite on top of the paper and the quartz crystal on top of that.

Step 4: Call in Higher Help

After placing everything, say the "Parenting Guidance Prayer" found earlier in this chapter daily for nine days without skipping a day. If you skip a day, start again at Day 1. Repeat this ritual as needed.

FOCUSED GRATITUDE FOR PARENTING

No matter what is going on in your life as a parent, gratitude for what is going right helps shift your mood and perspective and opens you up to solutions. Here are two gratitude exercises to help improve your parent-child relationship or any issues with behavior.

Exercise: Improve a Parent-Child Relationship
Gratitude

Has the relationship between you and your child hit a rough patch? Did you have an argument, are you engaged in an ongoing battle, or have you suffered a break in the relationship? Whether you are struggling with a toddler, tween, teen, or even an adult child, this exercise takes you back into the past to help you create more harmony, balance, and understanding in the present. Specifically, you will think back to the innocence of the baby you once held and fill yourself up with that love from head to toe. It not only shifts your energy, but it also shifts the energy between the two of you.

Step 1: Find Three Baby Pictures of Your Child
Whether it's a physical photo, one on your mobile phone, or one posted on social media, find three different baby photos of your child—up to the age of two or three—that have happy memories attached to them. This can be a birthday party, a holiday, or some other scenario in which you remember feeling joy and love.

Step 2: Reimagine the Scenes
Starting with the first photo, close your eyes, put a smile on your face, and go back to that time and memory. What was your child doing? What were they saying to you? Remember their excitement, how they made you laugh, how much you loved them, and how they snuggled into you, needed you, and loved you. Bring the memory back to your conscious mind as vividly as you can, and as you do, make positive statements in your mind about it.

For example, if it was the first time they visited a beach, you can say, "You loved the water, and we kept having to take you down to it to dip you in, and you would laugh and laugh. We had so much fun with you." Then stop and put your hands over your heart, and really feel the gratitude for that time, and for having that memory and capturing it in a photo. And feel gratitude for the life you brought into this world and the love you have between you.

Repeat this for each photo until you go through all three memories, spending about a minute or so on each one.

Step 3: End with an Affirmation

Once you are done, place your hands over your heart again, and finish with this affirmation as you look at the photos: "From my heart to your heart, I send you my unconditional love now and forever. May you be happy. May you be healthy. May you be loved. May you be at ease." Repeat the affirmation five times.

Step 4: Repeat

Do this at least once a day, if you can, twice, morning and night, until you feel the situation has been resolved. Each time try to bring up more detail and feel more grateful and loving toward this innocent and happy child. The child in these photos still lives within your child today, no matter how old they are now.

Exercise: Behavior Improvement Gratitude

Are you getting emails from your child's teacher about behavior issues in school? Are they not studying or are their grades dropping? Do you struggle with your child listening to you, picking up after themselves, having a bad attitude, or being disrespectful to you or others? Are they getting into trouble and making unhealthy choices for themselves?

As a parent, you want your child to do well. You want them to do the right thing, be kind, and succeed in all areas of life. You want them to be safe and happy. And when they make choices that lead them in the opposite direction of these things, it leaves you feeling frustrated, helpless, and stressed—especially when you've tried everything you can think of to change the situation.

But when you feel this way, anticipating the worst and in a constant state of worry, you just create more of what you don't want and perpetuate the problem. What if you could shift this in yourself—and flow that shift energetically to your child? That is where this exercise comes in.

Step 1: Dedicate a Notebook or Journal to Your Child

Find a notebook or journal and dedicate it to gratitude around your child's behavior. Keep this by your bedside to use each evening.

Step 2: List the Good

Each night, open to a blank page and put the date on top. Then, in your mind, go back through the day and think of everything that went right with your child. Did they listen the first time? Did they have a good day at school with no email or phone call from the teacher? Did they do well on a test? Did they do something sweet? What positive shift in behavior can you recall from that day? Write down anything that comes to mind from that day, and really feel the gratitude for the tiny shifts you see in your child.

NOTE: If there has been no shift or anything positive for the day, say the "Parenting Guidance Prayer" found earlier in this chapter each morning and trust that your higher helpers are on it. And feel grateful for the changes that are coming.

In the final chapter, you will find spiritual tools to help you partner with the Universe in order to strengthen your spiritual connection, open your intuition, and enhance your overall spiritual growth.

Chapter 11

SPIRITUAL CONNECTION

SPIRITUAL CONNECTION IS NOT SOMETHING you need to achieve. It's something you need to strengthen. You are already connected to the Universe or Spirit. You are a soul walking around in a human body in this physical world, and that soul can't disconnect from its Source. However, your connection can get frayed or muddied, and the signal may not come in as strong or clear as it could. Being in the dense energy of the physical world, there are many factors that dampen that signal, including negative thoughts, beliefs, and emotions, and negative or lower vibrational energy around you. However, there are higher helpers and simple spiritual tools you can use to combat this, strengthen that connection, and keep the channel open and clear.

The Universal energy of unconditional love, peace, and joy is only a breath and a thought away. The tools in this chapter help you tap into the flow of this energy, including opening and developing your psychic and intuitive gifts—something each and every one of us possesses—to better receive the guidance pointing you toward solutions for greater health, happiness, and ease in all areas of life. It also includes tools to protect and cleanse your energy so you can maintain a higher vibration and stronger connection to the Universe.

HIGHER HELPERS FOR SPIRITUAL CONNECTION

These higher helpers are called on for all aspects of spiritual connection, whether it's energetic clearing and protection, opening psychic and intuitive gifts, or assistance with spiritual growth and knowledge.

Archangel Aurora

As the twin flame to Archangel Uriel, she works with the solar plexus chakra and protects you from taking on emotions from other people and places. Archangel Aurora also assists with developing clairsentience or psychic feeling.

Archangel Christine

This archangel opens the crown chakra to allow higher wisdom and guidance into your consciousness. Archangel Christine also represents Christ consciousness, or the awareness of the higher self, and assists with this connection as well.

Archangel Faith

The twin flame to Archangel Michael, Archangel Faith protects and strengthens the aura and helps you develop trust and confidence in yourself and your intuitive abilities, as well as the Universe, angels, guides, and more.

Archangel Gabriel

Known as the angel of communication, Archangel Gabriel assists with receiving the communication and guidance coming from a higher source, whether for yourself or if you are doing intuitive work to help another person. He also helps with automatic writing exercises while communicating with or channeling information from angels, guides, and the higher self.

Archangel Haniel

Often depicted as a female angel, Archangel Haniel is the angel of intuition and Divine communication. She assists with developing intuition and connecting to the guidance within and aligns you with signs and synchronicities to recognize them when they arrive.

Archangel Jeremiel

Call on Archangel Jeremiel for help in developing clairvoyance, or psychic seeing, as well as receiving Divine communication and messages in dreams.

Archangel Metatron

A teacher of all things esoteric and metaphysical, Archangel Metatron provides help when acclimating to the ascension changes you may experience on the spiritual path and in all aspects of spiritual growth. He also assists with balancing the aura, adjusting to big energetic shifts in life, and opening your psychic or spiritual gifts.

Archangel Michael

Often depicted with a sword, Archangel Michael provides both physical and energetic protection. Empaths and those sensitive to energy work with him every day to protect them from absorbing energy from the places and people around them.

Archangel Sandalphon

Known as the tallest of the angels, his presence is said to stretch from the Earth into the heavens, endowing him with a connection to both the other side and the natural world. Archangel Sandalphon offers a strong grounding energy during any spiritual practice and assists you in opening up to signs and communications from the Universe, angels, guides, and more.

Archangel Uriel

As the angel of truth, wisdom, and faith, Archangel Uriel assists with connection to the Divine and obtaining and understanding spiritual knowledge and teachings.

Barbara Marx Hubbard

Cofounder and president of the Foundation for Conscious Evolution, Barbara Marx Hubbard was an author and speaker on consciousness, planetary evolution, science, and spirituality. As the author of several books, including *Conscious Evolution* and *Emergence,* she is called on for help with all aspects of the spiritual path, including expanding your consciousness and evolving spiritually.

Buddha

Known as Siddhartha Gautama during his lifetime, he is the founder of Buddhism and helps you stay consistent with spiritual practices. Buddha also assists with all forms of meditation and opening up to compassion and kindness toward others—especially those you find difficult.

Dr. Wayne Dyer

Bestselling author and spiritual teacher, Dr. Wayne Dyer taught about self-actualization, spirituality, manifesting, and a variety of other subjects to assist you in your spiritual growth. He provides guidance on the spiritual path, whether it's understanding and applying teachings, directing you to the right resources, or assisting with mindset and maintaining a state of love and peace.

Ganesha

This Hindu god is the remover of obstacles, and Ganesha removes any obstacles blocking your intuition, signs, and synchronicities; consistency in spiritual practices; or any aspect of spiritual connection and growth.

Goddess Hecate

As a Greek goddess who journeys between the worlds with ease, Goddess Hecate facilitates communication with loved ones on the other side and opens your awareness of the insights and guidance that spirits share in dreams. She also puts you in touch with your intuition or inner knowing when making decisions.

Goddess Iris

Goddess Iris is the Greek goddess of the rainbow and a messenger of the gods. Traveling between the physical world and higher dimensions, she delivers Divine messages to those on the Earth plane.

Holy Amethyst

The twin flame to Archangel Zadkiel, she also works with Archangel Michael to provide psychic protection. Holy Amethyst also assists in clearing your energy of negativity and psychic debris—transmuting it into love and light. She is called on to open and balance the third-eye chakra for the development of psychic gifts and intuition.

Jane Roberts

Author, medium, and intuitive channel, Jane Roberts brought forth the spirit of Seth and published several books based on her channelings including *The Seth Material* and *Seth Speaks*. She is called on for help with intuition, channeling, automatic writing, and opening up psychic gifts.

Lady Portia

Saint Germain's twin flame, Lady Portia is the keeper of the Sacred Heart Flame, which is the feminine aspect of the violet flame. She opens your psychic abilities, offers guidance in spiritual development and clears karma or blocks holding you back in this area.

Louise Hay

Bestselling author, spiritual teacher, and founder of the spiritual publishing company, Hay House, Louise Hay taught people to use affirmations, cultivate self-love, heal the body, and more, and assists in all aspects of spiritual growth and spiritual connection—including sending you the perfect resources to help.

Mahavatar Babaji

While some believe he was a real person and others a mythical figure, Mahavatar Babaji was introduced to a larger audience through Paramahansa Yogananda's book *Autobiography of a Yogi*. Mahavatar Babaji provides guidance on your spiritual path as well as assists with meditation and establishing a connection to the Divine.

Paramahansa Yogananda

As an Indian monk, yogi, and spiritual teacher who wrote the bestselling book *Autobiography of a Yogi*, Paramahansa Yogananda introduced many people to the practices of meditation and Kriya Yoga, which is a form of meditation. He provides direction on the spiritual path, helps you connect with your higher self and the Divine within, and provides guidance in meditation and spiritual connection.

Serapis Bey

Call on the ascended master Serapis Bey for help finding and maintaining self-discipline with spiritual practices in order to facilitate spiritual growth, ascension, and an acceleration of consciousness.

Sylvia Browne

New York Times bestselling author, psychic, and medium, Sylvia Browne helps open psychic and intuitive abilities and guides you to helpful resources in this area.

Thich Nhat Hanh

Spiritual leader, peace activist, and bestselling author, Thich Nhat Hanh taught on Zen Buddhism, mindfulness, and creating peace. He assists with spiritual practices, including meditation and mindfulness, as well as maintaining peace and a high vibration despite outside circumstances.

CRYSTALS FOR SPIRITUAL CONNECTION

Looking to protect and clear your energy, open your third-eye and crown chakras, boost your connection with angels and guides, raise your vibration, or go deeper into meditation? There are crystals to help! Here is a list of the best options related to all aspects of spiritual connection.

Amethyst

This multitasking stone is ideal to raise your overall vibration and is also associated with the third-eye and crown chakras. Amethyst assists with connecting to the Divine and its guidance and enhancing psychic abilities and intuition.

Angelite

This high-vibrational stone facilitates connection to the angelic realm, spirit guides, and higher guidance and knowledge. Angelite aligns the throat, third-eye, and crown chakras, and helps with opening psychic abilities and raising your vibration.

Apophyllite

This highly intuitive stone opens both the third-eye and crown chakras for expanding and developing intuition and inner vision, and also works with the heart chakra, allowing you to give and receive love with more ease. Apophyllite also helps to raise your vibration, facilitates a connection between the physical world and the spiritual world, and is ideal for meditation because it clears the mind and expands awareness.

Azurite

Azurite works to open the third-eye chakra to stimulate psychic abilities, including clairvoyance or psychic seeing, as well as to channel information from higher dimensions and spirit guides. It is also associated with the crown chakra and strengthening your connection to the Divine.

Black Kyanite

Black kyanite offers grounding and protective energy but is also used in a similar way to selenite because it clears the aura of negative energy and never needs to be cleansed or cleared because it doesn't hold energy. It also protects from energy vampires, or people who drain a person's energy, and shields the aura to deflect negative energy.

Black Obsidian

A very protective stone, black obsidian shields against negativity and psychic attack and absorbs negative energies in the environment. Connected to the root chakra, it grounds and anchors your spirit into your body.

Black Tourmaline

One of the best stones for energetic protection, especially for empaths and those sensitive to energy, black tourmaline is a grounding stone that blocks and absorbs negative energies and also protects you from electromagnetic fields (EMFs).

Blue-Green Kyanite

Combining both blue and green kyanite, this grounding crystal opens and aligns the chakras. Blue kyanite aligns with the third-eye chakra and green kyanite aligns with the heart chakra. This stone stimulates psychic development and assists in communication with the higher realms and guides. It's also a calming and stress-reducing stone, helping you to achieve a deeper level in meditation.

Candle Quartz (also known as Pineapple Quartz or Celestial Quartz)

A formation of quartz that looks like it has candle wax dripped down it, candle quartz is used to enhance intuition and connect with guardian angels.

Charoite

A stone said to be connected to ascended masters, charoite stimulates psychic abilities, intuition, and spiritual connection and grounds your energy when you're feeling psychically overstimulated. It's also helpful when trying to adjust to higher frequency energy.

Clear Quartz

Known as a master healer, this high-vibrational stone enhances psychic abilities, clears and balances your chakras, and raises your vibration. Clear quartz is known as a universal crystal because it is helpful in manifesting, healing, meditating, channeling, and more, and amplifies the energy of other crystals it is placed with or near.

Hematite

Not only can hematite protect you from negative energy, but it also dissolves it. Its connection with the root chakra makes it a very grounding and stabilizing crystal, and it also calms the mind and boosts confidence and self-esteem.

Herkimer Diamond

Referred to as the "stone of attunement," this high-vibrational stone opens the crown chakra to higher dimensions and guidance and heightens psychic senses and vision. As a specific form of clear quartz, herkimer diamond amplifies the energy of other gemstones.

Iolite

Helpful in developing intuition, iolite opens the third-eye chakra and helps you see clearly, viewing situations from a higher level rather than simply through the mind and emotions.

Labradorite

A stone to strengthen intuition and increase psychic abilities, labradorite opens clairvoyance and helps you notice signs and synchronicities around you. It bridges the gap between the physical world and the higher realms of consciousness and assists in spiritual awareness and growth.

Libyan Desert Glass

Found near the Egyptian–Libyan border in the Sahara Desert, this healing stone is said to be formed from a meteorite impacting and melting desert sand. Libyan desert glass resonates with the solar plexus and provides protection from energy vampires, those who drain energy, and prevents you from absorbing energy around you.

Lemurian Quartz

This stone features grooves or striations, almost like barcodes, in its appearance and helps with clairvoyance, telepathy, and intuition. Lemurian quartz also connects you to your higher self, angels, guides, ascended masters, and other higher-dimension beings and is ideal to assist in meditation, specifically entering a meditative state.

Moldavite

Formed from a meteorite crashing to the Earth, moldavite is a stone for spiritual awakening that stimulates the third-eye and the crown chakras. It helps you connect with and hear messages from angels, guides, and other high-vibration entities, including extraterrestrial ones.

Nirvana Quartz

Whether you are looking to open your intuition or heighten your connection with the Divine, nirvana quartz, sourced from the Himalayas, helps you reach a state of bliss or enlightenment. It is also helpful during meditation to create a spiritual connection with higher realms and bring in a feeling of peace and calm.

Phantom Quartz

This clear quartz stone with mineral inclusions is found in a variety of colors and heightens your intuition, helps to connect you with spirit guides and angels, and opens and unblocks the third-eye and crown chakras. Phantom quartz is also a stone of transition, assisting you in noticing the signs the Universe is sending, and it alleviates anxiety or fear around life changes.

Pietersite

Often called the "stone of truth," pietersite enhances psychic ability and as such is an ideal stone for doing psychic or intuitive work including oracle or tarot card readings. It allows you to see things clearly, activating the third eye, and helps you move to higher states of awareness and consciousness during meditation.

Prehnite

Boost prophetic and psychic abilities with prehnite, known specifically to enhance precognition and prophecy. It enhances visualization, lucid dreaming, and connecting with higher realms.

Selenite

Clearing energy and emotions, this calming stone creates a sense of peace within you when you use or wear it. It's perfect to assist in meditation and opens the crown chakra to access higher dimensions. Because it does not hold onto energy, it never needs to be cleansed and is used to cleanse other crystals and your aura.

Shungite

Although linked to the root chakra, this powerful grounding stone provides psychic protection and balances the left and right sides of the body, as well as masculine and feminine energies within the body. Shungite protects from electromagnetic fields (EMFs) and can be placed on or near electronics.

Sodalite

Not only does sodalite provide a calm energy and help bring order to the mind, but it's directly linked to the third-eye chakra to activate intuition. It's often associated with the energy of Archangel Michael and is beneficial to use during meditation as it calms the mind and running thoughts.

PRAYERS FOR HELP WITH SPIRITUAL CONNECTION

When it comes to maintaining a strong spiritual connection and opening your intuitive gifts to receive the guidance coming to you, there are many higher helpers ready to assist. Here are six prayers to help clear and protect your energy, open your intuition, help you stay consistent in spiritual practices, and more.

Prayer: Energy Clearing

Dear Universe, I call in my angels, guides, loved ones who have passed on, and all those in my soul society, only those of the highest vibration, to help me clear my energy of anything that is not beneficial or does not belong to me.

I call in Holy Amethyst to clear any negativity and psychic debris, transforming it to love, and I ask Lady Portia to use the violet flame to remove any karma or blocks holding me back from moving forward in any and all areas of my life now. I also ask Archangel Metatron and Archangel Faith to balance and strengthen my aura.

I now reconnect with my higher self and my own energy. And so it is.

Thank you, thank you, thank you. Amen.

Prayer: Open the Channel

Use this prayer prior to engaging in intuitive work.

Dear Universe, I call in my angels, guides, loved ones who have passed on, and all those in my soul society, only those of the highest vibration, to be with me now.

I specifically call in Archangel Michael to surround me in a bubble of light and love, and please prevent me from taking on any energy that does not belong to me. I also ask Holy Amethyst to provide me with psychic protection and open and balance my third-eye chakra, working with Archangel Jeremiel to open my clairvoyance or psychic seeing. Archangel Christine, please open my crown chakra to allow guidance from higher dimensions to flow to and through me, and please work with Archangel Sandalphon and Goddess Iris to help bring these messages through.

Archangel Aurora, please open my solar plexus chakra and help me connect with my clairsentience, and Archangel Haniel, Archangel Metatron, Lady Portia, Jane Roberts, and Sylvia Browne, I ask you to assist with opening all my intuitive channels so higher guidance and information can flow easily into my conscious mind.

Lastly, I call on Archangel Metatron to balance my aura and help me adjust to any energetic shifts as my energy and vibrations rise now.

Thank you, thank you, thank you. Amen.

Prayer: Open and Strengthen Intuitive Gifts

Dear Universe, I call in my angels, guides, loved ones who have passed on, and all those in my soul society, only those of the highest vibration, to be with me now, as I am seeking to open and strengthen my intuition and psychic abilities for assistance on my life path [or to work with and assist others].

Archangel Christine, I ask you to open my crown chakra to allow guidance from higher dimensions to flow to me and through me, and please work with Archangel Sandalphon and Goddess Iris to help me get the messages and guidance being sent. I also ask Archangel Aurora to open my clairsentience and Holy Amethyst and Archangel Jeremiel to open and balance my third-eye chakra to strengthen my psychic seeing.

I am also looking for help in boosting my confidence and trust in my intuitive abilities and the guidance I receive, and I ask Archangel Faith to assist me with this while also protecting and strengthening my aura.

Archangel Haniel, Archangel Metatron, Lady Portia, Jane Roberts, and Sylvia Browne, please help me open my psychic senses to communicate with the Divine and my angels, guides, and higher self, as well as become aware of the signs and synchronicities sent to guide me. I also ask Goddess Hecate to do the same for communications with loved ones on the other side.

I ask all of you to please send me signs and synchronicities to guide me to the people, teachers, classes, resources, and more to help me open and strengthen my intuition now, and please help me recognize them and act on them when they arrive.

Finally, I call in Ganesha to please remove any obstacles blocking me from opening my intuition and psychic gifts now.

Thank you in advance for all of your guidance and assistance now and in the future. Amen.

Prayer: Protection

Dear Universe, I call in my angels, guides, loved ones who have passed on, and all those in my soul society, only those of the highest vibration, to be with me now as I ask for protection for me and my energy.

I specifically call in Archangel Michael to surround me in a bubble of light and love and prevent me from taking on any energy that does not belong to me. Please allow it to bounce off of me and return to sender, or if it is negative, allow it to drop into the Earth and be transformed to love.

I also ask Holy Amethyst to offer me psychic protection, Archangel Faith to both protect and strengthen my aura, and Archangel Aurora to balance my solar plexus chakra and protect me from taking on emotions and energy that do not belong to me from other people and places.

Thank you for your help and protection now. Amen.

Prayer: Spiritual Growth and Ascension

Dear Universe, I call in my angels, guides, loved ones who have passed on, and all those in my soul society, only those of the highest vibration, to be with me now, as I am looking for guidance and direction on growing spiritually and expanding and raising my consciousness.

I am asking for help in opening my intuition so I can receive guidance to further me on my spiritual path, and ask Archangel Christine to open my crown chakra to allow guidance from higher dimensions to more easily flow to me. I also ask Archangel Sandalphon for help with receiving Divine communication and to assist me in staying grounded and centered in my body as my vibration ascends higher.

Archangel Uriel, I ask for your assistance with not only connecting with the Divine but also receiving and understanding the spiritual knowledge and teachings I am studying and learning now, and to please work with Lady Portia to assist in my overall spiritual development.

Additionally, I call in great spiritual teachers who have passed on from this physical plane, including Barbara Marx Hubbard, Dr. Wayne Dyer, Louise Hay, Mahavatar Babaji, and Paramahansa Yogananda, to provide me with guidance on my current spiritual path and send me to the right people, teachers, teachings, and resources that will help me grow and evolve for my highest good, and to please help me recognize and act on the signs and synchronicities when they arrive.

Finally, I call in Ganesha to please remove any obstacles blocking me from growing and ascending on my spiritual path.

Thank you, thank you, thank you. Amen.

Prayer: Staying Consistent with Spiritual Practices

Dear Universe, I call in my angels, guides, loved ones who have passed on, and all those in my soul society, only those of the highest vibration, to be with me now as I am seeking discipline, knowledge, and assistance in staying consistent with the spiritual practices to help me in my everyday life and expand my consciousness in this lifetime.

To help me with this, I call in ascended master Serapis Bey to aid me in maintaining the self-discipline I need to be consistent with my spiritual practices each day, including [explain what spiritual practices you are doing, such as meditation, gratitude, yoga, and other spiritual exercises].

I also call in help from Buddha, Mahavatar Babaji, Paramahansa Yogananda, Thich Nhat Hanh, and Dr. Wayne Dyer to assist me in this area and please send me the signs and synchronicities, ideas, people, resources, and opportunities that can help me with this now—and help me notice and act on them when they arrive.

Lastly, I call in Ganesha to please remove any obstacles blocking me from being consistent and engaging in all of the spiritual practices that will have a positive impact on my life.

Thank you in advance for your help, guidance, and assistance. Amen.

RITUALS FOR HELP WITH SPIRITUAL CONNECTION

Here are two rituals to help you clear and protect your energy each day using prayer and crystals and to ask the Universe for help in activating its energy to open your intuition.

Ritual: Daily Energetic Protection and Cleansing

Everything is energy, including you, and as you go through daily life, visit places, interact with people, and listen to and watch media, there is an effect on your energy and your vibration. Whether you identify as an empath or not, you are being affected by the energy around you. In fact, science calls this emotional contagion. This means you can "catch" emotions from other people the same way you can catch a cold.

This daily ritual protects you from being affected by the energy out-side of you, especially negative energy and vibrations that don't belong to you, so you can maintain a higher vibration and a stronger spiritual connection. It also helps cleanse you of any energy you may have unknowingly taken on. It makes a big difference in how you feel and the energy you are sending out into the Universe to create your future. Also, when you vibrate higher and your connection to Spirit is strong, you are more likely to notice the signs, synchronicities, and solutions the Universe is sending to help you move forward toward more success and happiness.

Items needed:

- One small tumbled protection crystal (just a stone or in jewelry) such as black kyanite, black obsidian, black tourmaline, or hematite
- One selenite or black kyanite wand

Step 1: Choose Your Crystals

You can either carry a protective crystal with you in your handbag or pocket or you can choose to wear it as jewelry, such as a ring, bracelet, necklace, or pendant. If you carry it with you, just choose one from the list above. If you would like to wear your protection as jewelry, you can use a combination of protection crystals together or a single stone. You can also wear jewelry that combines protection and cleansing crystals together, such as black tourmaline and selenite.

Also, choose either a selenite wand or a black kyanite wand to use every night to cleanse your energy.

Step 2: Cleanse and Program Your Crystals

Because selenite and black kyanite don't hold energy, you don't need to cleanse them, but you do need to use them to cleanse the protection crystal or jewelry you will be using. The easiest way to do this is to lay the crystal or jewelry on top of the selenite or kyanite wand. You can also use a round selenite plate to place them on top of as well, but you will also need the wand for Step 4.

The first time you do this ritual, place the stones on top of the selenite or black kyanite overnight. Then each night return the crystals you wore or carried with you to the selenite or black kyanite to be cleansed overnight before using them the next day. This can be done any time you feel the need for added protection or as a daily practice.

Step 3: Morning Routine

Each morning, reprogram your crystals. Simply hold them in your hands or hover your hands over the crystals and say the following either out loud or in your mind:

"I call in the energy of the Universe to clear any previous programming and energy from this crystal. I now command it to shield me from any negative energy or energy that does not belong to me, absorb it on my behalf, and keep me grounded and protected throughout the day."

Then either put the jewelry on or place the crystal in your handbag or pocket. Then say the following prayer for protection either out loud or silently in your mind:

"I call in Archangel Michael to surround me with a bubble of your white light of love and protection, and please protect me from taking on any energy that does not belong to me today. Please allow it to bounce off of me and return to sender, or if it is negative, allow it to fall into the Earth and be transformed to love. Amen."

Repeat this step daily.

Step 4: Evening Routine

Every night before bed, use the selenite or black kyanite wand to cleanse and dissolve any negative energy or energy that does not belong to you from your aura or energy field. Hold the crystal wand a couple of inches away from your body and, using a combing motion, move it down your arms and legs and around your head. As you do so, repeat the following:

I'm clearing any negative energy and any energy that does not belong to me. I ask Holy Amethyst to help clear any psychic debris I may be holding and Archangel Metatron to help me balance my aura. I release this energy now and reconnect with my higher self. And so it is.

Then place the protection crystal or jewelry you used onto the selenite or black kyanite overnight to be cleansed from any energy absorbed on your behalf during the day. Repeat this step daily.

Ritual: Open Intuitive Pathways

When it comes to your intuition, opening the top three chakras—the crown, third-eye, and throat chakras—is key to igniting its flow. An open crown chakra allows information, ideas, and concepts from a higher dimension to enter your conscious mind. The third-eye chakra is where your psychic vision, or images in your mind's eye, appear. And the throat chakra allows you to clearly communicate the information being received. When these chakras are open, aligned, and clear, intuition is heightened and guidance for yourself or another person can flow through more easily. This ritual focuses on opening these chakras to do just that.

Items needed:

- One sage bundle/incense, palo santo wood, or frankincense incense to burn; or your favorite energy-clearing spray
- One azurite or amethyst crystal
- One apophyllite crystal
- One angelite crystal

Step 1: Clear the Energy

It doesn't matter what room of the home you choose for this ritual. Burn the sage, palo santo wood, or frankincense (or use your clearing spray) to cleanse the energy in the room you choose, as well as the energy of each crystal. Clear the crystals by passing them through the smoke or spritzing them directly with a cleansing spray.

Step 2: Program the Crystals

Place your hands above the crystals and repeat this prayer out loud or in your head:

> I call in the energy of the Universe to connect with my highest self and clear all unwanted energy and previous programming from these crystals. I command and program them now to work with my energy and harness the energy of the Universe around me to open my intuition and psychic gifts and to open and balance my crown, third-eye, and throat chakras so I can better receive information, ideas, and inspiration from higher realms.

Step 3: Call in Higher Help

Say the "Open and Strengthen Intuitive Gifts Prayer" found earlier in this chapter on page 273.

Step 4: The Setup

Set a timer for ten minutes. Lie down flat on your back and place the apophyllite crystal a couple inches above your head. Then lay the azurite or amethyst crystal on top of your third eye, which is between and slightly above your eyebrows. Last, lay the angelite crystal in the center of your throat.

As you lie there, breathe normally in and out of your nose and imagine energy from the apophyllite crystal moving into the crown of your head and down into your third eye, activating the azurite or amethyst and opening this chakra. Then visualize the energy flowing from the third eye into the throat chakra, activating the angelite and opening this chakra. As you visualize this, repeat the mantra, "I am open to receive." Continue this for ten minutes. Repeat this ritual weekly, as desired.

FOCUSED GRATITUDE EXERCISES FOR HELP WITH SPIRITUAL CONNECTION

Here are two focused gratitude exercises to help you strengthen your connection to the Divine and open your intuitive gifts. They can be used together or separately, depending on your goals.

Exercise: Strengthen the Spiritual Connection Gratitude

Gratitude instantly shifts your energy and raises your vibration, and it's also the fastest way to strengthen your connection to the Divine because the energy of appreciation and love aligns with the highest energy in the Universe. Any time you shift to gratitude, you boost your spiritual connection, and the more you do it, the more you maintain that strong connection throughout the day. This exercise helps you do that, as well as retrains your brain and conscious mind to look for and focus on the good around you, which helps in every area of your life.

Step 1: Set an Hourly Alarm
From the time you wake up, set an alarm on your mobile phone or watch to go off at the top of every hour until the time you go to bed. If it allows you to put a note or word into the alarm, simply write, "Gratitude." If you don't have the option to set an alarm, do this exercise every time you look at the clock to check the time.

Step 2: Look for the Good
When the alarm goes off (or when you look at the clock), stop what you are doing and look for at least one thing to be grateful for in that moment. What has gone well or right in the last hour? If you can't think of anything from the last hour, then think of something you can be grateful for having, being, or doing from your life in general. Put your hand over your heart, put a smile on your face, and name the thing(s) you are grateful for in that moment, and really allow yourself to feel the gratitude of it inside your heart. For example:

- I'm so grateful my sister called me in the last hour with good news about X.
- I'm so thankful I got a reply email from X, who is going to help me with my project.
- I'm so happy there was no line at the coffee shop so I could get my morning coffee quickly and easily.
- I'm so very grateful it's Friday and I have the weekend off.

Step 3: Repeat Daily

Every day when you wake up, set the alarms and repeat the exercise.

Exercise: Intuitive Gifts Gratitude

If you are actively practicing and working to enhance your intuition and psychic gifts—using oracle cards, tarot cards, taking classes, or doing other psychic work—it's important to focus on and celebrate the intuitive hits you get and the progress you make. This not only increases your confidence and trust in yourself and your abilities, but it also opens you up to more. This exercise helps you track your progress and focus on the gratitude of your growing and expanding intuitive abilities.

Step 1: Dedicate a Notebook or Journal to This Exercise

Find a notebook or journal to use daily for this exercise, and dedicate it to gratitude and tracking your intuitive hits and successes.

Step 2: Record Your Success Daily

The goal of this exercise is to track your intuitive hits or any successes you have around psychic ability and intuition every day—including recognizing signs and synchronicities. For example, when you work with oracle or tarot cards for yourself or another, and they offer the perfect guidance or resonate with you or the other person—write it down. When you do an intuitive exercise, work with your pendulum, or do a reading for another person (even just practicing)—write down the successful hits. When you have an intuitive hit throughout your day and it turns out to be correct—write it down.

You can write them down at the time each event occurs, or you can do it each night by replaying your day and writing down anything that occurred around your intuition.

- Record the date.
- Explain what happened and what you got correct.
- Feel the gratitude in your heart, with a smile on your face, that your intuition is growing and expanding each day.

BONUS: Any time you feel doubtful about your intuitive ability, go back to this journal and remind yourself of the successes you have had in the past.

Conclusion

IT'S TIME TO CREATE
A LIFE YOU LOVE

YOU NOW HAVE ACCESS TO a method, tools, and techniques that continue to surprise and delight me every time I use them. I've had the pleasure of watching it do the same for others using them as well. Now it's your turn.

It's your turn to create magic, miracles, joy, and love in your life because anything is possible. We live in an endlessly abundant and creative Universe, and when we believe in it and ourselves, we can tap into this energy at any moment we choose. It's my hope that in using the Higher Help Method, you will know that you are not alone, you deserve all you desire, and with the Universe as your partner, you can create it—and in most cases, you can create something even better.

Any time you face a challenge, have a decision to make, or need a solution, and any time you desire positive change in some area of your life, I want you to remember you have an entire Universe of higher resources available to you to make the journey easier. I also want you to remember that no matter what happens, you will eventually figure it out, unearth the answer, and discover the perfect solution to any challenge. Why? Because you are always divinely guided and unconditionally loved by the Universe, your angels and guides, and all the higher helpers standing by to assist you right now.

May this book provide you with all you need to begin developing an intimate relationship with the Universe and your higher help team so they can take you places you never dreamed possible. I can't wait to see what you create.

ACKNOWLEDGMENTS

I HAVE TO START BY acknowledging and thanking my angels, guides, loved ones who have passed on, especially my mom, Maryann, everyone in my soul society, and all those I've called in from my higher help team for guiding me to create the Higher Help Method for myself and then for assisting me in writing this book so I could teach it to others who are looking to manifest positive changes in their lives.

In addition to my higher team, I also have to thank my Earthly helpers who all played a role in the creation of this book. To my amazing agent, Steve Harris, I thank you for always working so hard on my behalf and helping me find the perfect home for my work. To Diana Ventimiglia, Angela Wix, and the entire team at Sounds True, I am so grateful for your faith in me and my work and for your guidance in bringing the Higher Help Method to the world. And Angela, I'm so grateful the Universe continues to bring us together no matter where you roam.

To my husband, Ryan, for always reminding me I can do anything and for supporting me in all the work that I do and create, I thank you. The Universe brought me the perfect partner, and I'm forever grateful for you and your love.

And to all my readers, students, and clients, I thank *you* for allowing me to play a role in guiding you on your spiritual journey. If you have found me and my work, it is not by accident. There are no accidents in this Universe, and I am honored to share the tools and techniques in this book with you so you can create a life you love.

RECOMMENDED RESOURCES

ADDITIONAL BOOK BONUSES

Access audios of the meditations found in the book, along with additional prayers, rituals, and other bonus content at higherhelpmethod.com.

CLEARING LIMITING BELIEFS

For the Emotional Freedom Technique:

Gary Craig, *The EFT Manual* (California: Energy Psychology Press, 2011).

For the Sweep Technique:

Amy B. Scher, *How to Heal Yourself from Depression When No One Else Can* (Boulder, CO: Sounds True, 2021), youtube.com/@amybscher.

For the Sedona Method:

Hale Dwoskin, *The Sedona Method: Your Key to Lasting Happiness, Success, Peace, and Emotional Well-Being,* (Sedona, AZ: Sedona Press, 2003), youtube.com/user/TheSedonaMethod.

For Ho'oponopono:

Paul Jackson, *Ho'oponopono Secrets: Four Phrases to Change the World One Love to Bind Them* (South Carolina: CreateSpace Independent Publishing Platform, 2014).

Joe Vitale and Ihaleakala Hew Len, *Zero Limits: The Secret Hawaiian System for Wealth, Health, Peace, and More* (Hoboken, NJ: Wiley, 2008).

ENDNOTES

CHAPTER 2: ASK THE UNIVERSE FOR HELP

1 "Prayer May Influence In Vitro Fertilization Success," September 24, 2001, Columbia University Irving Medical Center, cuimc .columbia.edu/news/prayer-may-influence-vitro-fertilization -success.

2 Francesca Gino and Michael I. Norton, "Why Rituals Work," *Scientific American* (May 14, 2013), scientificamerican.com/article /why-rituals-work.

CHAPTER 3: SHIFT YOUR ENERGY

1 Christine Comaford, "Got Inner Peace? 5 Ways to Get it Now," *Forbes* (April 4, 2012), forbes.com/sites/christinecomaford/2012 /04/04/got-inner-peace-5-ways-to-get-it-now/.

2 Rick Hanson, "Confronting the Negativity Bias," accessed June 7, 2023, rickhanson.net/how-your-brain-makes-you-easily -intimidated/.

CHAPTER 6: PHYSICAL HEALING

1 David R. Hamilton, *How the Mind Can Heal the Body* (London: Hay House UK, 2018), 6.

2 Hamilton, *How the Mind Can Heal the Body.*

CHAPTER 7: EMOTIONAL HEALING

1   Mental Health America, "State of Mental Health in America: Adult Ranking 2022," accessed June 11, 2023, mhanational.org/issues /2022/mental-health-america-adult-data.
2   Substance Abuse and Mental Health Services Administration, "What is Mental Health," accessed June 11, 2023, samhsa.gov/mental -health.

CHAPTER 8: RELATIONSHIPS

1   Amy B. Scher, "Cut the Cord: Remove Negativity from Relationships," accessed June 11, 2023, reclaimajoyfullife.com/freebies.

BIBLIOGRAPHY

Alexander, Skye. *Your Goddess Year: A Week-By-Week Guide to Invoking the Divine Feminine.* Avon, Massachusetts: Adams Media, 2019.

Gray, Kyle. *Divine Masters, Ancient Wisdom: Activations to Connect with Universal Spiritual Guides.* Carlsbad, California: Hay House, 2021.

Stone, Claire. *The Female Archangels: Reclaim Your Power with the Lost Teachings of the Divine Feminine.* Carlsbad, California: Hay House, 2020.

INDEXES

HIGHER HELPERS

CRYSTALS

ABOUT THE AUTHOR

TAMMY MASTROBERTE IS A SPIRITUAL teacher and award-winning bestselling author of *The Universe Is Talking to You.* Through her books, membership program, and classes, she helps everyday spiritual seekers plug into the energy of the Universe and learn to spot the signs and synchronicities around them. Her work is designed to lead people into more joy, clarity, and peace than they ever thought possible. She has been featured in mindbodygreen.com, *Aspire Magazine, Authority Magazine,* Thrive Global, and more, and she speaks on radio shows and podcasts nationwide, including OMTimes Radio, Unity Radio, and iHeartRadio. She lives in New Jersey with her husband, stepson, two cats, and four goats. For more information, visit tammymastroberte.com.

ABOUT SOUNDS TRUE

SOUNDS TRUE WAS FOUNDED IN 1985 by Tami Simon with a clear mission: to disseminate spiritual wisdom. Since starting out as a project with one woman and her tape recorder, we have grown into a multimedia publishing company with a catalog of more than 3,000 titles by some of the leading teachers and visionaries of our time and an ever-expanding family of beloved customers from across the world.

In more than three decades of evolution, Sounds True has maintained our focus on our overriding purpose and mission: to wake up the world. We offer books, audio programs, online learning experiences, and in-person events to support your personal growth and awakening, and to unlock our greatest human capacities to love and serve.

At SoundsTrue.com you'll find a wealth of resources to enrich your journey, including our weekly *Insights at the Edge* podcast, free downloads, and information about our nonprofit Sounds True Foundation, where we strive to remove financial barriers to the materials we publish through scholarships and donations worldwide.

To learn more, please visit SoundsTrue.com/freegifts or call us toll-free at 800.333.9185.

Together, we can wake up the world.

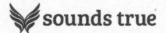